The Contradictions of
American Capital Punishment

Selected Titles

STUDIES IN CRIME AND PUBLIC POLICY
Michael Tonry and Norval Morris, *General Editors*

The American Street Gang
Malcolm Klein

Malign Neglect
Michael Tonry

Hate Crimes: Criminal Law and Identity Politics
James B. Jacobs and Kimberly Potter

American Youth Violence
Franklin E. Zimring

Gun Violence: The Real Costs
Philip J. Cook and Jens Ludwig

*Punishment and Democracy: Three Strikes and You're
Out in California*
Franklin E. Zimring, Gordon Hawkins, and Sam Kamin

*Maconochie's Gentlemen: The Story of Norfolk Island
and the Roots of Modern Prison Reform*
Norval Morris

Can Gun Control Work?
James B. Jacobs

The Contradictions of American Capital Punishment

Franklin E. Zimring

OXFORD
UNIVERSITY PRESS
2003

OXFORD

UNIVERSITY PRESS

Oxford   New York
Auckland   Bangkok   Buenos Aires   Cape Town   Chennai
Dar es Salaam   Delhi   Hong Kong   Istanbul   Karachi   Kolkata
Kuala Lumpur   Madrid   Melbourne   Mexico City   Mumbai   Nairobi
São Paulo   Shanghai   Taipei   Tokyo   Toronto

Published by Oxford University Press, Inc.
198 Madison Avenue, New York, New York 10016

www.oup.com

Oxford is a registered trademark of Oxford University Press

Library of Congress Cataloging-in-Publication Data
Zimring, Franklin E.
The contradictions of American capital punishment /
by Franklin E. Zimring.
p.   cm. — (Studies in crime and public policy)
Includes bibliographical references and index.
ISBN 0-19-515236-0
Capital punishment—United States.
I. Title. II. Series.
HV8699.U5 Z563   2003
364.33'0973—dc21
2002012490

1 3 5 7 9 8 6 4 2
Printed in the United States of America
on acid-free paper

For Gordon

Contents

————————

Preface

CAPITAL PUNISHMENT in the United States is an issue of great moral, political, legal, and practical importance. But the practice of executions in the United States in the early years of the twenty-first century is one other thing: It is a puzzle.

Why does the United States execute when every other developed Western nation has ceased to use the taking of life as a legal punishment? What elements of American history and culture create an affinity for state executions? What is the most likely future of the death penalty in the United States?

This book is my effort to resolve the puzzle of American capital punishment, to explain the contradictions in American culture that generate conflict over the death penalty and the changes that will be necessary to bring American capital punishment to a peaceful end.

My explanation revolves around three distinctive interpretations of capital punishment as an American phenomenon. I show that some of the same pressures that have led to the condemnation of the death penalty in Europe have produced instead its reinvention in the United States. The proponents of capital punishment have engineered a symbolic transformation over the last two decades. We now tell ourselves that an executing government is acting in the interest of victims and communities rather than in a display of governmental power and dominance. The net effect of this recent change is that the United States and the rest of the Western world are further apart on the death penalty than ever before, and in

more disagreement over capital punishment than over any other important political question.

But why do Americans reinvent what other developed nations abolish?
The origins of our current against-the-grain death penalty policy can be
found in the earlier history of nongovernmental violence that was present
in many parts of the United States but particularly rampant in the South.
Where nostalgia still exists for vigilante values, citizens are prone to identify with executions as a community process rather than as the activity of a
distant and self-interested government. This identification with punishment may lead citizens to be less worried about even lethal punishments by
government than they are about other governmental powers.

But there is a powerful contradiction in American culture because our
fear of government and due process tradition is also strong, as powerful a
tradition of distrust as that found anywhere in the world. So we distrust
government power, yet allow its maximum use. That contradiction is why
executions generate ambivalence and conflict. The prospect of not being
able to execute makes citizens angry, while executions themselves make
some of the same citizens worry about arbitrary and erroneous government power. The American ambivalence about executions is a product of
contradictory impulses about limits on governmental power.

The last section of this book documents the pattern of increasing conflict about executions in the United States a quarter-century after the U.S.
Supreme Court allowed their reintroduction in 1976. The contradiction
between due process values and the demand for executions grows more
problematic with every new year. The United States suffers domestic ambivalence about executions and is beset by a community of developed nations that regards executions as moral depravity. There is a defensive quality
to the justifications our politicians put forth in support of killing as criminal punishment. And there is no strong sense in current affairs that those
who support executions occupy any moral high ground in the debate over
capital punishment.

There are indications that the end game for the death penalty in the United
States has begun. Escalating domestic conflict and international hostility together guarantee that the execution of criminals will not become a routine
activity of American government. Tomorrow's elections and next week's
judicial appointments can bring the end of the death penalty in the United
States ten years closer or push it further away. But it will take abrupt and
regressive changes in both American political development and in the inter-
dependence of developed nations to rescue American executioners from the
permanent retirement that is now a generation overdue.

Acknowledgments

THIS VENTURE needed and received help from a staggering variety of people. Dedi Felman of Oxford University Press served as the agent provocateur of this project. Financial support came from the Boalt Hall Fund and the Criminal Justice Research Program of the Earl Warren Legal Institute. The principal research assistants were Monica Swanson and Tom Clifford. Amanda Packel, the Young Scholar in the Institute during 2002, helped to rehabilitate the book's references and edit the text. Toni Mendicino supervised the preparation of the manuscript. As the project encountered different needs in subfields of social science, I benefited from the wisdom of many colleagues. Robert Kagan and Jack Citron were guides to the political science of trust in government. Phoebe Ellsworth, Sam Gross, Merrill Shanks, David Sheaves, Tom Smith, Lois Timms-Ferrara, and Patricia Vanderwald provided help in the many adventures I had with survey research. Lawrence Friedman, Mark Leff, Harry Scheiber, and Tony Freyer provided historical guidance.

Several colleagues provided critical readings of the entire manuscript: Dedi Felman, Lawrence Friedman, David Garland, Sam Kamin, Deborah Leff, Mark Leff, and Robert Weisberg all read versions of the book and each provided important help in its improvement. Cristina de Maglie, José Luis Díez Ripollés, Jeffrey Fagan, Roger Hood, David Johnson, Michael Laurence, James Liebman, Norval Morris, and Eric Prokosch read and reacted to pieces of the manuscript as it was being written.

The Contradictions of
American Capital Punishment

I

DIVERGENT TRENDS

THIS INTRODUCTORY SECTION tells the story of the profound changes in perception and policy that have created the conflict between the United States and the rest of the developed West on the question of capital punishment. Chapter 1 provides a short description of recent activity in the United States, producing a snapshot of policies and the policy conflicts about capital punishment at the turn of the twenty-first century. Chapter 2 provides a longer account of the changes in death penalty policy in Europe over the period since the end of World War II. An important part of the current difference in outlook between Europe and the United States results from dramatic changes in the European view of the death penalty that have emerged only since the 1980s. How and why did capital punishment become a human rights question? Why do our friends and neighbors in the developed West now regard American capital punishment as fundamentally uncivilized? What can the recent history in Europe tell us about the potential for change in the United States?

Chapter 3 profiles the changing imagery of the death penalty since 1980 in the United States, searching for clues to explain why the policies in the United States differ by examining the way in which Americans talk to each other about the death penalty. Of particular importance in this search for explanations of current U.S. policy is the shift in images of executions from a governmental act to a service program for homicide survivors, a degovernmentalization of the execution that has been the most dramatic change in the popular imagery of capital punishment. The changes documented in Chapter 3 provide a basis for speculating about what differences in culture, temperament, and history make this new image of capital punishment in the United States more acceptable to public opinion.

1

The Peculiar Present of American Capital Punishment

THE UNITED STATES GOVERNMENT was about to make history in the spring of 2001, and it looked like a public relations bonanza for capital punishment. The pending execution of Timothy McVeigh seemed like an ideal case to launch a program of lethal injections as criminal punishment by the national government of the United States. The McVeigh case combined a terrible crime with a defiantly guilty defendant and none of the problems of discrimination and uncertainty that bedevil most executions. McVeigh had detonated the bomb that killed 168 occupants of the Oklahoma City Federal Building in 1995. The defendant had planned to kill hundreds of people he did not know to express his anger at the U.S. government's behavior two years before in Waco, Texas. He was adequately defended at trial by a team of competent lawyers, at a cost to government that exceeded 100 times what states such as Texas and Virginia pay for defense services in death cases. McVeigh had publicly acknowledged his guilt and moved up the date of his execution by abandoning legal appeals, thus providing a grateful federal government with a mass murderer of women and children for the first federal execution since 1963. Even better, this defendant was not retarded and was not a member of a disadvantaged minority.

By May 2001 there had been more than 700 executions since the U.S. Supreme Court allowed the death penalty back on American soil, but no other condemned criminal had presented credentials of this caliber for a feel-good execution, for a triumphant reaffirmation that government killing can be a good thing. There was unprecedented media attention not only throughout the United States but around the world. Perhaps executing the monster of Oklahoma City might even silence some of our foreign critics?

But then things started going wrong. Four days prior to McVeigh's scheduled execution date in May, the Federal Bureau of Investigation announced that it had just discovered several thousand pages of investigative documents of the kind that the government had promised to give to the defense before trial. An embarrassed Attorney General of the United States postponed the execution on his own initiative from May 17 to June 11, to give the defense lawyers time to review the newly discovered material. The media reported that this three and a half week delay created an overwhelming sense of anticlimax for the victims' families (whose psychological well-being was supposed to be a major reason for the execution) as well as for the media and the public. When the McVeigh defense team requested a longer delay in the execution to allow more review of the mishandled documents, the government refused to cooperate because there was no doubt of the condemned man's guilt. But why then the original delay in a case where the defendant had confessed in out-of-court statements? Why put the victims through one more emotional roller-coaster ride? The rescheduled lethal injection occurred on June 11, 2001. Ambivalence and a sense of anticlimax had infected even this exemplary execution.

A Matter of Timing

One accident of timing occasioned by the delay in Timothy McVeigh's execution concerned the travel schedule of the new U.S. President George W. Bush, whose first presidential tour of Europe began on June 13, 2001. The president's policy agenda on this trip would not add to his popularity in any of the capitals he visited: He was announcing that the United States would proceed with its own missile defense system despite objections on the continent, and he still opposed the Kyoto Treaty to control global warming that was supported by every major government in Europe. So demonstrations in the streets of London and Stockholm could be expected during the Bush tour. But the leading complaint on placards and in the streets in June 2001 was not global warming or missile defense or any other item on Mr. Bush's international agenda. It was capital punishment in the United States. And executions in America were condemned not only by street demonstrators but by the European governmental leadership. It was a matter of unfortunate timing that an American president was touring Europe that June, just after the American national government conducted its first execution in thirty-eight years.

For most European critics, however, the problem created by the execution of Timothy McVeigh was that it happened not in the wrong month but in the wrong century. By 2001, the United States and the developed nations of Europe and the former Commonwealth nations were further apart on the question of state executions than on any other issue. What the Council of Europe regarded as an option that should be forbidden to any civilized nation was the official policy of the national government of the United States and thirty-eight of its fifty states.

As we see below, the huge gulf that separates the United States and other Western nations at the turn of the twenty-first century is of very recent origin. Up until the 1970s, emerging policy trends toward capital punishment seemed similar throughout the developed world, and the United States did not seem out of step with the general trend. In the quarter-century after 1975, however, policy in both the United States and the rest of the developed West has been changing rapidly and in opposite directions.

The Singular American Present

At the beginning of the twenty-first century, the position of the United States on the law and practice of capital punishment is singular. Alone among the Western democracies, state governments in the United States authorize and conduct executions as criminal punishment and show no clear indication of a willingness to stop doing so. Alone among nations with strong traditions of due process in criminal procedure, criminal justice systems in the United States attempt to merge a system of extensive procedures and review with execution as a legal outcome. It has been an impossible task. The result has been a frustrating and lengthy process that combines all of the disadvantages of procedural regularity with unprincipled and arbitrary outcomes.

For much of the modern era, policy trends in the United States did not contradict the drift toward abolition in other developed nations. During the first half of the period after World War II, executions in the United States declined in much the same pattern found after World War II in Europe and the British Commonwealth and profiled in Chapter 2. Figure 1.1 profiles executions over time in the United States by year, combining execution totals from all states conducting them into a national aggregate. Between 1950 and 1965, executions steadily diminished from over a hundred a year to under ten.

By 1967, federal courts had imposed a prohibition on execution so that a series of challenges to the principles and procedures of capital punishment could be decided. The nationwide judicial moratorium on executions would last a decade. During the 1970s, the U.S. Supreme Court would first tiptoe to the brink of judicial abolition of capital punishment in 1972—when *Furman v. Georgia* invalidated all death penalty statutes that were then in effect—and then pull back, allowing states to administer somewhat more structured regimes of capital punishment in a series of decisions issued in 1976: *Gregg v. Georgia, Roberts v. Louisiana, Proffitt v. Florida,* and *Jurek v. Texas.*

All of the divergent elements of American policy that are evident in current international comparisons are based on changes in policy in the United States that have occurred since those 1976 Supreme Court decisions. While the rest of the Western world has been creating and attempting to enforce nonexecution as a human rights orthodoxy, the policy of the national government in the United States has shifted to the toleration of capital punishment by the states, and a series of capital crimes have been added by the federal Congress for the limited jurisdiction of the federal government. The result of these shifts in policy is reflected in the trends in the number of executions by year since 1977 displayed on the right-hand side of Figure 1.1.

Change or Regression?

By the year 2000 the volume of executions by American states had bounced back to levels quite close to those experienced during the early 1950s. The crude visual impression of Figure 1.1 is thus of an almost symmetrical policy pattern in the United States, with declines to zero in the first half of the postwar period and a return to a level of execution in the late 1990s quite close to the historical pattern of fifty years before. Was this just a return to the capital punishment policy of an earlier era?

There is a kernel of truth to the visual appearance of decline followed by return to a previous equilibrium, but the symmetrical national aggregate pattern over time since 1950 conveys two false impressions. In the first place, aggregate criminal execution levels for the United States as a whole

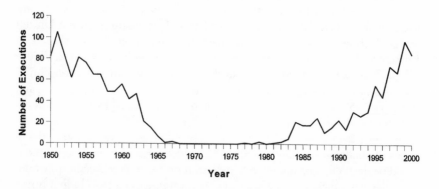

Figure 1.1. U.S. executions by year, 1950–2000. *Source*: U.S. Department of Justice, Bureau of Justice Statistics. Available at http://www.ojp.usdoj.gov/bjs.glance/tables/exetab.htm.

hide the enormous variations among regions and individual states that are one of the chief characteristics of American capital punishment. Twelve of the fifty United States provide no death penalty in their criminal statutes, and several other states have conducted no executions. South Dakota and New Hampshire are death penalty states that have executed no one in over half a century. The populous state of New Jersey legislated a death penalty in 1980 that has not produced an execution in its first two decades (Death Penalty Information Center 2002).

Several states in the American South are at the other extreme in the distribution of American executions. In the year 2000, for example, seventy-six of the eighty-five executions in the United States (89 percent of the total) were in the South, even though that region accounts for about one-third of the United States population and about 40 percent of the American states that authorize a death penalty. During the year 2000, two-thirds of all American executions were conducted in just three of the thirty-eight American states that authorize executions: Texas, Oklahoma, and Virginia. The state of Texas alone executes more people (forty in 2000) in an average year than had been executed in the quarter of a century after 1977 in the four most populous northern states that have experienced any executions: California (8), Pennsylvania (3), Illinois (12), and Ohio (1) (Death Penalty Information Center 2002).

With variations in death penalty policy within the United States that are enormous, there is no single "American pattern" to be represented in aggregate statistics. Appreciating the absence of a single national profile is the first step in understanding the causes and meanings of variation between the states.

A Different System

The second respect in which the similarity in numbers of executions between the 1950s and the late 1990s is misleading is that the capital punishment systems that produced these similar numbers of executions in the 1980s and 1990s had changed drastically from the systems that were functioning in the United States in the 1950s. The total population of condemned prisoners awaiting execution in the United States in 1953 was 131, compared with a total of sixty-two executions that year. The population on death row was thus about twice the annual total of executions. In the year 2000, by contrast, the eighty-five persons executed were drawn from a population of persons under sentence of death that exceeded 3500—more than forty condemned prisoners for every execution. Figure 1.2 shows the pattern for persons under death sentence and execution since 1953.

The current circumstances of capital punishment in the United States are distinguished from earlier eras by huge death row populations, very long delays between the sentence of death and the earliest that an execution might

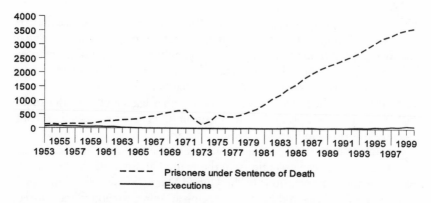

Figure 1.2. Prisoners under sentence of death and executions, by year, United States 1953–2000. *Source*: U.S. Department of Justice, Bureau of Justice Statistics, available at http://www.ojp.usdoj.gov/bjs/glance/tables/exetab.htm and http://www.ojp.usdoj.gov/bjs/glance/tables/drtab.htm.

occur, and a relatively small likelihood at current rates that a particular death sentence will lead to an execution.

The very high ratio of condemned prisoners to executions in many states—200 to 1 rather than the 40 to 1 in many northern jurisdictions—has meant that there is no longer a clear and proximate relationship between death sentences and executions. Being sentenced to death is, in most states north of the Mason-Dixon line, one modest step in a process that will produce a palpable risk of execution only after the passage of many years and several further legal contingencies. As later chapters of this book show, the variation between states in the risk that a death sentence will result in an execution is often vast.

The delay and uncertainty of the current system have produced anger and frustration. About seven in every ten death sentences are estimated to be invalidated by appellate review in the state or federal court (Liebman et al. 2000), but these aggregate figures again hide wide variation among American states. Some states reverse eight out of every ten death sentences on appeal, while other states affirm eight out of ten. And the current system of American capital punishment seems to be hated in equal measure by the opponents of capital punishment systems and by those who support execution but desire more certainty and less delay.

The Legal Framework

The laws and procedures that have produced the high rates of death sentences, the substantial delays, and the variations among states are the product of substantive legal changes put into effect by the U.S. Supreme Court over the past thirty years. This federal constitutional framework is the product of two contrasting precedents of the 1970s and a long series of subsidiary high court decisions.

The U.S. Supreme Court first ruled in 1972 in *Furman v. Georgia* that state laws that delegated to the jury the choice between imprisonment and execution for specific crimes without any clear guidelines were unconstitutional as cruel and unusual punishment in violation of the Eighth Amendment (*Furman v. Georgia*). Four years later, the Supreme Court ruled that legislative standards that provided mandatory death penalties for some types of murder were also unconstitutional (*Roberts v. Louisiana*; *Woodson v. North Carolina*). But in *Gregg v. Georgia*, *Jurek v. Texas*, and *Proffitt v. Florida*, statutes that provided a series of aggravating circumstances in the commission of murders to be weighed by juries against mitigating factors were upheld by the Court as acceptable structures for guiding the jury to choose in individual cases between life and death. Aggravating factors that could allow the consideration of the death penalty included the commission of multiple homicides, homicide committed during other felonies, torture, and contract killings. Mitigating circumstances that could allow juries and judges to choose imprisonment rather than death included youth, mental and emotional disturbance, and other factors.

The result of this search for guided discretion was a patchwork of decisions in the 1970s and 1980s on a wide variety of topics in which some rules were clear and others decidedly vague. States were allowed substantial variations in the circumstances that they could select to aggravate and mitigate murders, but the ultimate standards were always matters of federal law, and the ultimate judgment was that of federal courts.

The problem with approving the results in both the 1972 decision of *Furman v. Georgia* and the 1976 approval of guided discretion in the *Gregg v. Georgia* decision is that there are no observable differences between outcomes in the "standardless" discretion disapproved of in *Furman* and the "guided discretion" upheld in *Gregg*. It is much easier to support the result in one case or the other than to approve of both, but both decisions remain precedent and jointly have determined the course of the constitutional law of capital punishment.

One result of the decisions in *Furman* and *Gregg* was that federal courts became the ultimate authority on what circumstances and procedures could be used by the states in death cases. Whereas the Supreme Court of the United States had only rarely reviewed state death sentences in the century before the *Furman* decision in 1972, the substantive law and procedure in state death cases became the most frequent business of that court in the two decades after 1976.

But death penalty jurisprudence was not a specialization that Supreme Court justices welcomed. Most of the justices who heard cases in the last quarter of the twentieth century disliked administering a detailed code of constitutional standards for death cases and particularly resented serving as a last resort for appeals lodged by prisoners on the eve of execution. In the early 1980s the Supreme Court launched a campaign to loosen the links between federal constitutional law and the administration of the death penalty by the states, a judicial program that one scholar labeled "deregulating death" (Weisberg 1983).

To some extent, the easing of federal control over state capital punishment came from a loosening of the substantive rules that govern who could permissibly be executed. For the most part, however, the Supreme Court has loosened its controls over the capital punishment process by requiring clear evidence that constitutional errors have prejudiced a defendant before it will reverse death sentences and instituting or approving procedural limits on how, when, and how often persons sentenced to death could raise legal objections. The U.S. Supreme Court remains the primary architect of the constitutional law of capital punishment, but most of the justices on that court have no enthusiasm for law making in capital cases.

Public Sentiment

Public opinion about capital punishment is both complicated and ambivalent. Public attitudes toward the death penalty vary not only over time, but also on what sort of question is being asked. As a matter of principle, the American public believes that death is an appropriate penalty for murder, but the average citizen neither trusts nor supports the system that determines who shall be executed.

Figure 1.3 charts the changes over time in the proportion of respondents who support the death penalty for murder. I use available Gallup poll responses to the same question at five-year intervals, but substitute the closest available date in the mid-1990s and early 1950s where the question was not reported for the anniversary year.

The trend over time was a decline from the early 1950s to the mid-1960s, followed by an increase in public support that reaches two-thirds after the U.S. Supreme Court put the validity of the penalty in doubt in the 1972 *Furman* opinions. After a decade at two-thirds, the Gallup majority climbs during the 1980s, peaks at 80 percent in the mid-1990s and falls back to 65 percent at the turn of the century.

But it is not public support for the death penalty that separates the United States from nations that abolish the death penalty. The level of public support for capital punishment in the United States in 2001 was no greater than it was in democracies such as Great Britain, Germany, and Canada at the time that death penalties were abolished (Zimring and Hawkins 1986, pp. 12–15, 21). Indeed, a 1975 opinion poll in Great Britain found 82 percent in favor of a death penalty that had been abolished in 1965, yet that

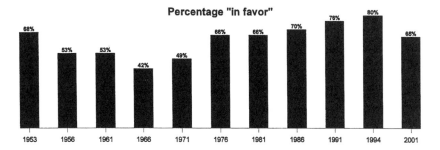

Figure 1.3. Trends in responses to "Are you in favor of the death penalty for a person convicted of murder?" from Gallup Polls. *Source*: The Gallup Organization, available at http://www.gallup.com/poll/topics/death_pen.asp.

level of public opposition did not produce a reversal in policy in any of the democracies that ended the death penalty. In European and Common-wealth democracies, the public seems to give in grudgingly to its leadership when the arithmetic of opinion polls would normally spell trouble.

American public opinion as measured in surveys that report support for a death penalty is typical of public opinion in developed nations just prior to or just after a suspension of executions, so that the poll numbers cannot explain why American policy has taken its exceptional course. If American support for the death penalty turns out to be distinctive, it is in the intensity with which people identify with the death penalty rather than in the proportion of respondents who express support.

Regional Patterns

There is one other respect in which the general poll support for a death penalty does not seem closely linked to the likelihood of governmental action. The difference between levels of execution in the South and else-where is vast, but there is no parallel increase in support when the regional pattern of public support is examined, as seen in Figure 1.4.

Public support for the death penalty is spread fairly evenly across regions. By contrast, executions are clustered in the South but are rare events in the Northeast. So two regions with similar levels of public support for death penalties—the South and Northeast—have levels of execution that vary in the first twenty-five years of the modern execution era by more than 100 to 1. There does not appear to be any close link between the breadth of public support for capital punishment and the use of capital punishment by region. Again, there is very little public opinion research on the intensity of feeling behind survey answers. Much more is known about the breadth of public support than about its depth.

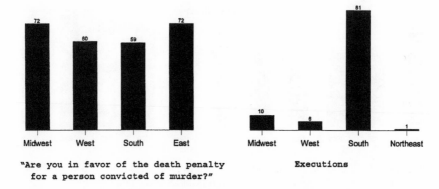

"Are you in favor of the death penalty
for a person convicted of murder?"

Executions

Figure 1.4. Regional patterns of public support for the death penalty, 2001, and number of executions, 1977–2000. *Sources*: U.S. Department of Justice, Bureau of Justice Statistics (executions) and the Gallup Organization, cross-tabulation of May 10–14, 2001, poll, question 19 by region.

The Dynamics of Ambivalence

When survey research shifts from "yes or no" items on the death penalty to more detailed questions, the average citizen who responds to surveys appears both ambivalent and concerned. An ABC/*Washington Post* poll released in May 2001 reported that 63 percent of the respondents supported the death penalty "when no other option is presented" (Langer 2001). When questioned about those aspects of U.S. capital punishment that pleased or concerned them, respondents selected the four sentiments profiled in Figure 1.5 more frequently than any others.

More than seven out of ten respondents regard the removal of the threat that "the killer might kill again" as an important benefit of the death penalty, but 68 percent regret that the current system results in "mistaken executions." More than six of ten respondents are concerned about the jurisdictional differences in death sentences and executions, but six of ten also think the system provides "closure." This set of profoundly mixed feelings about the death penalty suggests that public responses to death penalty surveys might vary importantly by the context and the wording of questions.

In the ABC News/*Washington Post* poll that reported that 63 percent supported the death penalty, the sample also supported a "national moratorium on the death penalty while a commission studies whether it has been administered unfairly" by a margin of 51 percent in favor to 43 percent opposed. So a majority of the sample supports the penalty of death, but a smaller majority wishes to stop executing while the system is studied. Again, how one asks the question has major influence on levels of public support. The Gallup organization reported in April 2001 that "the public's

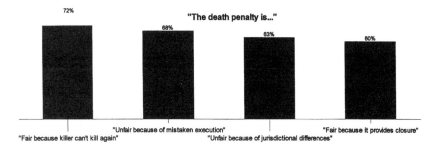

Figure 1.5. Public sentiments on capital punishment, 2001. *Source*: ABC News/ *Washington Post* poll, April 2001; available at http://abcnews.go.com/sections/us/ DailyNews/poll010504_deathpenalty.html.

support for a moratorium ranges between 53% and 42% depending on exactly how the concept is presented to them" (Jones 2001).

A second method of fine-tuning public sentiments is the effort to compare the public attitude toward death penalties with its view of legislation that would substitute life imprisonment without possibility of parole. This tactic produces an even split in public sentiment rather than the 63 percent who support the death penalty when there is no reference to a "life without parole" alternative (Langer 2001).

The phenomenon of mixed feelings itself is more significant than the way that public opinion divides on specific proposals such as life without possibility of parole or a death penalty moratorium. The death penalty appears to be a more important part of public life in the early years of the twenty-first century than in earlier eras, and more discomfiting as well. This pattern of public ambivalence may reflect a deeper conflict between cultural traditions that makes the question of capital punishment a special struggle on American soil.

Four Key Questions

This book is an attempt to answer four related questions about the character of American policy toward capital punishment.

1. Why did the United States reintroduce the death penalty after 1976 when the trend in most other developed democracies was to abolish the penalty as a matter of domestic policy and to press for the prohibition of capital punishment in all civilized nations?
2. What explains the many peculiar patterns of death penalties and executions that have emerged in the United States?

3. Why have the conflicts over the death penalty in the United States intensified rather than abated in the 1990s and at the turn of the twenty-first century?
4. How might the conflicts about the death penalty get resolved in the proximate American future?

Each of these questions is distinct from the other questions in the sequence. But finding a satisfactory answer to each question on this list also provides information essential for answering all of the other questions. So the aim of the book is to provide answers to all four questions and to use the different levels of analysis involved in considering each question to build toward a comprehensive vision of the special status of the death penalty in the United States.

Comparing the patterns of recent history in Europe and the Commonwealth with that in the United States provides a very important window into the question of why the United States is different. Without a strong sense of the pattern and the perceptions in other nations, we cannot identify what has been distinctive in recent American experience. So the second chapter of the book launches the study by providing a synthesis of the reasons why the death penalty ended in Western Europe and then throughout the Western developed nations and the rest of Europe.

Chapter 3 then compares the changing images of capital punishment in the United States since 1975 with the prior imagery of the death penalty in the country and with the images of execution in other nations. I find a degovernmentalization of the image of death penalties and executions in the United States, that is, an attempt to reimagine executions as a service that the government provides to the relatives of crime victims rather than as a manifestation of the power of the state. This becomes powerful, if indirect, evidence of how support for the death penalty can be protected in a political environment where government power is distrusted.

The second section of this book explicitly addresses the first and second basic puzzles of American capital punishment policy: American difference and the peculiar patterns of death sentences and executions. Chapter 4 shows the influence of the federal system on state power in death cases and the huge variation in execution rates that have been produced in the first quarter-century of reintroduced capital punishment. Chapter 5 uses the extraordinary patterns of execution in the United States as evidence that the cultural values that support executions are particularly strong in the American South and Southwest and particularly weak in the far North-central and Northeastern United States. These patterns demonstrate that executions are concentrated where the vigilante tradition is most respected. In Chapter 6, I present a model in which values of distrust of government and belief in due process protections (which are popular throughout the United States) are in constant conflict with a cluster of vigilante values also rooted in American culture but more concentrated in the South and Southwest. I construct a theory of death penalty policy as a high-conflict topic where inconsistent due process and vigilante sentiments pull the same citizens in different directions.

The final section of the book addresses the third and fourth key questions on American death policy: the chronicity of conflict and the prospects for future resolution. Chapter 7 shows how the conflicts between vigilante and due process values are reflected in the contradictory reform trends of the 1990s. Until these basic value clashes can be resolved, the conflict over the death penalty will not quiet down. Instead, as the rate of execution has increased, so has the public importance of the conflict over the death penalty.

Chapter 8 outlines some of the implications of my high-conflict model for American capital punishment policy over the long run. The end of capital punishment will be more important as well as harder to achieve because of the conflict of values that lies behind the death penalty debate. One of the two value traditions that collide in the death penalty arena must lose its hold on popular opinion before the angry conflicts over the death penalty will calm down. It will be very difficult to abolish executions in the United States without acrimony; it will be impossible to continue executing without provoking conflict. In essence, the country itself needs to change before controversy about capital punishment will cease to be a source of chronic societal friction.

2

More Than a Trend: Abolition in the Developed Nations

IN SEPTEMBER 1977, Hamida Djandoubi was led to his death by guillotine in southern France and so became an important figure in the history of modern Europe. His place in history was not a function of the enormity of his crime. Mr. Djandoubi was a Tunisian agricultural worker who had been convicted of murdering a female acquaintance, a garden-variety homicide in any nation. What set his execution apart, however, was that it was to be the last state execution in Western Europe in the twentieth century and perhaps for all time (Forst 1999, p. 112).

When compared with the recent events in the United States, the events in the other developed democracies in the last quarter of the twentieth century are remarkable in two respects. The first is that as recently as the late 1970s, the situation in the other developed democracies was not much different from conditions in the United States. In 1977, only one person was executed in the United States: Gary Gilmore became the first offender put to death in a decade. But that same year, France beheaded two homicide offenders.

As similar as conditions may have seemed in 1977, the second remarkable aspect of recent history is the great gap that now separates the United States and Europe in action and in ideology about capital punishment. One reason for the current difference between Europe and the United States on the death penalty is the enormous distance the Europeans have traveled in their views on the death penalty as a political issue. Until 1949, all the major powers in Europe had death penalties in their statute books and executions in their prisons. As recently as twenty-five years ago, death penalty policy was regarded in Europe as the prerogative of national governments, with no international pressures to conform to an abolitionist standard. By the year 2000, however, the death penalty had become a human rights matter of high import. This chapter tells the story of that change.

The last half of the twentieth century was a period when Western Europe experienced two great transitions in death penalty policy. The first twenty-five years after the conclusion of World War II was a period in which the nations in Western Europe and several in the British Commonwealth suspended and then abolished executions. This process was almost exclusively a matter of the internal politics of each nation without any international organization or government-to-government pressure animating the change in policy.

It was only in the last decades of the century that multinational organizations in Europe and a strong normative human rights emphasis came to play a major role in death penalty decisions in Central and Eastern Europe. This second transition accounts for the title of this chapter. Only quite recently has the abolition of capital punishment become more than a trend in government policy. A stand against capital punishment is now an orthodoxy in Europe and most Commonwealth nations, a moral imperative believed necessary to the status of any civilized modern state, and this morality is exported to other nations with missionary vigor.

The Decline of Capital Punishment in Developed Nations

Until rather recently, the penalty of death was a universal feature of criminal justice. Students of European ideas and institutions usually credit Cesare Beccaria's *Crimes and Punishments*, published in 1764, as the first detailed and influential criticism of capital punishment that expressly called for its abolition. The death penalty according to Beccaria was ". . . the war of a nation against a citizen. . . . It appears absurd to me that the laws, which are the expression of the public will and which detest and punish homicide, commit murder themselves, and in order to dissuade citizens from assassination, commit public assassination" (Beccaria 1764, pp. 48, 51).

Capital punishment was only one of many topics addressed in Beccaria's essay, but the focus on the capital sanction as a special area of concern and the forceful objection to its brutality attracted the attention of intellectuals and reformers in many places. By late in the eighteenth century, a variety of reform proposals directed at reducing death sentences had been introduced in Europe and in the United States (Zimring and Hawkins 1986, p. 12). A long, slow, and uneven decline in executions was in progress, but the actual abolition of capital punishment did not begin until the 1860s. By the end of the nineteenth century, however, five nations in Europe had ceased to conduct executions for nonmilitary offenses, but only three of these—Portugal, the Netherlands, and Italy—had formally abolished the penalty for ordinary crimes. Even before Portugal became the first Western European nation to abolish the death penalty in 1867, three states in the United States had ended the penalty by legislation at least a decade earlier: Michigan (1846), Rhode Island (1852), and Wisconsin (1853) (Hood 1997, p. 518).

In most developed nations, while the campaigns of the nineteenth century had established the death penalty as a punishment of special concern, both the penalty of death and at least occasional executions survived into the 1950s. The recently united Italy abolished its death penalty for ordinary crimes in 1889 but reinstated it in 1926. Norway abolished its death penalty in 1905, and Sweden and Denmark rendered Scandinavia a center of abolition by 1933 (Amnesty International reports). But the major European powers did not follow suit.

Still, the death penalty had become an exceptional punishment in all Western democracies by the start of the twentieth century, reserved for only the most serious of offenses, rarely imposed, and regarded as particularly problematic. In all the developed nations, other methods of punishment had replaced the executioner as the principal punishment for serious offenses. Executions remained a symbolically important extreme punishment, available for crimes of the order of treason and murder, but they had become rare and troublesome events in the conduct of criminal justice in developed democracies.

While the number of executions in Western democracies was declining in the first half of the twentieth century, the European total of executions probably increased substantially after 1925. In Europe, fascist and communist regimes in Germany and the Soviet Union used the penalty of death with promiscuous enthusiasm. Spain, Italy, and Portugal were minor players in this resurgence of state violence by comparison with Stalin and Hitler. But any less dramatic competition would consider these regimes serious retrogressions. Often, state killings in totalitarian regimes did not involve even the pretense of judicial process.

An important fact in the arithmetic of capital punishment is that one totalitarian state the size of the Soviet Union in the 1930s could execute more persons in one year than all of nonfascist Western Europe would sentence to death in a century. The division of Europe in the 1930s into totalitarian and nontotalitarian camps almost certainly increased the gross number of executions in that region many-fold. But this explosion of lethal force carried the seeds of its own demise. The summary executions and death camps of the first half of the twentieth century may have made both the symbol and practice of execution less palatable to democratic governments in the second half of the century.

The Postwar Years

For Western Europe and the nations of the British Commonwealth, the end of the Second World War also marked the beginning of the end of executions as a legitimate tool of democratic government. The first major nations to abolish capital punishment were the successor regimes to nations defeated on the battlefield. Italy had first abolished capital punishment in 1892 and halted executions again in 1944, shortly after the summary execution of the dictator who had reestablished an Italian death penalty. The Constitution of the Federal Republic of Germany of 1949 included a prohibition of capital punishment, and the Austrian government abolished the death penalty for civil offenses in 1950. Two other nations, the Netherlands and Belgium, had ceased to execute long before periods of German occupation but executed a number of wartime collaborators before ending their practice of capital punishment for good. But England and France, the major European powers on the winning side in World War II, kept the death penalties on the books and performed occasional executions for decades after war's end.

There are a variety of reasons why after a war the defeated nations might be quicker to abolish the death penalty than the victors. The losing powers in World War II experienced changes of regime at war's end, and the changing of governments can itself precipitate legal reforms that might take much longer to accomplish in stable governments.

A second potential inducement to rethink the death penalty in the former Axis nations was the experience of occupation, where the power to punish belongs to a foreign government. For Germany, a sustained occupation and the execution of substantial numbers of members of the prior regime as war criminals may have contributed to its policy turn away from capital punishment in the late 1940s. But the character of the previous dictatorship in Germany and Italy must also have played a role in wishing to restrict the power of any government to coerce its citizenry with extreme measures.

The published record available on the abolition of capital punishment leaves ample room for speculation about causes. The best-documented legal change was the German constitutional debate, in which unusual and ad hoc coalitions of interest groups carried the abolition of the death penalty. The Social Democrats on the left were joined by some hard-right elements with different reasons for distrust of a death penalty (Evans 1996). There was not much systematic debate on the issues and little in the debate to suggest that what would later be called human rights concerns played an important role in opposition to the death penalty. Yet that German debate took place less than five years after the most prominent documented use of a policy of mass killing by government against citizens in the history of Western civilization. While death camps and gas chambers did not inform much of the text of German debate, this history is more than likely an important subtext for the first new postwar abolition of capital punishment by a major European power. But if the experience was a motivating element in the enthusiasm of the Social Democrats for abolition, why was this not a topic of discussion?

The British Royal Commission

The British were the first major power of the victorious nations in World War II to give serious attention to the abolition of capital punishment. While the formal abolition of capital punishment in Great Britain was not put into legislation until 1969, the British did create a Royal Commission on Capital Punishment in 1949 that conducted the most thorough analysis of the capital punishment issue in the two decades after the end of the Second World War. The Royal Commission's report, in its own understated fashion, was the launching pad for rethinking capital punishment throughout the developed world.

The beginning of the British Commission of Inquiry on Capital Punishment came late in the five-year-long postwar labor government, famous for radical innovations such as the National Health Service and the foundational planning for the modern welfare state. An earlier effort in the Labor Party to suspend executions in 1947 had almost succeeded, and the Royal Commission was seen as buying time for a government that was sharply divided on the death penalty and in political trouble as well (Christoph 1962, chap. 3).

Measured against such major innovations as the national health system and the welfare state, the terms of reference of the Commission on Capital Punishment seem timid and confining. The commission was asked to consider "whether the liability under the criminal law in Great Britain to suffer capital punishment for murder should be limited or modified, and if so, to what extent, and by what means" (Royal Commission on Capital Punishment, p. iii). The commission's long, detailed, and meticulous 1953 report was structured wholly within these terms of reference. It contained extensive explorations of the criminal law of homicide, the defense of insanity, and the processes of clemency in Britain to determine whether changing parts of the criminal law of homicide could rationalize the use of the capital sanction. But the commission recognized that these substantive legal adjustments could not have a major impact on the death penalty in the middle of the twentieth century because "a stage ha[d] been reached where there is little room for further limitation short of abolition" (Royal Commission on Capital Punishment, p. 212). Unable to find "some practicable half-way house between the present scope of the death penalty and its abolition," the Royal Commission concluded that "the real issue is now whether capital punishment should be retained or abolished" (Royal Commission on Capital Punishment, pp. 212 and 214).

The Royal Commission took no explicit stand on that "real issue," but the tone of the commission's discussion of issues such as deterrence leaves little doubt about the abolitionist sentiments of the authors. The long sections of the report considering the advantages and disadvantages of hanging, electrocution, firing squads, and lethal gas were not intended to be the Royal Commission's gift to posterity. The report contained neither passion nor a forceful statement of the obvious orientation of the commission but was a document intended to provide a foundation for abolitionist ambitions by indirection.

Some modest reduced punishments for some homicides that had been considered by the commission were passed in 1957 by the Conservative government that had come to power two years prior to the commission's report. The next Labor government to hold power in Great Britain quickly created a five-year suspension of executions (in 1965) and then passed total abolition for civil offenses in 1969. Since a Conservative government was not likely to abolish the death penalty, there is no indication that the circumspection of the Royal Commission in 1953 delayed the end of executions in Great Britain. And the joint impact of the commission and the later abolition in Great Britain hastened the end of the death penalty in Canada and Australia.

The contemporary written record of the consideration of the death penalty during the quarter-century after 1945 is appallingly thin. Because the British Royal Commission report is the only sustained analysis to come out of the period just prior to the end of executions in Western Europe, it becomes necessary to search in its pages for clues to attitudes and rhetoric of death penalty discourse in 1954. In doing this, we should remember both the proabolition bias of the authors and the circumspection that was required both by the status of the report as one written by a Royal Commission and by the fact that the report was to be delivered to a Conservative government.

The Royal Commission as Death Penalty Dialogue

Very little that is present in the Royal Commission report is either surprising or discordant to a modern reader. The tone is pragmatic, utilitarian, and dispassionate. The data were meticulously gathered and analyzed in a simple and straightforward manner. The sense that the report conveys of the evolution of capital punishment in the administration of the English criminal law is accurate as far as it goes. Few committee reports from the world of 1954 have aged as gracefully in the light of subsequent events as this document.

But what is absent from the report when read with modern eyes is worthy of notice. Hardly anything that can be called "the political aspect" of the death penalty is discussed in this long and comprehensive document. Here was a government that had spent six of the prior fifteen years in mortal combat with Nazi Germany, and the whole of what had been learned from human extermination as government policy was missing from the commission's review of capital punishment. The operating assumption was that Nazi death camps have nothing to do with British criminal justice. The single oblique reference to the German experience found in the report is in its discussion of various forms of execution, where an argument against the use of gas chambers was developed in the following terms: "We must not forget that while hanging is tainted by the memory of its barbarous history, 'gassing' is tainted by more recent but not less barbarous associations" (Royal Commission on Capital Punishment, p. 256).

There was also no discussion of whether any conception of a right to life or any other category of human rights should be regarded as a limit on the execution of criminal offenders. Questions about human rights were not on the map of this comprehensive report.

France and Other Nations

France was the last great power in Europe to abolish the death penalty, with a last execution in 1977 and formal abolition in 1981. The tardiness of the French was not connected either to unusual patterns of public opinion about capital punishment or to any special political status of the death penalty. Instead, it was the long reign of the center-right parties in national politics that delayed abolition. When the left came to power, François Mitterand made the abolition of the death penalty an easy and early priority (Forst 1999, p. 113).

Table 2.1 sets out the dates of abolition of the major European nations to end executions in the three decades after the end of World War II and refers to the political circumstances that explain the timing of abolition in each country.

The major contingencies that separate the English, Portuguese, Spanish, and French over a sixteen-year period are domestic political events that were not caused by the issue of capital punishment. The order of abolition could easily have been reversed by election results or the earlier passing of right-wing dictators.

The Repetitive Pattern

The usual pattern for the end of the death penalty in developed nations over the first three postwar decades was what one commentator called leadership

Table 2.1.

The Timing and Precipitation of Political Circumstances
of Postwar Abolition in Europe

Nation	Date	Precipitating Circumstance
Italy	1944	Fall of Mussolini
West Germany	1949	Constitution for new state
Austria	1950	Socialists join governing coalition
Great Britain	1965[a], 1969[b]	Election of labor government
Portugal	1976	Transition from Salazar regime
Spain	1978	Transition from Franco regime
France	1981	Election of left government

[a]Five-year suspension
[b]Permanent abolition
Source: Compiled from Amnesty International Reports

"from the front" (Buxton 1973, p. 244). The end of the death penalty was engineered by governing elites at a time when public opinion still favored capital punishment for murder. In Germany, 74 percent of the public was in favor of retaining a death penalty for murder at the time the penalty was abolished, and only 21 percent supported abolition (Noelle and Neumann 1967). It took more than two decades after abolition for public opinion to be evenly divided on the issue in Germany, and more than thirty years before the German public supported a nonexecution policy by a 2 to 1 majority. In England, Canada, and Australia, public support for capital punishment for murder was 2 to 1 or better at the time of abolition. Indeed, an English poll found 82 percent in favor of reintroducing the death penalty in 1975, a larger majority than any American poll of the modern era (Gallup 1976, pp. 774, 1462).

Yet the majority opposition to the end of the death penalty in all these nations has not produced any reintroduction of executions. Abolition policies survived "free vote" procedures in Canada and England that were put on the parliamentary agenda when governments of the right succeeded governments of the left after abolition had been put in place (Wicker 1983; Witt 1987). Nowhere in Europe did the return of right-wing parties to power bring back the death penalty. Indeed, nowhere in Europe did the death penalty stay an important political issue for very long after abolition.

When positions supported by 2-to-1 majorities do not reemerge as government policy in a democracy, some explanation is necessary. Part of the story may be that the presence or absence of a death penalty may not be a very important issue to the man in the streets. The guillotine is not what politicians call a "pocketbook issue." Government policy that is contrary to public sentiment may be tolerated when the citizen is not deeply invested in a particular policy outcome.

Ambivalence about executions may also help explain public tolerance for the abolition of capital punishment even when substantial majorities say they want a death penalty to continue. There is a grudging respect for those in government who vote their consciences on death penalty matters, because many members of the public are conflicted and uncertain about the morality of executions. An ambivalent majority that supports a death penalty on the books may not be willing to spend time and treasure to secure an active execution policy. Particularly when the public support for bringing back the hangman lacks both moral leadership and the sanction of majority religious authorities, it is difficult to separate public grumbling from serious discontent. The adjustment to life without execution was swift and uneventful without exception in postwar Europe and in Canada and Australia.

The pattern in Western Europe in the postwar years appears to be a consistent and steady progression from sporadic execution to a continuation of death penalties but without executions to suspension or abolition of the penalty. Once abolition was secured, usually during a government of the left, it survived the reemergence of governments of the right. Through all the years when this pattern was playing out in Western Europe, there was no strong transnational organization participating in or coordinating an international campaign. Each nation considered the issue of the death penalty individually, as if its experience in considering the end of executions was unique and not part of a larger pattern. The momentum of all the other abolitions in Europe was not a major feature of the death penalty debate in any country in Europe except France, the last in Western Europe to abolish the death penalty.

The Narcissism of National Death Penalty Debate

There were two distinct aspects to the parochialism of the capital punishment issue in the postwar debates. The first was the extent to which each of the major European nations was preoccupied by its own history and experience in discourse about the death penalty. The extraordinarily thorough and well-prepared British Royal Commission did examine evidence submitted to it on the criminal law of murder in other nations and on homicide trends before and after abolition in other places that it thought relevant to discussions about deterrence.

But the political and social ramifications of starting or stopping executions in other nations were not examined, and not merely because this experience might not fit the commission's limited mandate. The British considered their own situation unique. The French discussed the problem of French public opposition to abolition as if this phenomenon was unprecedented in other democratic governments. Each incident of debating the end of a death penalty in a European nation was treated as if it were the first time in world history this reform was being contemplated, as well as the last. Most of the special interests involved in such debates, ranging from police organizations and prosecutors to leagues for penal reform, were national in their scope and in their ambitions. So the larger pattern of the decline of capital punishment in Western Europe was without any coordination or international plan at least until the late 1970s.

The second sense in which the first thirty postwar years of the death penalty reform process was parochial was the lack of any attempt to construct transnational standards of permissible penal conduct. Neither the friends nor the foes of capital punishment made any serious effort to build a position on the death penalty into a larger framework of human rights in either law or moral argument, and there was little effort to extend any principles or results from a national death penalty policy victory beyond the borders of that nation.

The absence of all these features is conspicuous only in retrospect. An international moral or legal standard argument would surely have been regarded as eccentric in the British discussions of the 1950s and 1960s because it was unprecedented. The earlier absence of a rhetoric of human rights seems quite remarkable in the twenty-first century because of the extraordinary changes in the discourse about capital punishment and in the political ambitions of the abolitionists that have been present since the early 1980s. The orthodox belief in current European politics is that the death penalty is fundamentally a question about human rights and the proper limits of government power rather than merely a question of the costs and benefits of a particular punishment. The human rights standard is one that Europeans seek to apply to all nations with any claim to civilization, and the modern goal is no less than the worldwide elimination of the death penalty. All of this developed in earnest only after Western Europe had become what current anti–death penalty groups like to call "an execution-free zone." While much of the rhetoric now enlisted in this cause harkens right back to Beccaria, there is a sharp divergence between the limited and national ambitions of the earlier abolitionists and the global claims of their successors.

There are two different ways to ask questions about the important reframing of the abolitionist movement since the late 1970s. Either one can ask why this new and global set of claims emerged so suddenly after the end of Western Europe's death penalties had been achieved, thus putting the emphasis on the novelty and lack of connection to earlier discourse that the modern movement exhibits. Or one can be astonished that the political and human rights dimensions of the death penalty were repressed for so very long even by those who were seeking to stop executions. This is an issue best considered after some introduction to the orthodox human rights perspective that is the official policy of the Council of Europe at the turn of the twenty-first century.

Change Without Discourse

One final note about the inexorable progress toward abolition in the decades after World War II was the extraordinary contrast between the steady level of political change that took place and the absence of high levels of intellectual discussion on questions about capital punishment policy. In the critical years of political change, there was little excitement and ferment in the abolitionist rhetoric and very little sustained debate between retentionist and abolitionist advocates. In that sense, the absence of a human rights dimension to the case against capital punishment was part of a more general intellectual torpor that afflicted both sides of the death penalty debate in the developed world. The issues on both sides of the public debate were the same after the war as before it. The inventory of arguments had an almost tired familiarity, and there was almost no detailed debate on the subject except in legislative settings where proposals were on the table.

It was as if the terms of the debate on the death penalty had been determined long before the fact of final legislative action, so that the intellectual debate had been conducted by a generation older than the leadership that finally changed legal policy in Western Europe. In the entire postwar generation, there was only the British Royal Commission and two international surveys. It was an era of change without discourse, a time when it may have seemed that there was nothing new to be said on this topic, no fresh perspective available to revive interest in this most extreme of punishments. All the more surprising, then, would be the sharp shift in orientation and the renewal of interest in the politics of abolition of the death penalty that closely followed the abolition of the death penalty in France in 1981.

Europe's Great Transformation

June 2001 was an eventful time in the modern history of capital punishment. It was the month in which the national government of the United States conducted its first two executions after thirty-eight years and it was the time of the first World Congress against the death penalty, hosted by the Council of Europe in Strasbourg, France, the headquarters of this official multinational body. The executions of Timothy McVeigh and Juan Garza in Indiana were in direct opposition to the three days of speeches and press conferences in Strasbourg on the desirability of capital punishment. But they shared one important feature: Both were acts of government.

How does it happen that the Council of European states in its official capacity creates an international pep rally to condemn executions by governments anywhere in the world? The mandate to hold that kind of congress flows directly from what I call the "orthodox position" on capital punishment that is the consensus policy of all Western European governments. There are three elements at the core of the orthodox position:

1. The question of capital punishment is fundamentally a matter of human rights, not an isolated issue of criminal justice policy.
2. For that reason, policy on the death penalty should not be governed by national prerogatives but by adherence to international human rights minimum standards.
3. Since there is no case where capital punishment can be justified under the international human rights standard, European citizens, organizations, and governments are fully justified in demanding the end of all executions by all governments.

This orthodoxy was stated with great economy in a joint "appeal" signed by the presidents of nine national parliaments to be released during the Strasbourg conference:

> We, the Presidents of national and international parliaments . . . [a]re convinced that the death penalty is a violation of the most fundamental of human rights—the right to life. . . .Convinced that the worldwide abolition of the death penalty would be a vital contribution to ensuring respect for human dignity and human rights, [w]e call on all States to introduce a worldwide moratorium on executions without delay, and to take steps to abolish the death penalty in their domestic law. (Appeal of Presidents 2001)

I have already mentioned one notable feature of this tripartite orthodox position: No element of it played a part in the domestic process that produced abolition of the death penalty in any of the European states in the 1940s, 1960s, and 1970s. The growth of the human rights position came *after* all the critical battles in the local wars about capital punishment. The newfound faith in the human rights position and its enforcement by the Council of Europe did produce statutory clean-up campaigns in the 1990s, so that in 1998 Great Britain dropped statutes authorizing capital punishment in time of war (Committee on Legal Affairs and Human Rights of the Council of Europe, p. 182) and Belgium, the all-time champion of de facto abolition, was finally persuaded to make its longstanding disuse of the guillotine into official policy (Toussaint 1999, p. 34). But all the heavy lifting had already been done without international organizations or international norms.

The late-blooming international campaign to view the death penalty from a human rights perspective was not so much a product of the struggle to end executions in Western Europe as it was an aftereffect of the triumph of abolition. Why was that?

The Right to Life and the Death Penalty

No international organization of consequence was involved in the various national death penalty debates until Amnesty International in the mid-1970s. Amnesty was novel both as an international association with no primary national headquarters and as an organization centrally concerned with government violation of individual rights. This new organization came to its concerns about capital punishment from a broader engagement with government power and its misuse. Michael Forst, the head of Amnesty International in France, has this retrospective view of the new emphasis at the 1977 conference:

> The conference highlighted the fact that not only was capital punishment used in a great many cases for political ends, but that it was by its nature a political instrument. . . . At the close of the Stockholm conference, Robert Badinter . . . said "Amnesty International's greatest merit is that it does not simply treat the death penalty as though it were a separate issue that could be resolved by abolition, without also mounting a constant and vigorous defence against attacks on fundamental human rights, of which the right to life is but the first." (Forst 1999, p. 111)

The "right to life" that provides the modern human rights linkage to concerns about the death penalty had earlier been the subject of attempts to frame it as a principle that would allow for some state executions. The European Convention on Human Rights, adopted in 1950, begins its second article with a paragraph declaring "that everyone's life shall be protected by law and that no one shall be deprived of his life intentionally, save in the execution of a sentence of a court following his conviction of a crime for which this penalty is provided by law" (Krüger 1999, p. 69).

The political compromise in this first statement of a right to life is obvious: exempt the practice of lawful execution, the major interest that states would seek to protect, in exchange for recognition of a right to life in all other contexts. The problem with that formulation is that it is difficult to derive a general principle or a consistent limit on government in the provenance of a right to life that places no limit on the state's prerogative to take life as a punishment for crime. Each side got a major concession out of the 1950 language. The human rights advocates got a new category of right and a name for it. The defenders of state execution received a categorical exemption for all executions as criminal punishment. What made that categorical exemption potentially vulnerable was the lack of any clear meaning or evident principle in this first approximation of a right to life. Whenever the issue of a right to life would be reexamined, the clash between the announced right and the capital punishment exception was sure to arise.

So the right to life with a general exception for death penalties turned out to be a time bomb in the 1950 statement, but a time bomb with a rather long fuse. The instability in the 1950 version of a right to life provoked a move at the expert level in the Council of Europe to "study the problems of capital punishment in Europe" (Krüger 1999, p. 70). But this did not produce any further movement in the council for twenty-eight years.

Indeed, a similar but more limited death penalty exception to a "right to life" was put forward in 1966 in the United Nations International Covenant on Civil and Political Rights (see Toscano 1999, p. 93) with further conditions attached to exempting executions from the protected scope of a right to life (i.e., when imposed "for the most serious crimes").

The key transition from a right to life that exempts state death penalties to a right to life that condemns state execution was contained in Protocol No. 6 of the European Convention on Human Rights, commissioned in 1982 and "opened for signature" in 1983. The first article of this provision states its mandate without equivocation: "The death penalty shall be abolished. No one shall be condemned to such penalty or executed" (Protocol No. 6 to the Convention for the Protection of Human Rights and Fundamental Freedoms, Concerning the Abolition of the Death Penalty 1983). The only allowed exception in the protocol involves time of war or the imminent threat of war.

At once, the human rights framework was extended to provide for mandatory abolition of death penalties for all of the European nations involved in the Council of Europe. And while every Western European nation had either suspended or abolished the death penalty before 1983, each nation had done so on its own initiative. Protocol No. 6 was an international norm, replacing state sovereignty (for those states that signed it) with an international human rights standard.

And the importance of the shift from viewing the death penalty as a criminal justice issue to regarding it as a human rights matter was not only that an international standard governed those nations that wished to subscribe to it. Once a group of nations agrees that the standards governing the death penalty policy of individual states should be international, this creates the mandate to judge other countries on death penalties, whether or not those other states agree with the standard imposed. So the 1983 protocol provides the foundation for external judgments about the penal policies of other nations. And while this is a proclamation of a transnational body with a jurisdiction limited to Europe, there is no such territorial limit on the human rights standard the protocol announces. The willingness and the ability of the organization to enforce its norms may have territorial limits, but the norms themselves are general and can be applied to states across the Atlantic Ocean just as easily as to those within the territorial boundaries of Europe. From 1983 onward, the potential impact of Protocol No. 6 on the international dialogue about capital punishment was enormous.

The immediate practical impact of the protocol on death penalty policy was minimal because it was preaching to the already converted. Only on the margins of Europe, in Turkey, was the prohibition of the protocol a challenge to a potentially active death penalty in a state with aspirations to join Europe. Other Western states may have delayed signing and ratification because of worry about the precedent of international norms controlling aspects of previous national sovereignty, but there was no nation in Western Europe wishing to execute criminals in 1983.

The practical impact of Protocol No. 6 would explode with the fall of the Iron Curtain and is separately considered in the next section of this chapter. My emphasis here is on the curious fact that the level of intensity of the crusade against the death penalty in Western Europe seems to have increased after its national policy goals had been achieved. What accounts for the fact that the death penalty seems a larger political concern in Europe two decades after the last national abolition than during the decades when the domestic policies of major Western European nations hung in the balance?

Part of the recent enthusiasm in Europe for abolition of the world's death penalties comes as a consequence of the issue being reframed as a human rights issue. Without doubt, the rhetoric of human rights has great appeal to audiences that usually do not concern themselves with criminal justice policy, particularly the criminal justice policy of other nations. But the violation of human rights is a credible basis for becoming involved in the actions of foreign governments. So the emergence of the death penalty as a human rights issue in the 1980s broadened the generality of the abolitionist appeal and made it more attractive to citizens not usually concerned with crime policy.

But if a human rights focus is an explanation of the recent enthusiasm for anti–death penalty activism, that raises questions about the timing and focus of the human rights emphasis in the death penalty discourse in Europe. The first question is why the transformation to human rights terms itself happened so late. The second question is why the death penalty, of all the human rights abuses evident in current events, has become such an important specific topic for human rights advocates. If capital punishment were such an obvious violation of a fundamental human right, why was this not recognized (at least by abolitionists) in the 1950s, 1960s, and 1970s? If the death penalty is not such an obvious encroachment on human rights, why is it now the focus of so much protest and activity among human rights groups?

That death penalties and human rights issues were regarded as separate categories at the close of World War II might be inferred from the widespread use of execution by national and international authorities to deal with war criminals and collaborators. But that might give too much precedential value to the angry aftermath of war and occupation. The historical record does not show any general justification for executions being urged on the basis of the postwar experience in Europe. Most of the national executions were a swift and unprincipled reaction that the Dutch, the Belgians, and the Italians were quite unwilling to use as precedent for any domestic policy. There was little sense of inconsistency in a policy of hanging Mussolini and then abolishing his regime's death penalty.

Only Nuremberg, with its extraordinary creation of crimes against humanity as a category together with its use of executions as a policy tool, might have been used as an argument that human rights and capital punishment could coexist. But the twenty-five years after the end of the war were not a period when the discourse about capital punishment took the human rights category into consideration and then rejected it on principled grounds. Human rights questions simply did not play a role in the debates. And the Nuremberg hangings have not been regarded as an important precedent of execution as an instrument of human rights at any time in the past half-century.

Nor could it be said that the right to life was entirely absent from the early conversations about human rights. The phrase was first used in the Universal Declaration of Human Rights of 1948 and is found in the International Covenant on Civil and Political Rights and United Nations Commissions in the 1960s and 1970s (Toscano 1999, p. 93).

What was missing for almost thirty years was a serious effort to confront the death penalty in Western democracies as a human rights issue. Article 2, paragraph 1, of the 1950 Convention for the Protection of Human Rights and Fundamental Freedoms announced: "No one shall be deprived of his life intentionally save in the execution of a sentence of a court following his conviction of a crime for which this penalty is provided by law" (Ravaud and Trechsel 1999, p. 79). The categorical exemption in the first Council of Nations charter provided a result without any reasoning. The right to life and the legal death penalty were separate entities and did not overlap. The promulgated right could be discussed in human rights dialog but need not be considered in discussions of the death penalty. In that sense, the exemption might be regarded as a jurisdictional arrangement rather than an attempt to create a coherent balance between personal rights and government interests.

The more detailed provisions in the later International Covenant on Civil and Political Rights are even more vulnerable to charges of incoherence. We are presented again with a "right to life," and this time the death penalty it will tolerate is more restricted. It can be imposed only for the most serious crimes, but there is no explicit criterion of necessity. Is this "most serious crimes" requirement a just-deserts limit to a right to life? The death penalty cannot be imposed on those under eighteen at the time of their offenses or on women pregnant at the time of their sentencing. These are important humanitarian provisions, but by what logic can they qualify a right to life, for that is a broader concept which presumably covers nineteen-year-olds, men, and women who are not pregnant?

So the balance struck in various human rights statements was vulnerable to even casual examination. But for decades, nothing of that kind happened. Why did human rights or the right to life not become part of the domestic politics of the death penalty in Great Britain, in Spain, or in France? Was it oversight? Or the political risk such a use would pose to the right to life? Or the risk of a backlash in domestic politics?

The least likely of these possibilities is mere oversight. The proximity of the Second World War and the then well-known genocides of the Third Reich make it hard to believe that simple oversight explains the failure to engage state execution as a human rights problem in the 1950s and 1960s in places such as Britain and France. That every early effort to frame a right to life encountered questions about the death penalty also makes it unlikely that those behind efforts to abolish the death penalty would not notice the nascent language and culture of a human rights claim against government execution. At least for those who desired the abolition of capital punishment in Western Europe, the human rights argument could not be missed by oversight.

It is much more likely that nonabolitionists would fail to see a linkage between human rights and criminal punishment. Those who work in a system that executes will not easily see themselves as violators of human rights. Judges, prosecutors, and police in democracies do not regard themselves as the peers of concentration camp commanders.

There is one instance of a heroic effort to consider the juridical branch of the history of capital punishment as separate from the actions of other parts of the state. When asked to estimate for a United Nations study the number of cases of innocent persons that had been condemned by the state, a German correspondent reported with Teutonic precision in 1960 that twenty-seven such death sentences (and three executions of the innocent) had occurred in the previous century (see Ancel 1962, p. 51). A student of Auschwitz or Buchenwald might think that number an underestimate by several million. Why did that not occur to the German correspondent? Can the tendency to consider separately the formal criminal justice category be that powerful a bureaucratic urge? Or is the psychology of denial necessarily implicated? And when can we impose an interpretation of denial on a record when there is no surface indication of awareness of the problem?

Of course, the German correspondent had a respectable legal argument. For those intent on compartmentalizing, the fact that genocide of Gypsies and Jews was not expressly authorized by law might separate the Nazi horrors from capital punishment in Western criminal law. But why was the effort not made by abolitionists to characterize the failure to involve Nazi atrocities in discussion of state death penalties as denial? How could an emphasis on right-to-life issues hurt the cause?

One possible weakness here might have been the vulnerability of the "right to life" category itself. Perhaps there was worry that the nascent human right could survive neither the scrutiny of skeptics nor the hostility of those tied to the retention of national death penalties. Yet if the appeal to citizens of the right-to-life concept was doubted, have subsequent events not proved the contrary? The right to life has had a spectacular success as an anti–death penalty theme in Western Europe in the 1980s and 1990s. And the popularity of the right to life as a political theme has thrived during its association with ending the death penalty.

But perhaps this association would have been more dangerous prior to abolition. The power and the recentness of the Nazi experience made a charge of governmental human rights violation into an allegation that could provoke anger as well as sincere denial in allied nations such as Britain and France that had long traditions of capital punishment. In the immediate postwar period, the emphasis was on contrasting good and bad governments rather than good and bad acts of government. And the contrast between good and bad governments in the postwar period much resembled a census of winners and losers. There were no war crimes trials of the victors in the Second World War, even though this category included a Soviet regime that had generated world-class horrors on an epic scale for the fifteen years prior to 1945. So whatever international standard had emerged from World War II was neither an obvious nor a neutral principle. And the political risk of asserting that one's government was violating human rights was not necessarily reduced by analogies to fascist regimes that might prove uncomfortably suggestive.

Capital Punishment as a Priority

Yet the political risk attached to using a human rights vocabulary for capital punishment seems to have vanished in Western Europe when the penalty was abolished. What is striking in retrospect about the 1980s is how quickly the death penalty became a focus for human rights activity in the Council of Europe. In a world with more than its share of political prisoners, torture, abuse of ethnic minorities, and suppression of free expression, the problem of state death penalties took a position at center stage as a human rights issue in very short order. What made the death penalty such a compelling target in the aftermath of Western European abolition?

One element that sets capital punishment apart from governmental practices such as torture and the persecution of political critics is that governments openly claim to be justified in conducting executions. Charges of torture and persecution are denied by governments and become the subject of messy factual disputes. Governments with any claim to civilization will not proudly assert the right to torture subjects. But the death penalty is the subject of a claim of right by sovereign states. The issue of the state's right to kill can be joined cleanly where there are such assertions.

There may be another factor at work. Where the question of state execution becomes a priority soon after abolition takes hold in domestic politics, there is also something that resembles the former sinner's repentance
that acknowledges after the fact the wrongness, in this case, of previous
domestic policy. Just as the born-again convert feels it is safe now to acknowledge the sinfulness of prior conduct, the born-again abolitionist regime is free to acknowledge the wrongfulness of actions it used to take.
And the analogy to religious fervor may not be misplaced. By the middle of
the 1990s, there was in human rights circles a passionate commitment to
abolition of the death penalty in many parts of Western Europe, and this
passion too seems to reflect an implicit judgment about prior domestic
policy. What we hear at the turn of the twenty-first century in Western
Europe is that state death penalties are not merely wrong but are very
wrong, the sort of moral issue about which young people should take to
the streets. It is difficult not to hear in this rhetoric the enthusiasm of the
recently converted.

Tomorrow the World?

The last two decades of the twentieth century saw a momentum in both
the international campaign against state executions and in the pace of national abolition of death penalties that is without historical precedent.

Figure 2.1 shows the crude trend in national-level death penalty abolition by tracking the Amnesty International reports on nations that have
abolished the death penalty for all offenses or for what they called "ordinary crimes," from 1980 to 2001. The "ordinary crimes" classification
allows for possible death penalties in military crimes and war circumstances. It is a popular sop to the possibility of reintroduction in emer-
gency circumstances.

The figure begins its story in 1980, two centuries after Beccaria began
the campaign against the death penalty and after every Western European
nation except France, Belgium, and Greece had abolished the death penalty. At that time, a total of thirty-seven nations had put a formal legal end
to capital punishment in their criminal codes. In the next twenty-one years,
the number of abolition states would more than double to a total of eighty-
nine nations. If one adds the twenty other nations not in the figure that
Amnesty classifies as abolitionist de facto because they have not executed
in more than a decade that brings the nonexecution total to 109 nations,
twenty-three more than the eighty-six nations that are listed as retaining a
death penalty and conducting at least one execution within the decade. For
the first time ever, the majority of the world's governments do not execute
any criminal defendants; more nations have abolished the death penalty
than practice it.

As one measure of the recent momentum of abolition, the figure reports that more countries have abolished the death penalty in the twenty-one years after 1980 than in the preceding 200.

While the rate at which nations formally abolish the death penalty has increased swiftly in the aggregate, different regions of the world have very different recent records. The most dramatic pattern of change in the period after 1980 has taken place in Eastern and Central Europe in the aftermath of the end of Soviet hegemony in those regions. By contrast, Asia, the Middle East, and nations governed under strong Muslim influence have shown little tendency to reduce or renounce executions (Hood 1996, pp. 22–26, 31–40).

Central Europe

The fastest and most complete regional abolition in history took place in the twelve states in Central Europe that had been under Soviet domination prior to 1989. Until 1987, all twelve of these states had death penalties for some ordinary crimes. By 1999, all twelve nations had enacted one of the two major varieties of abolition of the death penalty that are chronicled in Figure 2.1, a 100 percent transition in a dozen years. But while the eventual legislative categories were similar for all the former Iron Curtain satellite states, there were two very different patterns of motive for abolition.

The first group of states to abolish the death penalty after the end of the Soviet domination renounced the death penalty quickly and did so as a part

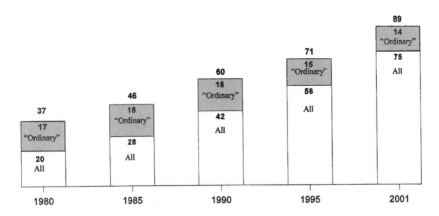

Figure 2.1. The prevalence of death penalty abolition, 1980–2001. "Ordinary" is ordinary crimes; "All" is all crimes. *Sources*: Amnesty International Reports, 1980, 1985, 1990, 1995, and 2001, and see Appendix A.

of drawing free from the previous political domination by the Soviets and
their collaborators. Abolition in Czechoslovakia, Hungary, and Romania
clearly followed this pattern of swift rejection of the policies of a prior
regime.

The penal changes happened very fast in such circumstances. The Romanian story was particularly dramatic because the summary execution of
several members of the Ceausescu family and retinue was swiftly followed
by formal abolition of capital punishment (Hood 1996, p. 17). What might
have seemed like inconsistent attitudes toward the capital sanction were
for those in charge just two emphatic methods of rejecting the Ceausescu
regime. This Romanian behavior just after the fall of the regime was a repeat
of the pattern in Italy after the fall of Mussolini.

Those Central European states that did not immediately abolish their
domestic death penalties just after the Soviet demise became targets for
European pressure to condition membership in the Council of Europe and
possible economic integration with the Western Europeans on abolition
of state death penalties. These incentives played a large role in abolition in
Albania, Bulgaria, Estonia, Latvia, Lithuania, and Poland.

The Central and Eastern European states emerging from Soviet control
were splendid prospects for political pressure and economic incentives from
Europe. Their much weaker economies and the great transitional costs of
emerging from the Soviet era made any economic integration with Western Europe necessary and attractive to all the former satellite nations. The
geographic proximity of Western European states meant that the only major
economies that could replace their previous linkages with the east were in
the Council of Europe, and there were no substantial local political obstacles attached to abolition in the rather fluid domestic policies of these
transitional states.

The strong appeal of the culture and politics of Western Europe to the
citizens of Central Europe also has assured the status of the Western powers among the citizens of the region. The nations and cultures of Western
Europe are what most citizens in Central Europe emulate. And whether or
not they agree with the death penalty standard, the high status of the cultures imposing it helped the anti–death penalty initiative.

While the rejection of capital punishment all across Central Europe was
a stunning political achievement, it probably did not reduce the level of
executions much in the region because very few had been carried out in the
period prior to abolition. In Poland, this was the consequence of a formal
moratorium after 1988, but all through the region execution had been un-
common for years (Hood 1996, p. 19).

However, the end to executions achieved by organized Europeans in the
Ukraine and Belarus and the moratoriums on executions in the Russian
republic had a much greater impact on levels of execution. The Ukraine
had conducted 212 executions between November 9, 1995, and March 11,
1997 (Committee on Legal Affairs and Human Rights of the Council of

Europe 1999, p. 181). (Still, the net effect of the breakup of the Soviet Union in 1991 on executions in the region was probably to increase them, because of the activity in newly autonomous governments under strong Islamic influence) (Hood 1996, pp. 22–23).

The swift progress of abolition in Central and Eastern Europe contributed to the morale of abolitionist activists in two ways. First, the sheer number of states shifting policy and the prospect of Europe as an "execution-free zone" was a substantial accomplishment. Second, the political credentials of those newly independent nations that had rejected executions as a matter of principle added to the reputation of the movement. To have the abolition of the death penalty as an integral part of the Czechoslovakian Velvet Revolution gives the movement a sense of holding the moral high ground. Once the abolition of the death penalty could be seen as an integral part of liberalization, something like virtue by association resulted from the support of Europe's political heroes of the 1980s.

The new regime in South Africa was the other striking instance of "virtue by association" in the abolitionist portfolio of the 1990s. The peaceful transition from the remains of a government based on racial classification and white suffrage took place in 1994. A new constitution was promulgated and elections produced an African National Congress majority with Nelson Mandela as state president. One year after this transition, the South African Constitutional Court ruled that the new Constitution's right to life prohibited any death penalty (Hood 1996, pp. 28–29). It is an understatement to say that this rejection of capital punishment was a break both with the policies of prior regimes in South Africa and with the traditions and expectations of government in sub-Saharan Africa. The South African exemplar created credibility for the abolition of capital punishment in a region that had not been hospitable to such appeals. Outside Africa, the South African undertaking seemed a conspicuous case of virtue by association, creating a linkage between liberal new regimes with broad political participation and abolition of the death penalty as a substantive priority.

Retentionist Regions and Nations

The momentum toward abolition of the death penalty was by no means worldwide in the 1990s. Asia and those nations in the Middle East and elsewhere under strong Islamic influence continue to be almost uniform in maintaining regimes with at least token levels of executions. In Asia, only Hong Kong, New Zealand, Australia, Cambodia, and Nepal have formally abolished the death penalty, and the first three of these nations are closely linked to the British in political values and institutions. The Asian continent at the start of the twenty-first century was almost an "abolition-free zone," the sharpest contrast in the world to Europe. But there are wide variations among different Asian states. It is estimated that China conducts about 80 percent of the executions in the world. India, by contrast, has about twelve executions a year, a rate of execution to population of close to one per 100 million (Hood 1996, pp. 37, 74). The execution rate in Texas is 300 times that high.

Japan is the only fully developed nation other than the United States that executes. The level of execution is low, but the small number of executions may underrepresent the level of commitment to the policy. Singapore and Malaysia have, by contrast, extremely high rates of execution for their small populations, and these nations execute drug offenders as well as murderers (Hood 1996, pp. 62-63).

While the prevalence of execution in Asia is high, the level of governmental commitment to death penalties varies widely. There is a big gulf between "soft" nations in their commitment to execution—such as India and perhaps Japan—and the aggressive practitioners found in Singapore, China, and Malaysia. There is no clear link in most of Asia between capital punishment and other elements of the core culture or religion of the communities governed. While the continent is monolithic in its support of death penalties, the variability of governments in current commitment to the death penalty and in susceptibility to a swift change in death penalty policy without fundamental change in government may make non-Islamic governments in Asia a better prospect for the missionary efforts of European lobbyists than are those governments in the Middle East and elsewhere with strong ties to Islamic fundamentalism. The Islamic nations, alone, have a moral claim to execution as government policy.

How quickly the Europeans can build on their clean sweep of their home continent will depend first on the priority that European governments place on the further export of abolition as a human rights norm. If strong economic incentives can be offered—such as aid in sub-Saharan Africa or trade in Asia—many states in both Asia and Africa may shift toward moratoriums if not abolition of execution.

The New World Map of Executions

The anti–death penalty activism of the last two decades of the twentieth century has produced a profile of capital punishment policy across the world that is different quantitatively and qualitatively from earlier patterns. The sheer number of nonexecuting nations and the fact that abolition is now a policy in a plurality of nations would not by itself be much of a force for change in those regions where most governments still execute. Taiwan is usually more influenced by U.S. trade restrictions than by Polish death penalty policy. But the qualitative changes are of great importance. Almost all of the First World is now adamant in its abolition sentiments. The status of the "leading nations" that now agitate for abolition as successful and powerful democratic states is one important element in the international effort.

But the near-unanimity of the economic powers of the First World makes the two exceptions to this pattern—Japan and above all the United States— into particular targets for the other developed nations. Without the United States as a First World standard-bearer for executions, the low status of most executing nations in both human rights and material wealth would probably undermine the claim that developed and politically progressive states might nonetheless have executions as policy. The hostile focus on the United States in much current European death penalty activities is in large part a product of this concern. Very few world governments will openly aspire to the status of Iraq or North Korea. But the United States provides a powerful and democratic profile on the international stage, and execution in the United States makes it more difficult to label the practice as the refuge only of primitive regimes.

Still, with the United States as a spectacular exception, the contrast between abolitionist and executing nations is clear on questions of human rights, political freedom, and respect for democratic institutions. This contrast is now more than a reflection of the fact that completely developed nations tend both to high standards of human rights and to abolition. Among the former Iron Curtain countries and in South Africa, the decisions of exemplary regimes to endorse abolition has added to the political reputation of abolition and the breadth of its appeal. The abolition of the death penalty in the South Africa of the mid-1990s was not a complacent gesture by a nation where violent crime was under control. It was a high-stakes statement of principle at a time when violent crime was one of the major threats to nation building after apartheid. Such exemplary abolitions helped the anti–death penalty voices take a monopoly hold on the moral high ground in the 1990s.

The other qualitative advantage that was secured for abolitionists during the last two decades of the twentieth century was the intensity of the anti–capital punishment crusaders. An extraordinary feature of the recent European campaign is that capital punishment has become a high priority among the human rights issues, a hot button issue among activists on the European scene. The death penalty in Oklahoma is not an issue of compelling salience for the average European citizen, but for a small number of intensely committed campaigners, the death penalty is near the top of the priority list, a brand new phenomenon in the international politics of the death penalty.

Some of the high-intensity enthusiasm invested in the death penalty may stem from the opportunity this issue presents to catch the United States in an indefensible human rights position. There is no doubt some pleasure taken in proposals to deprive the United States and Japan of observer status in the Council of Europe because of their persistence in conducting executions, given the other grievances that the European left has had with American power and American policies.

But much of the European energy and intensity on death penalties had been directed at successor regimes to the Soviet Union and its satellite states. For a core constituency in the human rights campaigns, there is something worthy of intense commitment in the current campaigns against capital punishment, and this concern is projected worldwide. This intensity of commitment among a core group provides some assurance that an emphasis on the death penalty will not soon fall out of fashion. It provides a sense of the importance of the mission, which is good for the morale of the activist campaigners and their less adamant supporters. It gives to the street protests and meetings the character of a crusade, and not just a youth crusade. The death penalty in Europe has become a modern morality play to be pursued on a world stage. In an age dominated by negotiation and pragmatism, abolition is one of very few issues that allows its adherents to hold on to a sense of transcendent virtue. This is no small matter in a world where so many rules and regulations are for sale.

Conclusion

Since the end of the Second World War, Europe has experienced two transformations in policy toward state execution. The first transformation was the gradual elimination of the death penalty from the criminal codes of individual states, a process that was completed in Western Europe by 1981, and that carried eastward quickly after the fall of the Soviet Union in 1989. The second transformation in European policy was the reframing of capital punishment as a violation of human rights that must be prohibited by civilized governments. This international standard emerged in Protocol No. 6 in 1983 and has become the basis for anti–death penalty evangelism worldwide.

The abolition of capital punishment across Europe was an indirect challenge to American policy, isolating practices in the United States and in Japan from the policies of other First World nations. The transformation of capital punishment into a human rights concern has become a direct challenge to the legitimacy of the death penalty in the United States.

The rhetorical transformation in Europe that started in the late 1970s has been extraordinary in two respects. The human rights focus did not emerge until after Western Europe had ceased executing criminal offenders. Yet it then became a prominent theme in human rights dialogue almost immediately. The broader concerns that emerged in the 1980s must have been close to the surface during the 1960s and 1970s, while the last states to give up their claims to execute were abolishing the death penalty. While abolition was a low-key and individual process in each nation, the aftermath of abolition has produced more intense political action and greater transnational activity than had preceded the end of capital punishment.

Two lessons from this remarkable European adventure should inform the study of American attitudes and policy. First, the rhetoric about capital punishment is itself both important and variable even when domestic penal policy is not on the brink of change. How people imagine and describe the process of state execution is an important topic for study that both reflects and eventually changes death penalty policy. One way then to examine what separates practice in the United States from that in other developed nations is to study the way that Americans describe the death penalty and executions. The attitudes and arguments of interested individuals and governmental actors are a neglected source of data that might explain changes in policy.

The second lesson from the European experience is that the relationship between what we say and what we do is complicated and not easily predictable. Would British elites have scoffed at a human rights argument in the late 1950s or would that argument have solidified opposition to capital punishment? Was the sudden surge of interest in abolition as a human rights issue in Europe evidence that such concerns were important motivations beneath the surface of death penalty debates long before they emerged in the aftermath of abolition? Interpreting the rhetoric of capital punishment is a highly speculative enterprise, and false leads are just as likely to appear as genuine clues are when we pay close attention to the ways in which attitudes toward the death penalty get formed and get changed.

3

The Symbolic Transformation of
American Capital Punishment

A STUNNING DEMONSTRATION of the great gulf that has opened between
the United States and other Western nations on the death penalty occurred
in March 2002, as the U.S. Justice Department was deciding to seek the
death penalty in its prosecution of a French national of Moroccan descent
named Zacarias Moussaoui. The American government had alleged that
Moussaoui was to have been "the twentieth hijacker" on September 11,
2001. This conspirator was prevented from filling out the five-person team
on United Airlines flight 73 that crashed in Pennsylvania only because he
was confined in jail for visa violations. The U.S. government wished to
treat this defendant as fully accountable for the program of mass destruction. It sought both a death penalty and the cooperation of the French
government in making its case against Moussaoui.

There was substantial sentiment for cooperation with American anti–
terrorist efforts in France after the events of September 11. The French
government had suspended its usual reserve and independence from
American concerns after the suicide attacks; French President Jacques
Chirac was the first foreign head of state to visit Washington with pledges
of support in September 2001, and observers were quick to note that
France had become "one of the staunchest public supporters of President
Bush's 'war on terrorism.'" Both President Chirac and the Prime Minister, Lionel Jospin, had pledged French "diplomatic, intelligence, and military support for a lengthy campaign to identify and destroy extreme Islamic
groups around the world" (Lichfield 2001). "'We are all Americans,' French

newspapers and politicians proclaimed in the aftermath of the attacks on New York and Washington" (Marlowe 2001).

Yet the concert of action that joined the French and American governments in the war on terror did not survive the American decision to seek the death penalty for Moussaoui's role in the September 11 conspiracy. In late March 2002, the French Justice Ministry wrote Attorney General John Ashcroft "reminding him that longstanding agreements between the two governments allowed France to end cooperation in cases in which a French defendant held in the United States faced the death penalty," and the French Justice Minister reported that she had asked Mr. Ashcroft "to assure that Moussaoui could benefit from a fair trial and that capital punishment not be sought against him" (Shenon and Lewis 2002). The day after this exchange was reported, the U.S. Justice Department nonetheless announced that it would seek the death penalty, and the French Ministry of Justice subsequently withdrew its cooperation in producing data on the defendant or his associations that could be used in a capital trial.

Three aspects of this conflict make it an excellent opportunity to observe the enormity of the perceptual differences on the death penalty that separate the United States from its European peers. First, the absence of French-U.S. cooperation on this very important prosecution had substantial practical importance. This was at that time the only case lodged against a direct participant in the worst mass killing in U.S. history, and it was reported that "a decision by the French to withhold evidence could be a blow to prosecutors since French intelligence agencies are reported to maintain a voluminous file on Moussaoui and his ties to Al-Qaeda and other militant Muslim groups" (Shenon and Lewis 2002). A Justice Department spokesman acknowledged, "[W]e'd obviously like to maintain access to it" (ibid.). There was every incentive on both sides to avoid a direct clash on the death penalty in a case of such importance, but it happened nevertheless. Why?

A second intriguing feature of this conflict was the air of disbelief it produced among some American observers that fundamental differences about state capital punishment could run that deep between other developed nations and the United States. After blaming the French decision on that nation's "typical arrogance," an editorial in the *Boston Herald* reasoned, "France abolished capital punishment in 1981. Evidently something permissible for France in 1980 is an abomination for America only 22 years later. Abominations, however, are not created that fast" ("When Death Is Appropriate" 2002). It might well seem to observers that fundamental differences in questions about death as a penalty should stem from longer gestation periods than the transformation described in the previous chapter.

But when closely examined, the decision of each government in this affair flows from the contrasting premises about the nature of capital punishment with the same inevitability we find in Greek tragedy. The Attorney General of the United States regarded the nation's choice in the Moussaoui matter as an appropriate criminal sanction for participation in an offense of unprecedented mass destruction:

> Following my instructions, the United States attorneys have filed a notice of intent to seek a sentence of death. In the notice, we have alleged numerous reasons—called aggravating factors—why we believe the death penalty is appropriate. Among these reasons is the impact of the crime on the thousands of victims. (Ashcroft 2002)

Earlier the Attorney General had presented an expanded characterization of the crimes:

> The indictment issued today is a chronicle of evil, a carefully documented year-by-year, month-by-month, day-by-day account of a terrorist conspiracy that gathered both force and intensity in the weeks before September the 11th. Zacarias Moussaoui is alleged to have been an active participant in this conspiracy, alongside the 19 terrorists who carried it out. Moussaoui is charged with undergoing the same training, receiving the same funding, and pledging the same commitment to kill Americans as the hijackers. (Ashcroft 2001)

Under these circumstances the Attorney General defended the decision to seek a death penalty by announcing the United States remains "committed not only to carrying out justice in this case, but also to ensuring that the rights of the victims are fully protected" (Ashcroft 2002).

The premises from which the Attorney General concluded that a death sentence is appropriate in the Moussaoui case begin with the assumption that whether execution should be permitted as a punishment is essentially a matter of criminal justice policy. The death penalty is to John Ashcroft one of a number of potential punishments available for criminal offenders, and the choice of punishments should be influenced by the harms inflicted by the crime and the culpability of the particular defendant. If these premises are correct, the decision to seek the death penalty seems natural, if not inevitable.

The French government's response to the prospect of a death penalty in this case addressed none of the elements that Attorney General Ashcroft put forward. Instead, the French Minister of Justice reclassifies the question to be considered as whether a civilized government could ever use the death penalty, and from this premise concludes that the French government cannot cooperate in producing evidence "if it can be used to back the case for the death sentence" ("France to Limit Legal Links . . ." 2002). The French Foreign Minister Hubert Vedrine said that his nation remained "in solidarity with the United States in their fight against terrorism," but that France must ensure that any evidence it provides "would not be used as the basis to request the death penalty, a conviction, or a sentence of that kind" (ibid.). The death penalty could not be justified in this case because the death penalty could never be justified.

The Great Divide

What is evident in the Moussaoui dispute with France now just as clearly divides the United States from all of Western Europe on the use of execution as a criminal sanction. It is not that the two sides differ on the answers to a common question; instead, there is a fundamental difference of opinion on what the key questions are that should determine whether governments should be allowed to kill citizens intentionally as a criminal punishment. In the United States, capital punishment is regarded as a question of criminal justice policy, to be decided by the same levels of government and in much the same way as other issues about the proper punishments of criminals. As a concession to the seriousness of executions, there are some special rules imposed by the federal Supreme Court since the 1970s, but in all other respects the policy ideal is that state governments should choose whether and for which offenders death should be available as a criminal punishment.

While the death penalty is an option that governments are free to choose or reject in this American account, the modern European view is adamant that no civilized state should be permitted the power to employ execution as a criminal punishment. In the European rhetoric, the absence of a death penalty is a defining political matter, a question of the proper constitution of a modern state, not a criminal justice policy choice. For France, cooperating in the execution of a criminal offender is as unthinkable as cooperating with other practices beyond the pale of Western civilization, such as slavery or cannibalism. Typical of the arguments one confronts in the modern Council of Europe literature is Andrei Sakarov's critique:

> The state in the person of its officials arrogates to itself the right to perform the most terrible and irreparable act—the taking of life. Such a state cannot expect any improvement in the country's moral climate. (Pristavkin 1999, p. 129)

This appeal to execution-free penal codes as a basic constitutional requirement for a civilized state performs a number of rhetorical functions for the international abolitionist. Seeking out the high ground of limits on government power renders all the traditional death penalty disputes about what terrible crimes and criminals deserve, about deterrence, about risks of error and fairness in administration, as literally beside the point. As soon as the human rights/limited government premise is accepted, the policy conclusion is automatic. There are no contingencies, no balancing of costs and benefits, and no reasons to consult public sentiments about crime as soon as the major premise of the human rights/limited government argument is accepted.

For this reason, once the limited government argument is conceded a place in the capital punishment controversy, it automatically achieves a status of priority. The contestants must first determine whether the claims for this constitutional argument are justified. If so, the debate begins and ends with the human rights/limited government claim. Only if that claim is rejected can the traditional topics for debate concerning the death penalty be given any serious consideration. This preemptive quality to the human rights/limited government perspective explains why many of the European activists who accept the human rights claim talk of nothing else. They do not have to. All the traditional controversies about capital punishment lose their legitimacy when a preemptive human rights strike succeeds.

The preemptive potential of human rights and limited government claims is one powerful reason why supporters of capital punishment would be tempted to ignore entirely the discourse about limited government and the right to life when considering capital punishment. Attorney General Ashcroft does not want to shift the terms of debate to the proper limits of government, and so he ignores the question. It is thus not a great surprise to discover that the whole of the political dimension of capital punishment as an extreme state power over citizens is simply ignored in the United States. The question of whether executions violate a human right recognized by international authorities (or any other human rights standard) is almost never debated in the United States.

The Missing Link

Half of the explanation for the absence of any human rights/limited government debate is easy to provide. Supporters of capital punishment are not pleased at the prospect of changing the death penalty debate from a punishment policy problem to an issue of the proper limits of government power or of human rights. The best way to avoid the preemption of traditional punishment concerns is for the political questions never to enter the debate.

But the other half of the explanation of this missing dimension of the American death penalty debate is harder to comprehend. Organizations that urge abolition of the death penalty in the United States, including some groups (such as Amnesty International) that stress political dimensions of the death penalty throughout Europe, do not emphasize such political appeals in their advocacy in the United States. This failure to press on a human rights or limited government theme in a nation where executions are taking place parallels the absence of these arguments in Western

Europe while England, Spain, and France went about the process of ending capital punishment. But the American situation would seem to establish that the absence of a human rights appeal is a conscious, tactical decision, because the same organizations are stressing political concerns in Europe but not in the United States.

Consider two pamphlets on the death penalty published by Amnesty International in 2000, one from London and the other from Amnesty USA in New York. The London version of the case against capital punishment begins its appeal with a five-paragraph affirmation of capital punishment as "A Violation of Human Rights," ending this by stating, "No matter what reason a government gives for executing prisoners and what method of execution is used, the death penalty cannot be separated from the issue of human rights. The movement for abolition cannot be separated from the movement for human rights" (Amnesty London 2000). The Amnesty USA pamphlet on the death penalty emphasizes, instead, the unfairness and irreversibility of the death penalty in the United States. None of the eight subsections in this death penalty appeal is devoted to a human rights analysis, but both a headline and a full paragraph of the text document that execution "costs more than life imprisonment. . . . [T]axpayers in Texas are spending an average of $2.3 million on each execution—while lifetime incarceration costs from $800,000 to $1 million" (Amnesty USA 2000).

Perhaps the human rights appeal is regarded as dangerous while an elected government is still executing. Yet the political arguments against the death penalty were made by Europeans including Amnesty in Russia and Central Europe in the late 1980s and 1990s during the campaign for an execution-free continent.

In the United States, rather than arguing that any government that wishes a death penalty should not be trusted, critics debate the fairness and accuracy of capital trials, the dangers of executing the innocent, and what later chapters describe as due process concerns. The argument thus focused on the criminal justice system rather than on a broader consideration of government powers and the reasons for limiting them. The unfairness of the system in particular cases is generalized to a systemic critique that doubts whether the death penalty system is or can be free of the risk of error. But the broader theme now dominant in Europe—that allowing a state the power to kill as criminal punishment is itself a fundamental political mistake—is not urged with any force by even the death penalty's mainstream opponents. Why has there been no effort to mobilize a broader distrust of government claims of power to execute citizens as a means to advance governmental interests?

The tactical judgments of experts in anti–death penalty rhetoric such as the Amnesty campaigners should not be questioned without good cause. Certainly, the human rights of a serial killer would be a hard sell in those areas of the United States where executions proliferate, the South and Southwest. But many of those regions and states most active in the execution of criminals are also places where distrust of taxes and other government regulation is prevalent. If distrust of government is a strong element of the culture of high execution regions, why can't this distrust be exploited by the supporters of abolition? The rhetoric is easy to anticipate: If you do not trust government bureaucracies with your tax dollars and racial policies in public schools, how can you trust them to choose appropriate targets for death sentences and believe that government officials can protect against the execution of the innocent? If the government screws up every other major responsibility it administers, why should the death penalty be any different?

There is nothing on the face of this type of appeal that seems inappropriate or unpromising. Yet anti–death penalty forces, desperate for a foothold in the high death penalty states, have not sought to tar the death penalty by association with other less popular exercises of government power or with a general distrust of states with extreme power over the lives of individual citizens. Why is this?

Perhaps the anti–death penalty advocates are making a mistake, missing a powerful appeal that would provide some leverage in states such as Texas, Virginia, South Carolina, Oklahoma, and Arizona. But in an age of focus groups and fairly sophisticated marketing, it seems unlikely that an operation such as Amnesty International would inadvertently pass up a promising limited government argument for use in the heartlands of American capital punishment. Yet it is not easy to find the logical flaw in an argument that links an extreme exercise of state power with other widely distrusted governmental powers. Why doesn't the negative reputation of government rub off on the image of executions in those areas where most executions occur?

If the absence of a limited government appeal in the American South and Southwest is based on consumer resistance to attacks on execution as excessive government power, the source of that resistance may be an important clue to the associations and imagery of capital punishment that makes the practice acceptable to a broad cross-section of citizens in the United States. So the complete absence of a political critique of government power may signal a peculiar characteristic in American culture that invites further inquiry. This issue is considered in detail in Chapter 5.

The Personal versus the Political

There is a curious symmetry in the symbolic profiles of the death penalty in Europe and the United States. While the American images of capital punishment lack the political dimension prevalent in Europe and the Commonwealth, the European account of the significant dimensions of the death penalty has none of the multiple personal linkages to homicide victims and their families who make appearances at capital trials and become a center of public attention as executions grow near. Thirteen American states provide by statute a right of designated relatives of homicide victims to witness the execution of an offender convicted of the crime. The next section of this chapter discusses the "victim impact" presentations established by many states in the sentencing phase of capital trials where evidence of the value of the deceased and the loss his loved ones feel is presented as an explicit argument that the jury should respond to this impact by choosing a death sentence rather than life imprisonment as a punishment. Victim interests have been consulted by public officials in choosing the administrative arrangements surrounding some executions, and victim psychology is referred to when executions are scheduled and when legislation intended to reduce the delay between death sentence and execution is passed.

The whole assortment of personal service symbolism in the American imagery of capital punishment is addressed in the latter part of this chapter, because it is the major change over time in the symbolic content of the death penalty in the United States. For present purposes, the important point is that all these significant linkages of the interests of victims to whether a death penalty should be imposed or to the time, place, and manner by which it is carried out had no precedent in centuries of execution in Europe. The personalized symbolism of capital punishment as a crime victim's prerogative has been important only on the American side of the Atlantic Ocean and only in very recent history.

There is therefore very little overlap in the symbols and subjects that are associated with capital punishment in the United States and in the rest of the Western industrial democracies. What other nations see as a basic political question about the proper limits of government is not regarded in the United States as a fundamental question of governmental structure. The death penalty instead is regarded as a policy intended to serve the interests of the victims of crime and those who love them, as a personal rather than a political concern, an undertaking of government to serve the needs of individual citizens for justice and psychological healing.

Chapter 2 established that the European focus on the political nature of capital punishment has a very short history. What the next section of this chapter shows is that the distinctive emphasis in the United States on victim impacts and psychology is also a recent phenomenon. The great symbolic divide between the United States and its developed Western neighbors was produced by a series of quite recent shifts—in opposite directions—on both sides of the Atlantic Ocean.

American Change

While other Western nations were reshaping the image of capital punishment in the wake of its abolition, the critical event that launched the change in image in the United States was the preparation in the 1970s to begin executions again after a decade-long hiatus. When the U.S. Supreme Court decided the *Gregg v. Georgia* group of cases in 1976, it not only signaled that capital punishment could be reintroduced in the United States, but also upheld a number of death sentences that meant executions might resume without a great delay. Suddenly, executions were just around the corner.

The two decades after 1976 were a period of innovations in both policy and image for the death penalty. The major shifts in the image of capital punishment during this period can be discussed under two headings: the modernization and the personalization of death penalty imagery. The long decline in rates of execution during the period after 1935 and the ten-year moratorium meant that the process of execution was reinvented rather than resumed in the 1980s and 1990s. The way in which the new symbols of capital punishment were assembled is an important indication of vulnerabilities that were believed to exist in the images of the death penalty at the end of the 1970s.

Modernization

One pressing problem confronting those who wanted to resume executions in the late 1970s was the antiquity and reputation for brutality of all the mechanisms that had been used to put criminal offenders to death. The last great wave of innovation in methods of execution in the United States had occurred late in the nineteenth century, when electrocution and lethal gas were introduced as modern improvements on hanging, the dominant means of inflicting death sentences in Great Britain and the United States (Death Penalty Information Center 2002). Whatever optimism had existed about the gas chamber and the electric chair as advanced and less brutal methods of execution had dissipated long before 1977. Even before court challenges to gas and electricity as cruel and unusual punishment gained a foothold in the courts, both the electric chair and the gas chamber had image problems that threatened to undermine social support for the resumption of executions. The gas chamber had been used as an instrument of mass murder by the Nazis, and the electric chair projected a visible aura of fiery brutality. More than this, all the traditional means of execution seemed anachronistic in the late twentieth century, a link to earlier times rather than a fitting symbol of a modern policy (Zimring and Hawkins 1986, chap. 6).

What was needed was a new method of execution that could appear to be both humane and efficient, a symbol of scientific progress in the service of modern capital punishment. The solution to this problem was the invention of lethal injection in the 1980s. While the injection of lethal drugs had been considered and rejected as a potential form of execution in the British Royal Commission report (Royal Commission on Capital Punishment, p. 261), a more proximate inspiration for lethal injection as an innovation in methods of execution was then-Governor Ronald Reagan of California, who said in 1973:

> Being a former farmer and horse raiser, I know what it's like to eliminate an injured horse by shooting him. Now you call the veterinarian and the vet gives it a shot and the horse goes to sleep—that's it. I myself have wondered if maybe this isn't part of our problem [with capital punishment], if maybe we should review and see if there aren't even more humane methods now— the simple shot or tranquillizer. (Schwarzchild 1982)

The image that Governor Reagan had in mind was a quick and painless chemical means of killing, a process that may have seemed particularly merciful in the veterinary setting, because the animal does not know what is happening. But even with the obvious distinction of a scheduled and known time of execution, what may have made the idea of injection appealing is that the untried practice lacked all of the brutal and anachronistic associations that hanging, gassing, and electrocution had accumulated. Some legislation authorizing injections as a means of execution lapsed into the language of advertising by referring to the chemical agent as "an ultra-fast-acting barbiturate" (Montana) or "an ultra-short-acting barbiturate" (North Carolina), which is usually preceded by administration of prescription tranquilizers (Zimring and Hawkins 1986, p. 112).

In the 1990s, some 396 of 478 executions or 83 percent were conducted by lethal injection (Death Penalty Information Center 2002), and there is no other method of execution that has been used in recent years as either an alternative or an additional option for states wishing to supplement or substitute methods of execution.

There has been no observational assessment of the pain, anxiety, or humiliation generated by lethal agents injected into a prone human subject as a means of execution. There has been no attempt to evaluate systematically the actual practice of lethal injection in the states that use it. As a matter of public relations, however, there is no doubt that the institutionalization of lethal injection has neutralized the reputation for brutality and anachronism associated with the electric chair and the gas chamber. While organized medicine is not party to executions, the physical apparatus of medicine—syringes and gurneys—have rapidly become the dominant physical representation of the execution process.

The Focus on Private Interests

The major change in the announced purposes of capital punishment in the United States in the last decades of the twentieth century was the transformation of capital trials and of executions into processes that were thought to serve the personal interests of those closely related to the victims of capital murders. The penalty phase of capital trials has become in many states an occasion for telling the jury its choice of sanction is a measure of the value of the homicide victim's life. Years after the trial is completed, the execution becomes an occasion to seek psychological "closure" for the family and friends of victims, when the tensions and uncertainties of the period leading up to an execution are resolved, and the concerned relative is supposed also to experience a resolution of feelings of grief and anger about the loss from the homicide. The symbolic victim focus at both trial and execution was almost wholly the product of legal innovations and new psychological language that followed the resumption of executions in 1977. The novelty of the emphasis on these aspects of the death penalty after 1977 would be difficult to overstate. The radical degovernmentalization of the death penalty was without important precedent in two centuries of prior American history.

THE FORM AND FUNCTION OF VICTIM IMPACT SUBMISSIONS

The trial of a murder case with a charge that can lead to a death sentence is typically composed of two stages. In the first stage, the issue is the proof of the facts supporting the capital charge. If the trier of fact (usually a jury) finds the defendant potentially eligible for the death penalty in this "guilt phase," a second proceeding, typically called the "penalty phase" of the trial, is launched in which the same trier of fact (again, usually a jury) must choose between the death penalty and the legislatively provided alternative punishment. The U.S. Supreme Court has provided a set of constitutional rules that make the penalty phase of a modern capital trial an open-ended and discretionary choice between imprisonment and death once the defendant's guilt of a death-eligible charge has been established. The first important constitutional rule was established in *Woodson v. North Carolina* in 1976, when the Court ruled that the states could not create capital offenses that carried only the death penalty. Because the defendant's guilt could never be a sufficient condition for a death sentence under *Woodson*, the second, or "penalty phase," trial would have to be concerned with facts other than the defendant's guilt of the capital charge. Factual guilt of a death-eligible charge was only the beginning of the process of choosing between imprisonment and death. Some alternative punishment must always be available, no matter what the crime.

A second ruling, *Lockett v. Ohio* in 1978, provided the defendant in a capital penalty trial with the right to present evidence and arguments on virtually any aspect of his life that was of potential importance in the choice between life and death. Chief Justice Berger concluded:

[A] statute that prevents the sentencer in all capital cases from giving independent mitigating effect to aspects of the defendant's character and record
. . . creates the risk that the death penalty will be imposed in spite of factors
which may call for a less severe penalty. When the choice is between life and
death, that risk is unacceptable. . . . (*Lockett v. Ohio* 438 U.S. at 605)

One reaction to the open-ended appeals to mercy authorized by *Lockett
v. Ohio* was the attempt in many states to create for death penalty prosecutions the ability to present information on not only the character of the
defendant's crime but on the nature and extent of the harm suffered by the
particular victims of the murder as well as by their relations. The method
of presentation of this information varies. In some systems, probation officers are charged with interviewing friends and relations of the victims,
and the probation officer's report becomes a record that is read to the jury
by the prosecutor in the penalty phase.

This type of summarized version of the particular victim impact was
used at trial in the Maryland case of *Booth v. Maryland*, as described by
Justice Powell in 1987.

Although the VIS [Victim Impact Statement] is compiled by the DPP, the
information is supplied by the victim or the victim's family. See §§ 4-609(c)(4),
(d). The VIS may be read to the jury during the sentencing phase, or the
family members may be called to testify as to the information.

The VIS in Booth's case was based on interviews with the Bronsteins' son,
daughter, son-in-law, and granddaughter. Many of their comments empha-
sized the victims' outstanding personal qualities, and noted how deeply the
Bronsteins would be missed. Other parts of the VIS described the emotional
and personal problems the family members have faced as a result of the crimes.
The son, for example, said that he suffers from lack of sleep and depression,
and is "fearful for the first time in his life." He said that in his opinion, his
parents were "butchered like animals." The daughter said she also suffers
from lack of sleep, and that since the murders she has become withdrawn and
distrustful. She stated that she can no longer watch violent movies or look at
kitchen knives without being reminded of the murders. The daughter concluded that she could not forgive the murderer, and that such a person could
"[n]ever be rehabilitated." Finally, the granddaughter described how the deaths
had ruined the wedding of another close family member that took place a few
days after the bodies were discovered. Both the ceremony and the reception
were sad affairs, and instead of leaving for her honeymoon, the bride attended
the victims' funeral. The VIS also noted that the granddaughter had received
counseling for several months after the incident, but eventually had stopped
because she concluded that "no one could help her." (*Booth v. Maryland*, 482
U.S. at 499–500 [footnotes and citations omitted])

A second type of victim impact fact presentation involves the direct testimony of those related to homicide victims about their suffering, or the

testimony of experts on the particular damage inflicted by a killing on the victim's close relatives. A famous example of this second sort of testimonial "victim impact" presentation and its use in penalty phase argument was considered by the U.S. Supreme Court in *Payne v. Tennessee* in 1991, a case involving the killing of a young mother, Charisse Christopher, and her two-year-old daughter as well as the stabbing injury of her three-year-old son Nicholas.

Here is Chief Justice Rehnquist's account of the penalty phase evidence on victim impact:

> The State presented the testimony of Charisse's mother, Mary Zvolanek. When asked how Nicholas [her grandchild] had been affected by the murders of his mother and sister, she responded: "He cries for his mom. He doesn't seem to understand why she doesn't come home. And he cries for his sister Lacie. He comes to me many times during the week and asks me, Grandmama, do you miss my Lacie. And I tell him yes. He says, 'I'm worried about my Lacie.'" (*Payne v. Tennessee*, 501 U.S. at 814–815 [citations omitted])

In each type of victim impact presentation, the prosecution is free to use the evidence of particular loss in arguments to a jury to the effect that only a death sentence will properly recognize the nature of the suffering of those who have been harmed by the defendant's acts.

In the Booth case, the prosecutor read the 1900-word summary of the emotional impact of the murder of this loving and long-married couple on their children and grandchildren. In *Payne v. Tennessee*, the prosecutor tells the jury about the killings of the mother and sister being witnessed by the three-year-old survivor:

> But we do know that Nicholas was alive. And Nicholas was in the same room. Nicholas was still conscious. His eyes were open. He responded to the paramedics. He was able to follow their directions. He was able to hold his intestines in as he was carried to the ambulance. So he knew what happened to his mother and baby sister.
>
> There is nothing you can do to ease the pain of any of the families involved in this case. There is nothing you can do to ease the pain of Bernice or Carl Payne [parents of the defendant], and that's a tragedy. There is nothing you can do basically to ease the pain of Mr. and Mrs. Zvolanek [adult victim's parents], and that's a tragedy. They will have to live with it the rest of their lives. There is obviously nothing you can do for Charisse and Lacie Jo. But there is something that you can do for Nicholas.
>
> Somewhere down the road Nicholas is going to grow up, hopefully. He's going to want to know what happened. And he is going to know what happened to his baby sister and his mother. He is going to want to know what happened. With your verdict, you will provide the answer. (*Payne v. Tennessee*, 501 U.S. at 815 [citations omitted]).

In each case, the victim impact material becomes a centerpiece of the penalty trial, a basis the legal system provides for choosing between death and prison.

The symbolism of this sort of victim impact presentation is of extraordinary importance in the transformation of the image of capital punishment in the United States. At one level, of course, all the victim impact statement provides is another tool for prosecutors to increase the number of death sentences in those few cases where government lawyers choose to seek death. After all, the victim's family members have no right to enforce any preference they might have for or against a death sentence on a prosecutor who wishes to settle a case for a lesser punishment. The victim's family's right to be heard on such questions is wholly dependent on prosecutorial choice to pursue a death sentence. But when the prosecutor does elect a capital trial, then the penalty phase is remade into what sociologists call a "status competition" between the offender (whose claims to sympathy and understanding are the subject of his penalty phase presentation) and those who were directly or derivatively injured by the crime. In *Payne v. Tennessee*, the prosecutor tells the jury that in selecting between a death sentence and life imprisonment, "There is something you can do for Nicholas. . . . He is going to want to know what happened. With your verdict, you will provide the answer" (*Payne v. Tennessee*, 501 U.S. at 815).

The pro–death penalty slant in this type of status competition is obvious. Victims and their families are much easier to identify with and offenders are usually horribly at fault. But the more profound transformation that has occurred is that the penalty phase of the trial is now presented as a competition between the claims of private parties. The prosecutor in *Payne* presents himself as *Nicholas's* lawyer instead of *the state's* lawyer. The jury is being asked to make its only choice in the penalty trial by vindicating and recognizing the loss of a little boy. The implication of this type of argument is that the selection of a sentence other than death in this phase of the trial would be a direct rejection of the interests of Nicholas Christopher.

The symbolic transformation of the death penalty trial into a private competition between the claims of those hurt by murder and appeals to mercy for the murderers makes a number of assumptions about the relationship between criminal punishment and the well being of those who suffered loss as a result of the crime. It is assumed that there is a "zero-sum" relationship between the welfare of the victim's relative and that of the offender: the greater the suffering to be inflicted on the offender, the better the victim's loved ones should feel. Perhaps a linkage of the selected penalty to the feelings of satisfaction of the victim's relatives becomes a self-fulfilling prophecy, with the relatives feeling rewarded (or punished) by the jury's choice of sanction.

But if the families of murder victims will feel satisfaction only from the symbolic vindication of a death verdict, the odds are against many victim families feeling rewarded by criminal homicide penalties. There are more than 15,000 criminal homicides that result from intentional attacks each year in the United States, and about 12,000 of these occur in states with death penalties. But the usual number of death sentences in the United States is about 225 a year (see Snell, Bureau of Justice Statistics 2001). Using this very rough arithmetic, it appears that the chance of a homicide generating a death sentence in a death penalty jurisdiction are less than one in 50. When the expectation is established that only a death sentence will adequately recognize the suffering of victims and their families, this will guarantee unhappiness in more than 98 percent of all homicides. The creation of an expectation that will satisfy the relatives of victims in fewer than one in every fifty killings would be problematic no matter what the priorities of the sentencing system. But to create such a formula for certainty of disappointment in the name of victim's rights is particularly ironic.

VICTIM REJECTION

The problem with imagining the death penalty decision as a measurement of status is suggested by the following account of a Missouri case in April 2002:

> A Kansas City man who killed his stepson and four other men in 1999 will serve life in prison instead of being put to death, a judge ruled on Thursday. The man, Gary Beach, 59, attributed his crimes to mental illness and anger over drug use by his victims, and pleaded guilty in February to five counts of first-degree murder and armed criminal action. After hearing extensive testimony, Judge Charles E. Atwell of Jackson County Circuit Court handed down the life sentence, in a decision that stunned the victims' families. (Napolitano 2002)

But why were the families stunned in this case? If the lesser sentence was the result of the guilty plea or the defendant's mental illness, there is no logical reason to connect the punishment with any judgment about the victims. But what about the drug use by the victims? The danger here is not only disappointment on the part of victims' families, it is the distortion of a process that should be about a defendant's moral fault into an evaluation of the social worth of victims of homicide. In the usual case where a noncapital sentence is the result of prosecutorial decisions rather than those of a jury or a judge, a strong association of the death penalty with the evaluation of victim impact is an invitation for loved ones to take any diversion from the road to a death penalty as a personal insult. If they do take the process personally, the odds are not in their favor.

THE IMPACT OF VICTIM IMPACT

However badly the ambition for death sentences serves the interests of victims, it does succeed in raising the status of the death penalty and associating the moment when a death sentence is issued with the satisfaction of crime victims. Creating the felt need to commemorate a victim's loss with a death sentence is bad for most homicide survivors but good for the death penalty. It also obscures the essential governmental nature of both death sentences and executions.

The current circumstances of victim influence in the jurisprudence of American capital punishment are a combination of minimum power and maximum symbolism. The relatives of murder victims can control neither the trial nor the punishment of the decedent's killer. Agents of the state decide who will stand trial for a capital offense without any review by other branches of government. But relatives of victims whose death does not produce a capital sentence—the "unlucky" 98 percent of total cases—are made to feel that their terrible loss has not been properly recognized. Once the punishment of murders becomes a status competition, victim families are manipulated into positions of maximum disappointment. While the symbols used in this process sound close to the basic themes of contemporary appeals to victim's rights, the role of the relations of homicide victims is wholly dependent on prosecutorial powers beyond their reach.

FROM VENGEANCE TO CLOSURE:
THE PRIVATE SYMBOLS OF EXECUTION

The attempt in recent years to create a prominent role for victim families in the execution process is, in some respects, more remarkable than the transformation of trials into ways to measure the social status of the suffering of victims. Trials, after all, are public, but executions are located in governmental punishment facilities closed to the public. An earlier era of public execution ended in the United States in 1936, and there was no belief that there was social benefit to exposing ordinary citizens to the spectacle of hanging, gassing, electrocution, or lethal injection (see Banner 2002). Execution was regarded as a spectacle that most respectable citizens need not witness. Relatives of the condemned could be allowed to witness the execution to provide some comfort to the subject of the execution and to reassure those who care for the condemned offender's welfare that no gratuitous suffering is inflicted.

Several states provide by statute and most by discretionary practice that persons close to the victims of a condemned criminal also have a claim on witnessing the execution, but the function of this kind of witness is not easy to discern. For the distrustful, observing an execution is one way to make sure that the killing takes place, of course. A more important reason to include those close to victims is so that they do not feel slighted or ignored by the government. Again, the issue of symbolic recognition is a major explanation for inclusion of victims in the ceremony of execution. So including representatives of victims makes sense as a way of not disregarding victim interest. But what is supposed to be the incentive for the victims, the benefit that execution brings?

One thing that those who lost loved ones might wish from the execution of the murderer is revenge, a feeling of satisfaction in witnessing the suffering of a person who has inflicted pain on the witness. But to identify vengeance for those related to victims as a principal public purpose of executions would be problematic for two reasons. First, many of those who have suffered the most from homicide do *not* wish revenge nor will they feel either pleasure or satisfaction when offenders are put to death. Certainly, little Nicholas, whose suffering was the reason for the death penalty in *Payne v. Tennessee*, does not sound like a candidate for revenge, nor do the relatives of Mr. and Mrs. Bronstein, the victims in *Booth v. Maryland*. While some of those most injured by murder might welcome an execution as an opportunity for vengeance, the constituency for this movement would not be as broad as supporters of a death penalty would want. Many of those most injured by the loss of a loved one might resist executions explicitly designed as revenge in their name.

Many citizens would worry about whether the facilitation of private vengeance is a proper goal for state punishment. The connotations of terms such as vengeance and revenge are primitive and anachronistic, not the best combination for a broadly appealing public image. Even more than the methods of execution, the personal objectives for victims in executions require modern and refined-sounding labels. Purposes of punishment such as deterrence and incapacitation are not closely related to the personal needs of those who have lost loved ones. They are public purposes. Vengeance is an anachronism with a bad press. Something new, something personal, and something that sounded both civilized and refined would be the best candidate for an appealing label for personal involvement in executions.

From this perspective, the evocative term "closure" was a public relations godsend. The term "closure" has a long pedigree in popular psychology but was not used by the printed mass media to describe a major objective of the death penalty until 1989, more than a decade after executions resumed on American soil (combined U.S. news sources [Lexis-Nexis]). The psychological notion of executions as closure is not that of the primary dictionary description of the term, "to stop operation," but, rather, the further *Cambridge Dictionary of American English* description: "the satisfying feeling that something bad or shocking has finally ended." Without doubt, when executions happen, there is some strong sense of ending for those close to the victim who have paid careful attention to the trial and appeals of a capital case. For most such relations, there will be a strong sense of relief that the uncertainties of outcome, disturbing public attention, and traumatic media revisiting of the facts of the murder will end after an execution. What is not known is whether pending death sentences delay the mourning and psychological closure associated with the loss of the homicide victim or whether the death of the offender in some sense accelerates the positive closure of relatives in relation to the victim's loss. The relief a relative feels when an execution takes place may simply mean that the additional pain and uncertainty inflicted by the death penalty process has come to an end. It has been said that the nice thing about repetitively hitting one's head against a stone wall is that "it feels so good when you stop." But that kind of relief would not make execution into a net benefit for survivors because the additional hurt that happens prior to an execution could also be avoided if the entire capital punishment process were not launched.

A TERM OR A CONCEPT?

Two elements of the way in which the term "closure" entered the lore of American capital punishment conspire against us ever finding a precise meaning for it or being able to distinguish sharply between "closure" and other terms such as "revenge" or "satisfaction." In the first place, the term has no official function in legislation or legal proceedings, so there is no definitive source that can be consulted for a definition. Closure is a term found only in the *unofficial* discussion of the purposes of capital punishment in the United States. The second problem is the sound-bite quality of discourse on the death penalty. The standard reference to closure is one or two sentences long, with no attempt to append a specific denotation to the term. Closure just seems to mean something good that execution brings to those mourning the murder of a loved one.

Even at this epic level of imprecision, there are some clear indications that the public meaning of closure is rather different than terms such as retribution and vengeance. There is no need to feel anger or any need to observe the offender's suffering to benefit from closure. The execution-cum-closure is not the grand climax that victims' families await as a vindication of hurt or in the name of a homicide victim's suffering. It is the pain of the relative, the grieving of the living that is to be addressed in this version of the psychological benefits of a death penalty, not any enjoyment of the suffering of the wicked. That is the theory of closure as a distinct psychological phenomenon, in any event.

The empirical support for such a theory is quite thin. It is not known whether there are psychological advantages in mourning the loss of a loved one when that loss leads to an execution, nor is there any indication that the adjustment to loss of a loved one in a homicide is any different in death penalty states than in non–death penalty states. But despite these unknowns, the term "closure" has come to play a prominent role in both the media coverage of executions and in the political debates about death penalty policies.

Figure 3.1 traces the number of news stories that link the term "closure" to the subject of executions in a broad sample of print media in the United States over the sixteen years from 1986 to 2001.

Prior to 1989, the term does not appear in death penalty stories in the United States. Its first and only mention in 1989 was followed by a year in which two stories use the term. By 1993, ten stories a year combine the topic "death penalty" and the word "closure," and thereafter the combination of "capital punishment" and "closure" grows almost geometrically to more than 500 stories in 2001.

This sharp expansion in the association of "closure" with capital punishment is not the result of any legal or criminal justice events external to the media stories. It was a shift not in how or why prisoners were put to death but in how the practice was talked about, a change not in the practice of capital punishment but in the language of capital punishment. Indeed, the institutionalization of the term "closure" in discussions of the death penalty is as close to an example of pure symbolism as can be found in the recent American past. There was no change in legal proceeding that comes with it (as there was with victim impact presentation), no change in the method of putting to death (as there was with lethal injection), only a shift in the language used to describe the benefits that the relatives of victims were thought to obtain from executions. So the story of the ascendency of closure is an example of the power that changes in language alone can have on the image of a penalty and on public attitudes toward the practice.

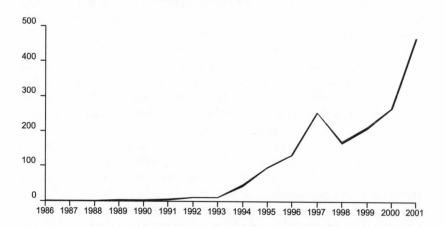

Figure 3.1. Number of stories mentioning closure in print media coverage of the death penalty, by year, 1986–2001. *Source*: Combined U.S. News Sources (Lexis-Nexis).

The semi-official status of "closure" as the presumed public benefit of executions was confirmed in April 2001 when the notion of closure was identified as a central objective of the death penalty system in the following ABC News/*Washington Post* poll statement: "The death penalty is fair because it gives satisfaction and closure to the families of murder victims." A total of 60 percent of the respondents agreed either strongly or somewhat with that sentiment, 37 percent disagreed, and only 4 percent expressed no opinion (Langer 2001). As noted in Chapter 1, this concept was supported by half again as many citizens (60 percent versus 40 percent) as general deterrence as a reason for executing criminals.

THE POLITICAL USES OF CLOSURE

One peculiar characteristic of the ABC News/*Washington Post* poll question accurately reflects some of the political logic in the current death penalty debate. The respondents in the poll were asked whether "the death penalty is fair" because of the benefits of closure that it might confer, but this phrasing represents either a very unusual definition of fairness or a non sequitur. As Chapter 7 shows, the dominant reservations about the fairness of the death penalty in the 1990s were concerns about racial disproportion, about the risk of executing the innocent, and the greater vulnerability of the poor and those with bad legal representation. It seems a matter of mixing apples and oranges to regard the prospect of closure as responsive to these problems.

Yet the uses of closure as a rhetorical tool in the political conflicts about capital punishment are many. Efforts to cut off time for appeals that were justified on grounds that survivors need closure were one of the first political uses of closure arguments in the debates in the federal Congress about the 1996 Effective Death Penalty Act. This appeal to closure transforms what would be the government's self-serving efforts to hasten executions by reducing the ways in which governmental mistakes can be rectified into a plea for executions as psychotherapy for survivors.

Indeed, any act that slows the pace of executions can be opposed as countertherapeutic on closure grounds. In Nebraska, the state legislature enacted a moratorium on executions in 1999 pending study of the fairness and reliability of that state's death penalty system. In vetoing the moratorium law, Governor Michael Johanns tells us, "I feel strongly that part of my role as Governor is to do all I can to carry out the law for the benefit of the victims and their families.... The moratorium would be just one more roadblock to bringing closure for them" (Tysver 1999).

The year before, then-Governor Pete Wilson of California used the presumed victim benefits of execution to object to the plea of guilty and life sentencing of Unabomber Ted Kaczynski in the following terms: "I am deeply disappointed and disturbed by the federal government's decision to plea bargain away a jury's right to decide whether multiple murderer Theodore Kaczynski should have faced the death penalty. The relatives of Kaczynski's victims have been cheated out of [their opportunity for] closure" (Salter 1998).

Governor Wilson's argument takes the notion of private claims to the death penalty to a double extreme in attacking the federal government's use of its prosecutorial power to accept a noncapital sentence. Surviving relatives have been "cheated out of" their evident right to "closure" by the government (the argument assumes that only the execution of offenders can bring about that status). The never empaneled jury has had *its* "right to decide whether Kaczynski should have faced the death penalty" bargained away by the federal government.

Governor Wilson's compound fantasy of survivors with entitlements to death penalties and would-be jurors with rights to hear all potential capital crimes bears no resemblance to the legal structure of capital punishment in the United States or to the way death penalty systems operate in fact. But this construction is based on an imagery of the death penalty that is widely present in the public domain. In this fantasy kingdom, the execution of criminals is exclusively a government service for the benefit of private parties. The duty of a governor in this kind of death penalty state is "to carry out the law for the benefit of victims and their families," as Governor Johanns said.

This symbolic transformation of execution into a victim-service program provides three powerful functions for the death penalty in the United States. First, it gives the horrifying process of human execution a positive impact that many citizens can identify with: closure, not vengeance. Second, this degovernmentalization of the rationale of the death penalty means that citizens do not have to worry about executions as an excessive use of power by and for the government. When "closure" is the major aim of lethal injections, the execution of criminals becomes another public service, like street cleaning or garbage removal, where the government is the servant of the community rather than its master.

The third function of the transformation of execution into a victim service gesture is that it links the symbolism of execution to a long American history of community control of punishment. The United States is not far removed from its age of vigilante punishment, and the nostalgia for many of the symbols and sentiments of punishment as a community rather than a government enterprise is quite powerful in many parts of the modern United States. When Pete Wilson of California speaks of victims feeling "cheated" by prosecutors' decisions and of juries having rights to decide on punishment no matter what the government resolves, he is embracing an authentic but frightening vigilante strain of American sentiment, a phenomenon that is explored in Chapter 5.

So the imagery and political uses of closure protect the death penalty from fears about strong government while linking modern sentiments about private rights to punishment with earlier claims that communities have the rights to exact their own punishments.

The spontaneous reframing of executions as closure in the 1990s demonstrates the ability of language and language alone to alter public perceptions. There will be no empirical studies of the impact of death penalties on homicide victims because no studies are needed. Closure is not important as a behavioral phenomenon; it is, instead, a belief system, a justification built on a foundation of faith. Even citizens who are usually distrustful of government are invited to believe this account of governmental motive and policy impact with no supporting evidence. To date, this campaign has been an unqualified success.

Conclusion

The imagery of the death penalty has been changing rapidly in the United States since the mid-1970s, as proponents of capital punishment struggle to make executions broadly acceptable. The attempt to create an image of a modern method of putting people to death and the many different ways that trials and executions have been portrayed as helping victims are remarkable testimony to the importance of imagery in the political career of a penal policy.

Of course, the mere fact that theories of victim impact and closure for survivors came to play such an important role in the public image of capital punishment is not evidence that death penalty policies benefit survivors or that the interests of private parties really play a role in the government's decisions about capital punishment. The public images of recent years are the stories Americans tell themselves to put the practice of execution forward in the most favorable light possible. So the practice is imagined as we wish it to be.

But just as dreams and aspirations may be a powerful window into the psychological character of the dreamer, the wishes expressed about capital punishment in the images of victim service and psychological closure are a window into what might make Americans uncomfortable about executions. The strenuous effort at degovernmentalization of the reasons for execution is a signal that many citizens feel uncomfortable watching governments kill to achieve solely governmental purposes. It is far more comfortable to imagine the executioner as the personal servant of homicide survivors than to accept the legitimacy of a government killing for its own purposes.

But why are most Americans not also discomforted by the idea that the principal objective of a program of state executions is to make the survivors of homicide feel better about their status in the community and to speed their psychological recovery from the trauma of losing loved ones?

Welcoming the image of community and personal stakes in the death penalty suggests a link to earlier years when individuals and groups would literally take the responsibility of punishing criminals into their own hands.
Those aspects of the death penalty that Americans seem to admire in the
modern image of capital punishment suggest that the sentiments behind
current support for the death penalty, the support that sets the United
States apart from other developed nations, may have its roots in the claims
of individuals and groups to demand punishment for their own private
purposes. After considering the role of federalism and deference to state
power in the way current death penalty policies have evolved in Chapter 4,
Chapter 5 introduces the vigilante tradition as one significant historical
precursor to the private service imagery of modern American execution.

II

EXPLAINING THE AMERICAN DIFFERENCE

TWO DIFFERENT KINDS of questions can be asked about the death penalty in the United States. One inquiry concerns the whole of the history and the function of the death penalty: why American governments use it, why most citizens support it, why some groups oppose it, and so forth. A detailed account of the whole of this history will cover many topics and will also overlap with the history of capital punishment in other nations. The history of capital punishment in one developed nation will be similar in its content and timing to the story in other developed nations.

The second sort of question that can be asked is, What sets the United States apart from the pattern of recent history in the rest of the Western world? This inquiry will not emphasize all of the common elements in the history of capital punishment in the developed nations; it searches instead for those exceptional elements in American history and governmental structure that account for why the United States is pursuing a different policy at the beginning of the twenty-first century. Does this separate course have causes that we can identify? This type of analysis implicates a narrower range of issues. The chapters that follow concern this second, more specific sort of question.

The next three chapters develop an explanation for the exceptional status of the death penalty in the United States. Two elements of American culture and government have jointly caused a revival of executions in the United States in the last years of the twentieth century. One is the federal system of government, which grants states extraordinary powers in the choice and in the administration of punishments. Chapter 4 profiles the conflicts around who controls the unique federal death penalty system that has caused monumental delays while failing to ensure minimum standards of justice in the states.

The second key ingredient in explaining why the United States is the scene of state execution in the twenty-first century is a strong tradition of vigilante values, which is found in all parts of the United States but is most powerful in the South and the Southwest. Chapter 5 shows the close link between a history of vigilante conduct early in the twentieth century and the propensity to conduct executions in the 1980s and 1990s. The vigilante tradition is important in current history as a counterweight to the strongly held attachment to due process of law and to distrust of government power, which are also deeply ingrained American values. Using lynching as the extreme example of vigilante values, the chapter shows a link between the excessive communal force at the dawn of the twentieth century and the propensity to execution a century later. The states and the region where lynching was dominant show clear domination of recent executions, while those states with very low historic lynching records are much less likely than average to have either a death penalty or executions late in the twentieth century.

Chapter 6 concludes this part of the book by giving an account of the fundamental conflict between due process and vigilante values that dominates emotions and conduct about capital punishment. The due process and vigilante value systems were each strongly held throughout the earlier history of the United States, and each tradition inspires the respect of contemporary citizens. But these two mindsets are also fundamentally inconsistent. That the death penalty conflict is a proxy war between two more general value systems makes the capital punishment question more important in the United States than elsewhere, less susceptible to satisfactory compromise, and more likely to require one or the other of the clashing value systems to drop from favor before there is a peaceful and stable solution to the controversy.

4

Federalism and Its Discontents

A CHAPTER on federalism seems more appropriate for a textbook on government than for an attempt to explain the extraordinary pattern of executions in the United States. But the system of allocating power to different levels of government in the United States is one defining element of the unique policy environment of capital punishment. The current system of processing capital cases is incomprehensible without information on federalism. And the large and systematic differences between states in execution policy are also important clues to identifying what sets America apart on the death penalty. So any serious study of American capital punishment must do its homework on the federal system of government and its manifold impacts on capital punishment policy.

But the capital punishment arrangement discussed in this chapter is certainly not garden-variety American federalism. There is little resemblance between the way that federal and state systems govern together on death penalty cases and the pattern of federal/state coordination on issues such as education, health care, highways, or water pollution. In part, these special death penalty problems have been generated because the federal controls that can be enforced only by federal courts must be superimposed on a system of criminal law that was complete and self-contained at the state level. But the conflicts and ambivalence that are caused by the death penalty itself are also a major feature of the dysfunctional present of the death penalty in the American federal system.

Here are four questions that cannot be answered without understanding the peculiar style of federalism that has developed for capital punishment:

Why do capital cases take a decade and much more between a death sentence and its execution? Why are there 3700 prisoners under sentence of death in the United States but only one in forty is executed each year? Why is a condemned prisoner in Texas or Virginia more than thirty times as likely to be executed in a six-year period as a resident of death row in California or Ohio? Why do seven out of ten death sentences get reversed at some point in the system of judicial review? Answering these questions is the task of this chapter.

The major issue of governmental organization in the death penalty branch of American federalism concerns which level of government should have the power to decide when death sentences can be carried out. For most of American history, state governments had almost complete authority over criminal justice policy, including capital punishment. During the 1970s, the U.S. Supreme Court imposed federal standards that governed the acts, levels of culpability, and procedures that must be established before an execution could meet the requirements of the Eighth Amendment. The federal rules designed to guarantee principled use of the death penalty were unique in the federal governance of state criminal justice proceedings. These new standards offended the interests of states to control their own punishment processes, and the federal rules have been compromised repeatedly by Supreme Court decisions and legislation. The resulting system combines most of the costs of federal rules and review with few of the benefits.

This chapter is organized in three unequal installments that tell the story of how the Supreme Court has fashioned a Frankenstein's monster out of death penalty cases in the past quarter-century. A brief first section outlines the historical division of authority between federal and state government on criminal justice generally and the death penalty in particular. A longer second section discusses some of the ways in which federal-state division of responsibility has influenced the kinds of death penalty policy that have evolved in the last fifty years of American history. The final section of the chapter addresses what the study of state level differences can teach us about the substance of death penalty policies.

Crime and Punishment in American Federal Government

Defining and punishing crime is the exclusive province of state government in the United States, with two exceptions. The first exception is that the national government also has the power to pass its own criminal laws. A second national limit on state control is the federal Bill of Rights and a few other federal legal standards that state laws cannot contradict.

For most of American history, the influence of the federal government on matters of criminal justice has been quite modest. States have had more authority in matters of crime and punishment than in most other governmental domains except education. The states currently account for about 95 percent of all state and federal criminal convictions, and state and local governments house more than 95 percent of all prison and jail inmates. This near monopoly on prisoners shows the modest impact of independent federal criminal law. The administrative dominance of state and local government extends as well to police, where more than 85 percent of all police jobs are state and local (Zimring and Hawkins 1996, p. 17, table 1).

For most of American history, the administration of criminal justice by the states was also not restricted much by the federal courts enforcing doctrines of federal constitutional law. The procedural requirements for criminal cases in the Bill of Rights were not applied full-force to state criminal proceedings because the Bill of Rights was held not to apply against state government. Only if the state's criminal processes fell below those necessary to a standard of ordered liberty would federal constitutional courts nullify state court criminal convictions. Until the middle of the twentieth century, federal courts would nullify state court criminal convictions only if the state's criminal processes fell below those "essential to a standard of ordered liberty."

In practice, the states were free to choose the conduct subject to punishment as well as the punishments to be imposed, and this discretion extended as well to the penalty of death. There were no special federal restrictions on capital punishment in the United States for the first 150 years of constitutional government. Each state decided whether to have a death penalty, the crimes for which a death penalty might be imposed, and the range of special procedures (if any) that would be provided when a defendant faced the death penalty.

The first shadows across complete state hegemony over criminal proceedings came in the mid-1930s, in *Powell v. Alabama* and *Brown v. Mississippi*. The *Powell* decision required that indigent defendants must be provided legal counsel if the state sought the death penalty. For almost three decades, this right to counsel obligation of the states applied only to capital cases. The *Brown* case forbade the introducing into evidence those confessions that had been violently coerced by police.

By the mid-1960s, the federal Supreme Court had extended the reach of constitutional controls to state policing and trial procedures including searches, interrogation, and indigent felony defendants' rights to counsel at trial and on appeal. About the same time that this expansion of the scope of review of state criminal procedure was in progress, the U.S. Supreme Court began to hear a series of constitutional challenges to capital punishment in the states in the late 1960s. While two previous attacks on state death penalties were unsuccessful, the court's 1972 decision of *Furman v. Georgia* struck down the death penalty provisions in every then-current state law. The *Furman* case decided that allowing juries in first-degree murder cases to choose between imprisonment and death for convicted offenders without any further legal guidance was cruel and unusual punishment forbidden under the Eighth Amendment (Zimring and Hawkins 1986, chap. 3).

The *Furman* decision had the immediate effect of implying a new set of federally determined principles that state death penalty laws would have to satisfy to conform to the requirements of the Eighth Amendment. The content of this new layer of federal law did not receive much immediate attention at the time of *Furman*, because it was widely thought that no state death penalties would survive Supreme Court scrutiny. If no death penalty could satisfy the requirements of the Eighth Amendment, then there need not be any detailed set of federal standards for judging state death penalties. However, when the Supreme Court reviewed a range of new state statutory systems four years later, it approved two types of nonmandatory death penalty procedures that provided some guidance to the jury on the choice between prison and death sentences.

The two-step process of striking down open-ended discretionary systems in 1972 and then approving some state systems in 1976 created the need for a detailed set of substantive principles that would have to be determined by the federal courts on a case-by-case common law method. Could the states provide a death penalty for rape if no death resulted? What about rape of a child? If the death of a victim is required before a death penalty will be permitted, need the defendant, to qualify for the capital sentence, have intended the victim's death? If not, need the defendant have been more than negligent? Can fifteen-year-olds who commit murder be properly sentenced to death? If not, what about mentally retarded adults lacking the cognitive capacities of the average eleven-year-old?

The Eighth Amendment and the authority of *Furman v. Georgia* made each of these questions and many more into elements of a new federal constitutional criminal law of capital punishment. Each new answer and its reasoning would beget more questions.

Several factors made death penalty jurisprudence a particularly problematic area of American constitutional law. The first problem was that there was no real substantive core to the principles on which the supreme constitutional court had to build this new law. It is very hard to identify the distinction between the laws that were struck down as cruel and unusual punishment in 1972 in *Furman v. Georgia* and those that were approved in *Gregg v. Georgia, Proffit v. Florida*, and *Jurek v. Texas* in 1976. Indeed, six of the eight justices of the Supreme Court who sat for both cases would probably regard the majority results in the two decisions as irreconcilable. Only Justices White and Stewart voted to strike down the penalties in *Furman* and upheld them in *Jurek, Proffit*, and *Gregg*. Others might consider the two sets of results as a political compromise worth supporting but not a principled compromise, so that it is hard to reason from the two sources of authority to any clear conclusions on the authority of *Furman v. Georgia* and the *Gregg* trilogy.

The second problem with a detailed federal code of substantive death penalty law is that it creates tension with the deference to state and local judgments, which is the emotional center of federalism. The detailed regulation of what a state may or may not put in its capital punishment penal law is the type of micromanagement of state criminal law deeply resented by the states and disliked as well by sitting justices of the Supreme Court, including Rehnquist, O'Connor, and Kennedy. In some ways, the detailed regulation of the operation of state systems is more continually intrusive on state government than would have been a flat ban on executions.

There is a third problem with constructing a set of principles of criminal law that state laws providing death must meet. Several justices on the Supreme Court in the 1970s and 1980s did not want to impose standards on the states and also hated last-minute death penalty litigation. Several justices grew to resent the Supreme Court being the last stop before an execution, and Justice Powell chaired a committee to cut down on last-minute death penalty litigation (Zimring 1999). Making the Supreme Court the last stop before an execution means that the judges will either have blood on their hands if the appeal is turned down or appear to be obstructing state justice systems if they grant an appeal. The effort to ban "last-minute litigation" is an attempt to create rules that do not blame the justices for the execution.

There is one further problem with the use of national standards by the Supreme Court to reduce the variability of state systems on aspects of the death penalty: It doesn't work. The Supreme Court itself will issue an opinion in fewer than one in a hundred capital cases, and the lower federal courts vary more than substantially in their inclinations in death cases as well as in the level of scrutiny they are willing to apply to the operations of state government. Adding a federal-court layer to the review of capital cases does not guarantee any uniformity of outcome in capital cases, as we see below.

The Fruits of Federalism

The three main impacts of the post-*Furman* federal system on capital punishment are: (1) huge variation in death penalty policy, (2) procedural complication and delay, and (3) the commingling of sentiments about capital punishment with the politics of localism and the rhetoric of states' rights. These three trends, taken together, have produced a pattern of procedures and outcomes that is almost universally detested in government, among practicing lawyers, and by interested observers. But the universal unpopularity of current procedures does not lead to any easy reforms, for reasons best examined after the role of the federal system in creating the federal Frankenstein's monster has been explored.

Diversity in the Federal System

In one important sense, the notion most foreign critics have of a national policy toward the death penalty in the United States is false. State policy toward the death penalty varies widely in both theory and practice. Over the first quarter-century after *Gregg v. Georgia* was decided in 1976, more than 99 percent of all death sentences were imposed by state rather than federal government, and all but one of the first 716 executions were conducted by state governments. But many U.S. states have no death penalty in their criminal codes; others have legislation on the books but do not conduct any executions; and a small number of states conduct the majority of executions (Hertz and Liebman 2001).

Documentation of the variation in death penalty policy begins with the basic question of whether the penalty of death is in a state's penal code. Thirty-eight of fifty states in the United States provide some death penalty, while twelve states provide no capital punishment. Many of the American states without a death penalty abolished capital punishment long ago, and those American states that had dropped a death penalty for a sustained period prior to 1960 have remained abolitionist since then. The state of Michigan abolished the death penalty in 1846, more than a century before France and England took any serious steps toward ending executions. Populous states such as Wisconsin and Minnesota have remained stable in their abolitionist posture for almost a century, even though public opinion in these states is as concerned about violent crime as elsewhere in the United States.

But the division between abolition and death penalty states is only the beginning of the many ways in which the fifty U.S. states differ in policy toward the death penalty. In addition to the twelve states without any death penalty, another seven states provide for a death penalty but have not executed any offenders in the quarter-century since *Gregg v. Georgia*. Small states such as South Dakota and New Hampshire are in this category; neither has executed in over fifty years. But large states such as New Jersey and New York have also not executed anyone. In New York's case, a death penalty has been in force only since 1995, but in New Jersey the penalty has been in effect for two decades without a resulting execution (Death Penalty Information Center 2002).

At the other extreme in execution policy are several states in the American South with very high numbers of executions. While only about 40 percent of the states with death penalty legislation are in the Southern region, 76 of the 85 executions that took place in the United States in 2000 were in the South, or 88 percent of the total.

Figure 4.1 provides summary statistics on how the fifty U.S. states can be divided on capital punishment. While only one-quarter of U.S. states are without execution by law, 38 percent of the states in the United States have not had any executions in more than thirty-five years, and only one-quarter of all states have averaged more than one execution every other year since 1977.

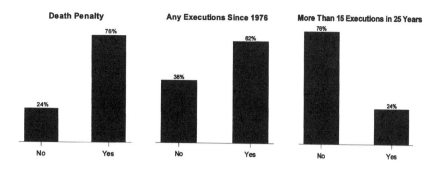

Figure 4.1. The division of American states by capital punishment records, 1977–2001. *Source*: Death Penalty Information Center 2002.

There is a pronounced regional pattern associated with variations in death penalty policy among U.S. states. All of the highest levels of execution reported in Figure 4.1 are in the South, except Arizona and Missouri, and no Southern state lacks either a death penalty or some history of recent execution. At the other extreme in regional pattern are the states in the Northeastern sector of the United States, where higher than expected concentrations of non–death penalty, nonexecution, and low rate of execution states are found. On a regional basis, the Southern states have generated an execution rate per million citizens more than a hundred times the level in the Northeastern states, and these regional totals hide state-to-state variations that are even more drastic. Figure 4.2 presents rates of execution over the period 1977–2000 per million state residents in the year 2000 census for the twenty largest American states with a death penalty statute in effect for at least fifteen years after 1976.

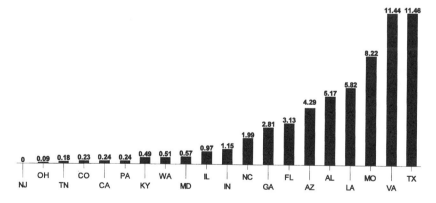

Figure 4.2. Execution rate per million population (20 most populous death penalty states), 1977–2000. *Note*: New York is excluded because it did not have a death penalty statute until 1995. *Sources*: U.S. Census, 2000; Death Penalty Information Center (http://www.deathpenaltyinfo.org/percapita.html).

Every state in Figure 4.2 has a population of more than 4 million and a homicide statute that provides a death penalty for roughly similar types of aggravated first-degree murder. But the variance in execution frequency can only be called extraordinary. The first interesting feature of Figure 4.2 is the state-to-state variance, with states such as Texas and Virginia executing at rates nearly fifty times those of Colorado, California, and Pennsylvania. The second striking feature of the figure is that there is no meaningful "average" state in execution rate. The fifth highest state in this distribution has ten times the execution rate as the fifth lowest. The median rate per million is only about a third of the mean rate.

THE SIGNIFICANCE OF INTERSTATE VARIATIONS

The facts of state-to-state variations are easier to determine than to evaluate. When and why is substantial difference in death penalty policy between the states a good thing in a federal union, and when and why not? The key to evaluating the significance of state-to-state differences is determining the ambitions and assumptions behind the Supreme Court decisions in *Furman* and *Gregg*. Some of the variations this section has shown are precisely what was hoped for in *Gregg v. Georgia*: Different states that have different legal policies toward capital punishment that produce the outcomes intended.

The clearest example of this benign variation is the contrast between abolitionist and death penalty states. Wisconsin has no executions because it does not believe in capital punishment, and Texas has executions because the Texas legislature wishes to punish some forms of murder by death. The statistical differences in outcome produced by this contrast in legislative policy is exactly the variation that *Gregg v. Georgia* approved.

At the other end of the spectrum are large contrasts in execution policy where the legal standards of two different states are quite similar. There is no great difference in the definition of capital murder in the penal codes of Texas and California. Each state allows juries to select death in a wide variety of murders with "special circumstances" such as a collateral felony, a multiple killing, or a special class of victim (California Penal Code §3600; Texas Penal Code §19.03). The majority of death row inmates in each state are sentenced for robbery killings, rape, multiple victim killings, or killing one of a special class of victims.

With all this similarity, and with federal standards and federal courts to police the appropriateness of death sentences, the contrast in death sentence outcomes between Texas and California has been quite striking. On January 1, 1995, Texas had a death row population of 391, while California had a death row of 386 (Death Penalty Information Center 2002). Over the next six years, from January 1995 through December 2000, a total of 154 executions occurred in Texas while a total of six executions were carried out in California. Texas executed twenty-six times as many prisoners for its death row population as did California. If we use these numbers to estimate the chances of execution for a prisoner on death row in Texas over the six years after 1995, the odds of being executed are higher than one chance in three. In California, the chances of execution over the same period were about one in sixty-five. This type of wide variation that has no explanation in legal terms would seem problematic under the assumptions of *Furman* and *Gregg*.

While there are no clear indications that the large variations in the types of operational systems found in states with different death penalties is a response to different styles of state legislation, there is abundant evidence that regional differences are extremely important to the variations in risk of execution found from state to state. Figure 4.3 computes, for every U.S. state that had more than fifty inmates on death row at the beginning of 1995, the number of executions over the next six years as a rate per 100 persons on death row in 1995. By restricting the comparison to states with big beginning death row populations, there is an increased likelihood that differences noted between the states are not mere chance variation.

The variation in execution rate per 100 death row prisoners is greater than 100 to one, with Ohio killing fewer than one in 100 condemned prisoners and Virginia's executions during the study period exceeding its death row population at the outset. The major Eastern and Midwestern states are clustered at the low end of the distribution, while all those states at the high end are in the South, with the exception of Arizona. But Southern states such as Georgia and Florida have execution rates less than one-sixth that of Texas and South Carolina and less than 5 percent of the Virginia rate, so the variation within the region is very substantial. The Illinois

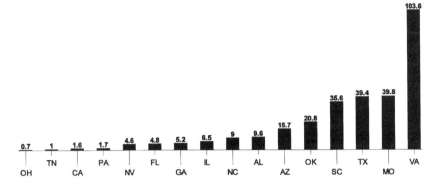

Figure 4.3. Number of persons executed, 1995–2000, per 100 offenders on death row in January 1995, in sixteen largest death row population states as of 1995. *Source*: U.S. Department of Justice, Bureau of Justice Statistics, Capital Punishment 1995; Death Penalty Information Center.

execution rate was more than four times as great as in the other northern states with large death row populations, even though the scandals in Illinois halted executions there in 1999.

When reviewing the very substantial range of rates reported in Figure 4.3, it should be remembered that the focus here is on the death row population as the beginning of the analysis, so that state-to-state differences in homicide rates, death penalty prosecutions, statutory coverage, and jury willingness to impose death sentences do not influence the different rates found. Figure 4.3 shows only the state-to-state differences in transforming death sentences into executions. Further, both the substantive standards that govern and the court system that provides the ultimate review of all these cases are federal—so that the same law and the same courts are governing outcomes. Under such circumstances, a range of rates that covers two orders of magnitude should be quite surprising. And this wide range is not the result of one or two states at the far end of an execution risk distribution. Twenty-five percent of states execute fewer than one in fifty of their condemned prisoners, and 25 percent of the states in Figure 4.3 execute more than one in three, so that the fourth-highest state (South Carolina) had an execution risk twenty times greater than the fourth-lowest state (Pennsylvania).

While the operating elements that produce these huge differences are not well understood, the significance of the degree of variation should be beyond controversy. The capital punishment systems in these different states cannot be using the same system of review in examining for errors in capital cases and in responding to errors identified in death penalty appeals. Being under a death sentence was 150 times as life-threatening in Virginia as in Ohio, forty times as dangerous in Texas as in Tennessee.

The main lesson of the huge range of execution risks in Figure 4.3 is that the law in action on the death penalty differs widely even when the law on the books—from death penalty statutes to federal Eighth Amendment standards and doctrine—is quite similar.

The timing of this extreme diversity in execution rates is a puzzle. All this variance is found after two trends pushed the formal legal principles of capital punishment law in the states that retained a penalty much closer together. The first homogenizing force was the federal standards that control so many issues after *Furman*, *Gregg*, and scores of later Supreme Court death penalty decisions. The second unifying influence was the court's approval of only a few particular formulas for death penalty legislation that were then widely emulated. For example, when the U.S. Supreme Court opinion in *Gregg v. Georgia* gave a favorable evaluation to the mitigating and aggravating factors outlined in the Model Penal Code, a large number of state legislatures adopted these standards to assure the validity of their statutes when challenged before the Supreme Court. So directly and indirectly, the expanding role of federal law and federal courts in the death penalty process made state death penalty systems more similar doctrinally.

But the operational differences in executions between regions and states remain vast, and by some measures these differences are higher after *Gregg v. Georgia* than in the earlier period without national standards. Figure 4.4 provides a comparison of the regional distribution of executions during the period 1950–64 with the parallel distribution for the two decades after 1980.

The two time periods in Figure 4.4 are before and after federal standards. The surprising conclusion is that the concentration of executions in the Southern states increases rather than decreases after federal standards are imposed. In the years before the federal rules, three out of five executions took place in the South, and the ratio of Southern to non-Southern executions was 1.5 to one. In the years after federal rules, four out of five executions took place in the capital punishment confederacy, which means that the ratio of Southern to non-Southern executions has been four to one. There was no major shift in the distribution of either death penalty states or population to explain this shift. There was continuity in both the number and location of death penalty states in the United States during the period. The Southern state share of total population increased 5 percent between 1960 and 2000.

To put the puzzle of increased concentration by region another way: Knowing the proportion of the U.S. population in a region, the number of states with a death penalty, and the homicide rate in the region will tell the observer *less* about the rate of execution in that region after the federal standards are in place than before. That factors such as legislation have less predictive value on execution rates would seem to disappoint the assumptions if not the ambitions of the justices who decided *Gregg v. Georgia*. But quite apart from its normative significance, the greater concentration of execution in the Southern states in the decades after *Gregg v. Georgia* is important for understanding and explaining the dynamics of capital punishment in recent times. As a descriptive matter, why are four-fifths of all

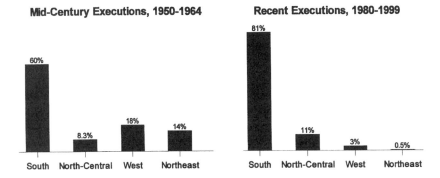

Figure 4.4. Regional distribution of executions, 1950–1964, versus 1977–1999. *Sources*: Death Penalty Information Center, http://www.deathpenaltyinfo.org; Espy and Smylka 1988.

executions in the South? If it is because the judicial hurdles are lower in Southern states, why might *that* be the case, and why does the concentration increase further when federal standards and federal courts are added after *Furman* and *Gregg*? If federal courts are also "easier" in the South or "harder" everywhere else, how does this happen and what are the ways in which it becomes manifest? Regional and individual state variations are of extraordinary magnitude in the United States, and explaining how they are determined is a quite significant part of understanding the American career of capital punishment.

Deference, Delay, and Resentment in the New Federal Death Penalty System

While the Supreme Court of the United States imposed a number of federal standards on state death penalties, the actual trial of all state charges takes place in state courts rather than federal courts. And all defenses and objections reasonably available to a capital defendant must be raised in the state courts by a defendant who must also work his way through all state appellate processes before he may file a writ of habeas corpus in a federal district court, the first sustained look at a case by a federal court for the more than 99 percent of all death cases where the U.S. Supreme Court does not hear a direct appeal from a state supreme court. Requiring a defendant to "exhaust state remedies" prior to federal habeas corpus is a method of giving deference to state courts, allowing them to correct errors even on federal questions, and exposing the case to federal judges only after all state remedies have been pursued (Hertz and Liebman 2001).

But deference in the federal system comes at a price, and that price is delay in completing the appellate review of state death penalty cases for many years. Because of the comprehensive portfolio of federal questions in death cases after *Furman* and *Gregg*, this means that the federal courts may not encounter the all-important federal questions in death penalty litigation until a decade after a death verdict has been rendered. The two-step process, in which federal review of federal issues cannot begin until all stages of state review have ended would be associated with long and complicated appellate judicial review even without any substantial incentives for delay. Here is the central reason why any realistic prospect of due process requires extensive delay: Most of the important constitutional issues in death cases are federal questions. But no federal court can even begin to examine arguments on these questions until all the proceedings in the state system have concluded. If the federal courts are going to take the constitutional provisions in death cases seriously, then the most important parts of giving a defendant a review on federal questions will not even start for many years. The federal courts cannot force the states to speed up the process. So the only way the federal courts can reduce delay is by cutting back the time and resources they devote to making sure that what the state system did meets the federal standards of fairness.

Add to this procedural redundancy the incentive that defendants have to stay alive by prolonging the judicial processes associated with a death penalty appeal. Because any legal review would be a mockery if the defendant were to be executed before the appeal was complete, the system must keep the defendant alive until the legal process is concluded. Defendants and their lawyers therefore have strong incentives to extend the appeals as long as possible.

For prosecutors, the lengthy appeal process generates resentment and frustration that is the unique function of death penalty cases. If a defendant who has been sentenced to prison is serving his sentence while he appeals his conviction and tries after appeal to reopen his criminal case, the prosecutor may not enjoy whatever work the extended litigation will produce, but the defendant is not avoiding his punishment through the appeal process. The defendant is being subjected to the prescribed punishment in his case while he appeals to the courts. When death is the chosen punishment, it cannot be enforced until the judicial system has finished. For that reason, the prosecutor will feel cheated of reaching the desired punishment by the appeals themselves. This is particularly the case when the critical federal court reviews do not even start until many years after the death sentence was issued (Zimring 1999).

There are several ironic twists to the special vulnerability of federal review processes to the resentment that delay in execution produces during appeals. First, the time consumed by state processes determines the totality of delay, but the federal reviews are more vulnerable to becoming targets of resentment because they are last in line. Second, cutting back on these "last-in-line" federal reviews would increase the power of individual states to control outcomes independent of the federal standards that were the substantive reason for the two-stage process after *Furman* and *Gregg*. So the most vulnerable stage of the review process is also the most critical stage for any of the quality controls on state capital punishment outcomes that were supposed to rescue the systems from the arbitrary lawlessness that *Furman v. Georgia* struck down. Responding to delay by reducing the federal stages of the process is much more like cutting off the head of the quality control process than trimming its tail. The third irony is that those states that hurry their own appellate processes the most would enjoy the greatest benefit from reduction in scrutiny, but these are exactly the places where federal review is most needed.

The genuine dilemma of appellate review in state death penalties is that the prisoner's strategic incentive for delay never diminishes, but there is no safe way to cut off a defendant's strategic delay without also increasing the chances of erroneous outcomes. For federal appellate review, one cannot cut fat without also cutting muscle.

The causes of excessive delay in death penalty cases are deference to state courts in the federal system and the incentives that capital defendants have to put off execution by lengthening appeals. But the target of resentment becomes the federal courts, because they have waited until the state system has finished. If the federal review is to be an independent effort to assure that constitutional standards have been observed, that effort will already be the object of deep local resentment. There is much natural hostility to federal norms and federal law enforcement in many American states, but the frustration of executions being put off ten or fifteen years and then put in jeopardy by thorough habeas corpus review is a particular enticement to fury. But there is also a strategic incentive to blame the federal standards and to push for a reduction in federal review. Reducing independent federal review increases the state power to control the death penalty process.

The hostility of prosecutors and other local officials to appellate review in death cases is an extreme example of the conflict of interest that tugs at government actors who simultaneously wish to punish crime and conform their own conduct to legal norms. The greater the emphasis on tactical advantage and adversary values, the larger becomes the temptation for prosecutors to cut corners to achieve punishment objectives. These pressures are by no means confined to death penalty prosecutions, but the conception of the appeal process itself as the enemy of the state's penal purposes is confined to cases where the state's punishment objective is the offender's death. And the special hostility toward federal courts here continues a tradition of resentment toward federal courts in the South and the Southwest particularly.

THE LATENT FUNCTIONS OF DELAY

Those sentenced to death are not the only actors in the system who have incentives to slow down the legal process and thus avoid executions. Courts and executives in states without a strong appetite for executions can reduce the pressure to execute by slowing the legal process. Indeed, slowing down the legal process is less risky politically than reversing large numbers of death sentences because there is no direct affront to prosecutors and no easy place to fix blame for particular delays in a system where procedures are both complicated and seemingly endless. Because there are no differences in state or federal appellate reversal rates or death sentencing rates that come near to explaining the 40-to-1 and 100-to-1 differences in state execution rates noted in Figure 4.3, the larger delays in Northern and Northeastern state and federal courts all but certainly contribute to the huge gap in rates of execution.

The subtle and low visibility impact of delay can be illustrated with a chapter out of the multipart saga of the death penalty and the California

Supreme Court. After three judges on the California Supreme Court were removed by the voters in a recall election that featured attacks on death penalty decisions, the newly constituted state supreme court under Chief Justice Malcolm Lucas affirmed more than 80 percent of all the death sentences appealed to it, a record very close to the Virginia Court's 90 percent affirmance record, the highest in the nation (Kamin 2000, chap. 2). But while Virginia has executed a very high proportion of its condemned offenders, California has accumulated the largest death row population in the nation while executing only six men in six years. And the tardiness of the California courts in appointing appellate attorneys and preparing trial records for appeal has added years onto the beginning phases of each inmate's direct appeal. Four- and five-year waits for the process to start in earnest will of course postpone the later stages of state appeal on direct review and habeas corpus and lengthen the entire combination of federal and state proceedings. In this way, the same supreme court that was publicly upholding death sentences in most of its appellate decisions was postponing the reckoning with death for most of California's condemned.

THE EFFECT OF DELAY

In theory, if state A's appellate courts take twice as long to dispose of cases as state B's, that should reduce state A's rate of executions for only a fixed period of time, after which the execution rates of the two states should move closer together. If two states condemn the same number of prisoners to death each year but the state B process takes eight years and state A's takes sixteen, by year sixteen each state should be executing a similar number of prisoners each year. In this pattern, the delay does not serve to suppress execution rates permanently.

Where, however, one of the objectives of delay is to reduce executions, we can expect patterns of delay to increase rather than stay fixed so that rates of execution stay low. As time passes, the backlog of cases puts more pressure on those who seek reductions in execution through procedural delays, but there is no mathematical point of reckoning where time extensions cease to achieve a slowing of executions. All through the late 1980s and early 1990s, the differences in rates of execution between Northern and Southern states have been maintained, suggesting that no day of reckoning or even of sharply diminished returns has yet been reached in the complex set of processes that have produced huge differences in rates of execution per 100 death row prisoners. If the only delay differences between high and low execution states were the fixed intervals between death verdict and execution, the large gap in execution rates noted earlier in the chapter should have started closing in the 1990s. It has not.

There is evidence, then, that the same endless processes of review detested by many in the system may also serve the interests of governments in moderating rates of execution without being visibly lenient.

Capital Punishment, States' Rights, and the Politics of Localism

The reaction to *Furman v. Georgia* was immediate. Those states that had death penalties before the decision quickly passed new death penalty legislation, while states that had no prior legislation did nothing. There can be no better demonstration of the states' rights flavor to the shape of death penalty legislation, because only those places that had experienced federal court rejection reacted. The enactment of new forms of death penalty in prior death states was generally a swift process without protracted debate or large political importance. This pattern is evidence that most of the states were responding to a federal court decision rather than to public opinion about the death penalty.

The legal status of the death penalty after *Furman v. Georgia* was in striking contrast to the political sentiments about capital punishment in most states and of some of the justices on the Supreme Court. After *Furman*, which crimes and procedures might be a permissible basis for executing a criminal defendant was a matter of federal constitutional law not only in basic precedents such as *Furman, Gregg, Woodson*, and *Roberts v. Louisiana*, but also in the discussion of specific subsidiary issues under this set of national restrictions: *Coker v. Georgia* (nonlethal rape of an adult), *Thompson v. Oklahoma* (defendant under sixteen at the time of the crime), *Eddings v. Oklahoma* (requirement of intent to kill), and many others. Even the details of what could be punished by death became a question of federal law.

But the prevailing political sentiments were in favor of state controls, so that the structure of the post-*Furman* death penalty—with federal definitions and enforcement—was a direct contradiction of the states' rights rhetoric that *Furman v. Georgia* had generated in the nation and on the Court. Whether federal controls might have worked better in another environment cannot be known, but the deference to state interests that was the subtext of *Gregg v. Georgia* was a terrible handicap for any federally enforceable national standard of proportional justice for the death penalty.

Implications for the Study of Capital Punishment

How can insights about federalism in the organization of American government contribute to an understanding of death penalty policy in the

United States? This concluding section addresses the interplay between federalism and attitudes about capital punishment.

The Two Faces of Federalism

There is an important contrast between federalism as a formal system of distributing government power—what I call structural federalism—and federalism as an ideological or emotional orientation in the political culture of American life. The ideological baggage of federalism and states' rights is much more than a preference for state versus federal governmental power. Often the rhetoric of states' rights argues for sharp limits on federal governmental power, but the hostility to federal power is not matched by any real enthusiasm for centralized power and programs at the state level. Instead, the people and ideologies that are hostile to powerful government generally enlist on the side of states in a state versus national government competition.

But these people take the side of the states only because this structure produces less powerful and therefore less oppressive total governmental intervention in the functioning of individual and community lives. State government is selected as the lesser of evils when in competition with national power. These antigovernmental federalists need not be radical individualists or libertarians. Often in American history, the alternative to strong formal governmental control was governance by informal social groups.

The great variety of different types of ideology that can join together to oppose strong national government make it prudent to distinguish between *positive* and *negative* federalism in the American political landscape. Positive federalism is a commitment to strong state government as an instrument for the general welfare. Negative federalism is a commitment to a rhetoric of states' rights primarily as a means to limit national governmental powers. The negative federalist supports state power only when in competition against the common enemy of national sovereignty. When state government becomes the alternative to local governmental control, or to no governmental power, the negative federalist feels no allegiance to the claims of state power.

Throughout American history, negative federalism has been a much more powerful force than positive federalism. The Civil War was a conflict about legal and social systems rather than about the powers of various levels of government. Those Southern and Western states most resistive to federal power now are not more active in government activities at the state level than other states. By some measures, such as levels of taxation and regulation, strong support for "states' rights" in a state is probably negatively correlated with the strength of state government: the higher the support for states' rights, the lower the expected levels of state taxes and state regulation. This is no mystery—it is negative federalism at work. Those citizens who wish limited federal government power also desire less state governmental power.

By standard measures, the state level of government is nominated as "most trusted" less often than local government and, depending on the time of the survey, the national government (Jennings 1998, p. 224, fig. 9.3). Where regional distributions are available, the profile of responses in the South on trust and satisfaction with state government are typical of the pattern for other regions (ABC News/*Washington Post* polls, 1995 and 1996). Evidently, the state level of government does not occupy a preferred position for residents of the South.

Thus, the "states' rights" association with the swift reenaction of the death penalties wherever they had been struck down does not tell us that supporters of a death penalty believed in powerful state governments. This was a classic case study in negative federalism, a coalition united by its opposition to the exertion of federal power. It is quite likely that the negative federalists who supported death penalty legislation were also suspicious of the state level of government when it taxed and regulated citizens. Why, then, were they not terribly concerned with the taking of human life as an act of state governmental power?

The answer is not that the level of government was closer to home than Washington, D.C. Austin, Texas, is a long way from Corpus Christi and El Paso. The negative form of federalism by itself offers no structural reason to favor capital punishment or to trust *any* level of government. Indeed, in other developed democracies, distrust of government is often linked to distrust of governmental power to kill as a criminal punishment. Is something missing from the political culture in the United States that is present everywhere else in the Western democracies? Or is there an additional element in American values and traditions that provides impetus to execute when other nations have rejected executions? That is the question addressed in the next chapter.

Some Lessons from State-Level History

When the current pattern of variation among American states is compared against the historical record of each state, a striking contrast emerges. There are huge differences in policy and in execution risk among the states of the Union, differences so great that it seems foolhardy to talk of "an American policy" on the death penalty. There are states that have rejected the death penalty for a century and more. Among large states with death penalties now on the books, some have conducted no executions, while others average more than ten per year.

But while the differences between states and regions are great, the pattern over time is quite stable for most states. There is a strong tendency for states that have traditionally been at either extreme in death penalty policy to stay in that position. All the states that had abolished a death penalty by 1960 do not have a death penalty in 2003. All of the top twelve executing states in the 1950s resumed executing in the 1970s and 1980s, and the relatively small number of states that dominate execution statistics in the current era were high among the leaders half a century ago (Zimring 1991).

This continuity of policy at the state level, which statisticians would call the "path dependence" of current death penalty policy on the historical record of a state, warns us that the particular origins of the very different execution policies among American states are not to be found in current events or recent history, but rather in differences between states that are at least half a century old. This extraordinary continuity also warns us against attributing the revival of the death penalty in the United States to shifting values or changed social conditions in the 1960s and 1970s. When the pattern of which states returned to executions and which states did not is examined, the course of policy choices in the 1970s and beyond seems strongly linked to conditions and events of an earlier time. The immediate precipitants of death penalties and executions may have included rising homicide rates and anger about crime, but only in those places with a recent history of capital punishment. States with a long history of abolition weathered the storm of the late twentieth century with their abolitionist credentials intact.

There are, however, two respects in which the events of the 1980s and 1990s do not continue earlier patterns. The first difference is that executions are now more concentrated in a very few states than in previous eras. The early 1950s and the late 1990s had about the same nationwide execution numbers. In the early 1950s, the top four executing states accounted for 43 percent of the national total. In the five years after 1996, the top four executing states conducted 68 percent of all U.S. executions (see Appendix B).

The higher concentration of executions in a very few states is a result of a second key difference between the older and newer patterns of death penalty policy: the more attenuated link in recent years between death sentences and executions. In the 1950s, the number of death sentences in a jurisdiction was a much better predictor of the number of executions that would result than in the post–*Furman v. Georgia* and *Gregg v. Georgia* death penalty system. When the level of death sentences is no longer a strong predictor of executions, this will usually produce a larger concentration of executions in a very few states. States with higher resistance to executions produce large death row populations that have not produced any sharp increase in execution rates by the turn of the twenty-first century. This is the usual pattern in Northern industrial states, such as Pennsylvania, Ohio, and New Jersey, and in California. Even though the number of executions in the late 1990s was almost equal to that in the early 1950s (370 from 1996 to 2000 vs. 407 from 1951 to 1955), the clustering of recurrent executions in a very few states narrows the base of states fully participating in executions (Bureau of Justice Statistics). One key question about future trends is whether this concentration will persist.

A Strategy of Research: The Federal Laboratory

The patterned differences between states and regions are both a puzzle and an opportunity. With so much variation between American governmental entities, why not use the fifty United States as a laboratory to test hypotheses about which elements in American character or government might explain the persistent attachment to the death penalty and the different ways in which the penalty is viewed? There is good reason to suppose that theories capable of explaining variations within the United States might also explain differences between the career of the executioner in the United States and in other developed countries.

The two central policy puzzles of the past quarter-century are the persistence of the death penalty in the United States when other developed nations have rejected it, and the absence of fear of government as political motive for opposing capital punishment. Perhaps understanding the differences between Texas and Virginia, on the one hand, and Ohio and Michigan, on the other hand, can help explain why so many American states retain and use a death penalty. The assumption is that what makes Virginia so much more likely to execute will also explain why so many U.S. states differ from other Western governments.

The second issue—searching for an explanation of lack of worry about excess government power as a major theme in the American death penalty debate—is a concern that comes from the materials considered in Part I of this book. Distrust of governments that claim the right to kill seems to be a concern that comes from the "human rights" emphasis on capital punishment. Why is there almost none of this element in the debates about the death penalty in the United States?

So the issues for exploration come from transnational comparisons, but the policy differences to be studied can be found among the United States. In this sense, American federalism makes possible an empirical dimension of the search for the American difference that a more unified governance of death penalty policies would not allow.

THE APPROPRIATE MEASURE OF POLICY

If variations in state death penalty policy are an important laboratory for testing the elements in American values that encourage a death penalty, there is a preliminary question of methodology that is raised by some of this chapter's previous findings. The key question is, Which elements of state death penalty policy are the most important? Is it the presence or absence of a death penalty in the criminal law? The number of death sentences issued? The number of persons on death row? The number of executions?

We already know that executions are much more concentrated in the United States than capital statutes or even death sentences. Figure 4.5 contrasts the percentage distribution of persons condemned to death in 2001 by region with the percentage distribution of executions over the first twenty-five years after 1976.

Southern states, which have just over half of all condemned prisoners, are responsible for four out of every five executions in the United States. The West, by contrast, has a quarter of all condemned prisoners but performs only 3 percent of modern executions, and the East has one out of twelve death row prisoners but has conducted only one out of 200 modern executions. Taking regional averages, this means that a death sentence in the South has been about twenty-four times as likely to produce an execution as a death sentence in the East over the two decades after 1980. It would not be prudent under such circumstances to use death sentences as the primary measure of death penalty policy and to assume that death sentences in different regions carry the same probability of actual execution. While each element of death penalty policy, from the presence of a statute to death sentences to affirmances to execution, provides some evidence of a political commitment to the death penalty, the execution itself is the hard currency of state death penalty policy and is the best overall measure of political commitment to a fully operational capital punishment system.

Figure 4.5. Percentage distribution of executions and death row populations. *Sources*: U.S. Department of Justice, Bureau of Justice Statistics (executions), available at http://www.usdoj.gov/bjs/cp/htm; Death Penalty Information Center, available at http://www.deathpenaltyinfo.org/DRowInfo.html#state.

Conclusion

The current system of controls for capital punishment combines all of the costs of attempting to impose national standards on state capital punishment decisions with few of the benefits. The system is slow, redundant, and expensive yet produces very little evidence of quality control or consistent principles in the selection of those criminal defendants who are sentenced to death or eventually executed. The huge variations in death penalty policy that occur may not make sense as punishment policy, but they do provide an excellent opportunity to search for the causes of death penalty support in the extraordinary variation of executions among the states in the American federal union.

5

The Vigilante Tradition and Modern Executions

THE SUBSTANTIVE FEATURE of American experience that has encouraged executions and protected them from being associated with excessive government power is a mythology of local control that appears to be linked to historical traditions of vigilante violence. This chapter shows a striking parallel between the practice of capital punishment at the end of the twentieth century and the practice of lynching a century earlier. Those parts of the United States where mob killings were repeatedly inflicted as crime control without government sanction are more likely now to view official executions as expressions of the will of the community rather than the power of a distant and alien government. For this reason, modern executions are concentrated in those sections of the United States where the hangman used to administer popular justice without legal sanction. Of equal noteworthiness, those areas of the United States where lynchings were rare a century ago are much less likely now to have a death penalty or to execute. In this important respect, the propensity to execute in the twenty-first century is a direct legacy of a history of lynching and of the vigilante tradition if it is still a part of regional culture.

Lynching: A Brief Statistical History

The story and legacy of lynching is an extraordinarily important chapter of our history with lasting impact on American character and culture. The term "lynching" usually refers to the killing of one or more people by groups of citizens without government authority. The method of killing was most often hanging, but death by other types of lethal mob action—shootings, beatings, and stonings—are also lynchings. While mob action of this kind has precedent in the history of many places, the term "lynching" is American, named after Charles Lynch, a justice of the peace who presided over extrajudicial executions of suspected Tory sympathizers in the Revolutionary War period (Dray 2002, p. 21).

What distinguishes the saga of lynching in the United States from most other examples of mob violence in Western history are the volume of killings, the length of the period lynching was practiced in the United States, and its linkage to racial repression. Rather than a series of unconnected episodes of group violence, lynching in parts of the United States was a regularly occurring event that was the expression of an institutional social structure that generated repeated lynchings for many decades (Brundage 1993, pp. 2–8). It is the lynching tradition as a historical institution that seems to have lasting influence on capital punishment in parts of the United States; it represents a still-honored tradition of vigilante justice that has never been completely exorcised from American culture.

Some vital statistics on American lynching establish its significance in American history. The archives at Tuskegee Institute report a total of 4,743 deaths by lynching in the United States during the period 1882 to 1968. Some 98 percent of these lynchings occurred before 1936, and 88 percent of the total were recorded between 1889 and 1918, the years we study in detail below. While 44 of the original 48 states recorded at least one lynching after 1882, recurrent and institutionalized lynching was a Southern and to a lesser extent Western practice. The victims of lynching were overwhelmingly African American (73 percent) and many others were Native Americans. The first year after 1882 when no lynchings were reported in the United States was 1952 (Dray 2002, p. viii).

My detailed analysis of institutionalized lynching in the United States by region comes from a 1919 report assembled by the National Association for the Advancement of Colored People (NAACP). This report was a contemporaneous document, and the thirty years covered were the peak periods for vigilante killings. Figures 5.1 and 5.2 show the regional concentration of lynch mob killings during this period. Figure 5.1 reports the distribution of killings by region without any control for population differences.

As Figure 5.1 reports, 88 percent of all lynchings took place in the South, while 7 percent happened in the Midwest and 5 percent in the West. Only nine killings occurred in the Northeastern United States in the thirty-year peak period of the lynching phenomenon, less than half of 1 percent of the total for the nation.

Figure 5.2 uses data from the census of 1900 to compare rates of lynching for the total period per million population in that middle-of-the-

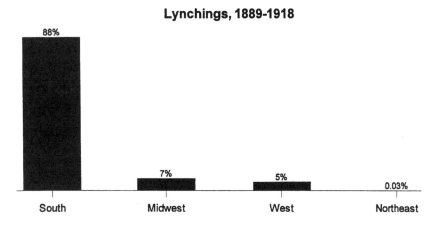

Figure 5.1. Regional percentage distributions of lynchings. *Source*: National Association for the Advancement of Colored People 1919.

period census. This calculation gives us a rough-and-ready estimate of the rate of lynching over this thirty-year period of the four regions.

The most striking contrast in pattern in both figures is that the South is at the high extreme and the Northeast at the low extreme. The Southern states were the capital of lynching as a social institution, accounting for almost nine out of ten such killings and a rate per population more than three times that of the West and fifteen times that of the Midwest. The Northeast is a firm anchor at the low end of the distribution. Controlling for population, for each vigilante killing in the Northeast, there were 290 lynchings in the South, 90 killings in the West, and 20 in the Midwest.

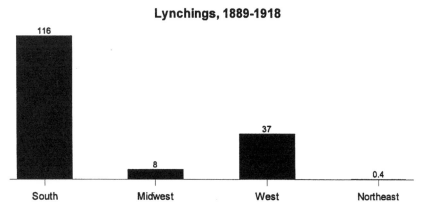

Figure 5.2. Regional lynching rates per million population from 1889 to 1918 (using 1900 census population). *Sources*: National Association for the Advancement of Colored People 1919; U.S. Census, 1900.

These extreme values in Figure 5.2 represent one region with a clear tradition of vigilante execution and one region without such a history. The sparsely populated West has a much higher rate per million than the Midwest, but each of these regions is substantially removed from both extremes in reported rates of lynching.

But might these sharp contrasts simply represent regional variation in crime or different attitudes toward the punishment of death? I test this theory with Figure 5.3, which shows the regional distribution of official state executions in the United States for the same period that Figures 5.1 and 5.2 reported lynchings.

When rates of state execution are the basis for comparison, the South is still substantially higher than other regions, but the gap between the high and low extremes is much smaller. When further controlled for population differences in the 1900 census, the rate of legal execution during the period of comparison is 2.1 to 1, South to Northeast, while the concentration of lynchings is almost 300 to 1. So the difference in lynchings is more than a hundred times as large as the difference in execution rates.

Behind this great statistical difference there is a substantive distinction between official and vigilante executions at the turn of the twentieth century: The vigilante system was functioning as a continuing element of community life throughout the South, but there was no such system or expectation in the American Northeast. By contrast, the state executioner was a continuous presence in all regions of the United States during the period 1889–1918, a regular part of government activity in all regions. The Southern states had a clear culture of vigilante violence that seems well measured by rates of lynching. The values and behavior of the late nineteenth and early twentieth century generated a vigilante tradition in the South that was not reflected in vigilante violence in the Northeast.

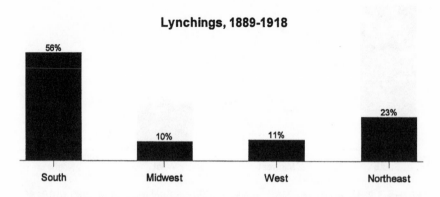

Figure 5.3. Regional percentage distributions of executions, 1889–1918. *Source*: Espy and Smylka 1988.

Which Past Is Prologue?

When the regional patterns of both executions and lynchings of a century ago are compared with the geography of recent executions, it is the lynching pattern rather that the earlier distribution of legal executions that best approximates the extremes found in the 695 executions recorded from 1977 to 2000. Figure 5.4 profiles the three distributions.

During the first twenty-four years of executions in the United States, states in the South conducted more than eight out of ten executions, while the Northeastern states had a total of three executions, or less than half of 1 percent. The ratio of Southern to Northeastern executions was 188 to 1, with the Midwest and Western states in the middle. The South to Northeast contrast in official executions is more than eighty times as large as the contrast in state execution rates between the same two regions near the turn of the twentieth century. The West, with a year 2000 population that is 63 percent of the population in the South has one-tenth as many executions in the period from 1977 to 2000 (United States Census 2002).

As the last chapter showed, the extraordinary concentration of executions in the South and the remarkable absence of them in the Northeast illustrate the wide gap between having a death penalty and killing prisoners in the new American capital punishment. We learned in Chapter 4 that the majority of states with death penalty laws are outside the South, and large states in the Northeast, such as Pennsylvania, Ohio, and New Jersey, have substantial numbers of death sentences. The gross disproportions we discover when comparing actual rates of carrying out death sentences have no parallel in the distribution of death penalty statutes, rates of murder, or even death sentences.

But why might these striking modern regional differences relate to patterns of lynching a century ago? And how can the legacy of lynching influence the wide range of practices that determine the current regional distribution of executions: differences in death penalty laws, variations in the quality of publicly provided defense attorneys, and levels of judicial scrutiny found in state and federal courts. Any plausible explanation of the huge variations in execution risk that the modern system generates must account for subtle and pervasive differences between states and regions. After a review of the execution records of individual states at the high and low ends of lynching history, I will turn to explaining how a vigilante tradition can have modern importance.

Some Data from Individual States

Might the link between lynching history and recent executions in individual states add to the regional patterns just explored? The forty-eight

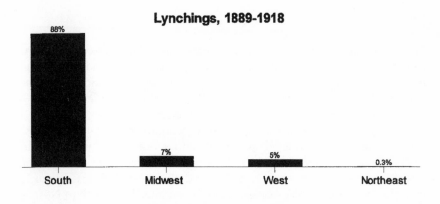

Lynchings, 1889-1918

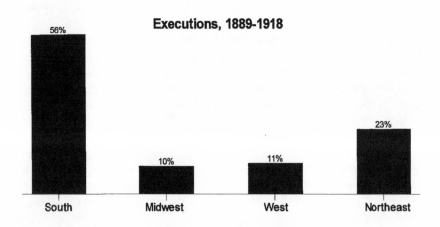

Executions, 1889-1918

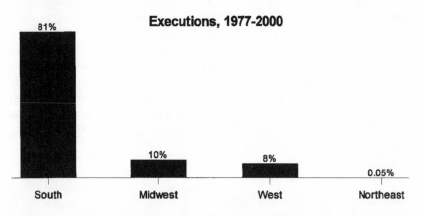

Executions, 1977-2000

Figure 5.4. Regional percentage distributions of lynchings and executions. *Sources*: Death Penalty Information Center; Espy and Smylka 1988; National Association for the Advancement of Colored People 1919; U.S. Census, 1900.

contiguous states in the Union can be divided into three rough groupings for the period 1882-1968, which is covered by the archives at the Tuskegee Institute. I use the aggregated Tuskegee Institute data here to maximize the number of lynchings for each individual state. (The Tuskegee and NAACP 1919 rankings of states are in very close agreement, as shown in Appendix A.) Fourteen states recorded 100 or more lynchings in the registry, ranging from a low of 100 in Virginia to a high of 581 in Mississippi. Using the round number of 100 as a cutoff, these will be my group of "high lynching" states. At the other end of the distribution, only fourteen of the forty-eight U.S. states recorded fewer than ten lynchings, and these become a "low lynching" group of equivalent size. The remaining twenty states are a middle group, with lynching totals ranging from nineteen to eighty-four. Table 5.1 compares the execution histories of these low- versus high-lynching states during the period from 1977 to 2000.

Eleven of the fourteen states with the lowest lynching histories have no executions in the twenty-five years after 1976, and seven of the low group have no death penalty statute. The fourteen states in the aggregate had a total of twenty-two executions, 3 percent of the 695 in the United States during the period. These states had 27 percent of the U.S. population in the 2000 census. As shown in Appendix A, the statistical patterns in the low-lynching states show much lower execution propensity than all other states in the Union. If the only contrast we made was between low-lynching

Table 5.1.

Executions 1977–2000 in High- versus Low-Lynching States

14 High-Lynching States	Execution Records 1997–2000	14 Low-Lynching States	Execution Records 1977–2000
Alabama	23	Connecticut	None
Arkansas	23	Delaware	11
Florida	50	Maine	None*
Georgia	23	Massachusetts	None*
Kentucky	2	Michigan	None*
Louisiana	26	Minnesota	None*
Mississippi	4	Nevada	8
Missouri	46	New Hampshire	None
North Carolina	16	New Jersey	None
Oklahoma	30	New York	None
South Carolina	25	Pennsylvania	3
Tennessee	1	Rhode Island	None*
Texas	239	Vermont	None*
Virginia	81	Wisconsin	None*

*No death penalty in effect throughout period.
Sources: Death Penalty Information Center (http://www.deathpenaltyinfo.org); U.S. Census, 2000 (http://www.census.gov).

history states and all other states, the difference in modern death penalty policy would be substantial.

By contrast, all of the highest lynching states in the earlier period have both death penalties and executions in the first twenty-five years after *Gregg v. Georgia*, and these fourteen states include all ten of the states with the highest volume of executions from 1977 to 2000. The fourteen states in this high-lynching category together account for 35 percent of the U.S. population in the 2000 census and for 85 percent of the first 695 executions after 1976. The median number of modern executions in a high-lynching state is twenty-four; the median number of modern executions in a low-lynching state is zero.

The statistical contrast between these two groups of states shows that they occupy the same extreme positions on the distribution of two distinct varieties of lethal violence in the United States separated by almost a century and the formal participation of government authority in the killing. Those states that had the most extensive lynching histories in the past now execute without exception and collectively dominate the nation's execution totals. Those states that were in the lowest levels of the lynching records are with only two exceptions at the bottom end of the distribution of modern executions. For the year 2000, the rate per million population of execution in the high-lynching states is twenty-two times the rate in the low-lynching states. Figure 5.5 reports the modern execution records and current population for the low, high, and middle groups of lynching states.

With just over one-third the U.S. population, the high-lynching-history states account for 85 percent of all modern executions. The lowest lynching states are responsible for only 3.2 percent of all executions, and the middle group of twenty states accounts for 12 percent of recent executions, a rate

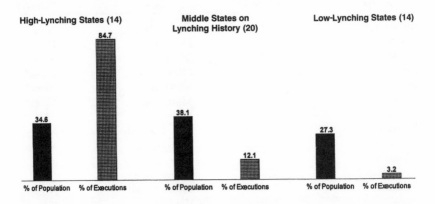

Figure 5.5. Percentage distribution of recent executions, 1977–2000, and year 2000 population of three categories of states by lynching history. *Sources*: Death Penalty Information Center 2002; National Association for the Advancement of Colored People 1919; U.S. Census, 2000.

per population about three times greater than the lowest lynching states but about one-seventh the rate of the highest lynching history jurisdictions.

The first difficulty with drawing a causal inference from the statistics on lynchings and later executions in Table 5.1 relates to the very strong overlap between regional differences and the high extreme in the lynching distributions. After all, all of the fourteen highest states are either Southern or border states. Doesn't the comparison made by Table 5.1 merely restate the Northeast-versus-South regional contrast mentioned earlier in the chapter?

There are two important dimensions that the state-by-state analysis adds to the regional distribution of modern executions presented earlier. First, while the high-lynching states are mostly Southern, the low extreme on the lynching distribution includes a group of Midwestern states as well as Northeastern states, and the same dramatic tendency of low-lynching history linking to zero execution experience in the current era holds for the low-lynching Midwestern states. Only Nevada and Delaware, with small populations during the lynching era, show any energy expended toward modern executions.

The fact that half of the lowest lynching states have no modern death penalty and the difference in execution rates between these states and the rest of the Union provide clear evidence that sharp differences in modern death penalty policies do not depend on the high rates of execution in Southern states. Extreme values at the low end of the lynching tradition predict very low modern execution records, even when the special status of Southern states is ignored. When the proportion of the low-lynching states without death penalties or executions is contrasted to the rest of the United States, the difference is statistically quite striking (see Appendix A).

This low-end linkage to modern death policy is a second, independent indication that lynching history predicts modern executions. Further, this non-Southern link between lynching history and executions makes it more likely that lynching history has an influence on modern executions at the high end. Merely to correlate Southernness with high rates of capital punishment begs the question of what in Southern culture might cause these extreme values. A wide variety of theories of Southern specialness relate to high rates of male interpersonal violence, but few of them specifically address the propensity to execute. A vigilante theory developed later in this chapter might explain the high regional propensity. Of course, it would help to test this notion statistically if two or three Southern states had low-lynching histories, but that is not the case. Instead, it will be important to identify a plausible theory of why a tradition of lynching might influence rates of execution in modern times, to create a logical connection to go with the statistical correlation.

The individual state patterns also put us on notice that the historical record on lynching does not inevitably determine the level of execution in later years. States such as Mississippi, Tennessee, and Kentucky have had a few modern executions but nowhere near the level that their earlier lynching histories might predict. Virginia, with 100 lynchings, was not in the top ten for the earlier period but has accumulated the second-highest execution total in the modern era. Delaware is a low-lynching state with lots of executions for a very small state. The American West had high lynching rates for the low population at the turn of the twentieth century but few executions in modern times. Lynching history is by no means an inevitable determinant of late-twentieth-century execution experience.

It seems plausible that a high historical commitment to vigilante justice may be a necessary but not a sufficient condition for a social and governmental climate that generates high levels of official execution in the late twentieth century. The low levels of execution found in larger states with no strong lynching history may signal that some element of the social tradition that supported lynching is necessary by the late twentieth century to support regular state execution. But how can these historical traditions account for such sharp variations in official conduct almost a hundred years after the peak of American lynching? The answer to that question may come from considering the conflict between traditions that animates current policy toward the death penalty in the United States.

How Vigilante Values Operate

I do not think that the major influence of the vigilante precedents on contemporary capital punishment comes from any inherited enthusiasm for killing as a form of social control. Instead, the tradition of regarding the punishment of criminals as a local concern acts to remove one major argument against the death penalty where the punishing agency is regarded as a government that may itself be a potential adversary to citizen interests. If this is the case, viewing punishment as a community rather than state response should leave a citizen less worried and conflicted about executions even though his or her general view of governmental power may be distrustful. If this is the operative difference in places with a strong vigilante tradition, it should produce specific patterns of citizen responses in survey research. The argument that execution is dangerous because it gives a potentially tyrannical government great power should receive more support in surveys in low-lynching regions than in high-lynching regions, even though the level of support for the death penalty itself might not vary much or at all. The strategic significance of viewing harsh punishment as communal may influence the intensity of support among supporters by removing a source of second thoughts and conflict. Easterners and Southerners may answer "yes" on death penalty poll questions in equal proportions, but the Southerners—less worried—are less conflicted supporters.

The critical significance of a vigilante tradition in this account is not that it increases the approval of killing or the appetite for lethal revenge, but that it neutralizes one powerful argument against allowing the state to kill its enemies: the fear of unlimited government power. The citizen who has positive feelings about vigilante values will identify more closely with the punishment process, will think of punishments as a community activity rather than the conduct of a governmental entity separate from community processes. The psychological mechanism that facilitates this identification process might be a form of transference, where the affective bond from communal social control in earlier times is transferred to state authority for executions and other serious punishments. Whether the psychoanalytic nomenclature is merely a metaphor for the closer identification I am suggesting in the vigilante tradition or is an accurate representation of the process is not known.

The closer identification with the agencies and acts of execution should make the identifying citizen much more receptive to the rhetoric of victim impact statements and psychological "closure" for relatives of victims in the modern merchandising of capital punishment. Stronger identification with punishment as a community process should also produce more hostility to legal controls on punishment.

Some elements of this account of how identification with a vigilante tradition can influence attitudes toward and acceptance of modern execution are easier to test than others. Finding out whether identification with the death penalty as a community response is associated with support for the death penalty and lower levels of concern about governmental mistakes in the death penalty process is not a difficult task. Finding the causes of such attitudes in individuals and groups and linking those attitudes to historical antecedents is much more difficult.

Contemporary Evidence of Vigilante Influence

No matter how dramatic the link between lynchings and current rates of execution, there is a time gap of nearly a century between the two that demands attention. What evidence do we have (other than variations in execution rates) that the lynchings of a century ago have any influence on modern attitudes, policies, and values? And if we can measure vigilante influence on contemporary conduct and belief, is there evidence that these modern traces of influence are stronger in areas where executions are more frequent?

Survey Research

This section describes my search for data on attitudes and behaviors that may relate to vigilante values. The most obvious place to search for sentiments about vigilante activities is in the extensive archives of public opinion polls in the United States. A search for polling questions explicitly mentioning vigilante behavior produced five in the Roper Center for Public Opinion Research at the University of Connecticut and two additional questions found in the Harris poll archives at the University of North Carolina (see Appendix D). One 1937 Gallup question was excluded leaving a total of six modern questions regarding vigilantism to be considered here.

A tour through the survey data begins with three differently worded questions asked by the Harris poll in the 1970s. The question was asked in 1973 whether "Vigilante groups such as the Minutemen, White Citizens' Council, and the Ku Klux Klan did more harm than good." In this version of the survey found in the Roper archive, 21 percent of the sample thought the groups did more good than harm, and 79 percent believed they did more harm than good. No breakdown on this question was available by region. Three years earlier, Harris had asked the slightly different question of whether "Vigilante groups such as the Minutemen, White Citizens' Council, and the like are helpful to the country, harmful, or neither helpful nor harmful." This earlier version was found in the Harris archive of the University of North Carolina. The national profile on this question is provided in Figure 5.6. In this multiple-choice format, six out of ten Americans regard such groups as harmful. The archived data on this question is cross-tabulated by region in Figure 5.7.

Outside the South, the proportion of the public regarding such groups as harmful averaged just over 60 percent, while the Southern respondents chose that description at a 53 percent rate.

A third Harris poll question asked respondents in 1975 whether "Citizen vigilante groups who train people to handle guns [constitute] a major contributor to violence in this country, a minor contributor, or hardly a contributor at all?" This survey did not mention specific groups, but did emphasize gun training. The pattern of responses is given in Figure 5.8.

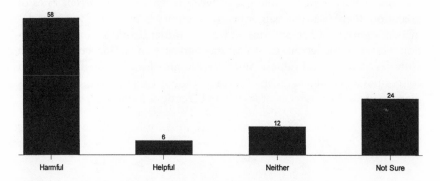

Figure 5.6. "Are vigilante groups such as the Minutemen, White Citizens' Council, and the like harmful, helpful, or neither?" *Source*: Harris poll, 1970, Louis Harris Archive, University of North Carolina (see Appendix D).

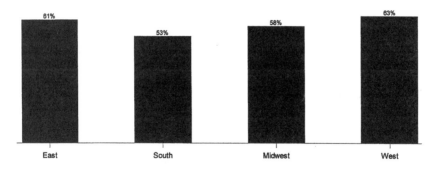

Figure 5.7. "Vigilante groups such as the Minutemen, White Citizens' Council, and the like are harmful," by region, 1970. *Source*: Harris Poll, 1970, Louis Harris Archive, University of North Carolina (see Appendix D).

The archived data on this question allowed a cross-tabulation by region, and only 27 percent of Southern respondents regarded vigilante groups as a major problem, at least 10 percent below the proportions of the population that rated such groups a major problem in the other three regions (see Appendix D).

A second pair of questions asked by the Gallup poll was inspired by the publicity surrounding the shooting by Bernard Goetz of four youths who accosted him in a New York subway. After describing the Goetz episode, the Gallup Organization asked "Whether incidents like these—taking the law into one's own hands, often called vigilantism—are sometimes justified by the circumstances, or are never justified?" When this question was asked in February 1985, some 72 percent of the respondents believed that "incidents like these" were sometimes justified, and 17 percent responded that such conduct was never justified. A slightly different version of this

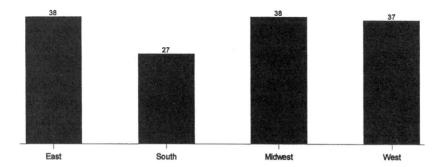

Figure 5.8. "Do you feel that citizen vigilante groups who train people to handle guns are a major contributor to violence?" October 1975.
Source: Harris Survey 7586, Louis Harris Archive, University of North Carolina (see Appendix D).

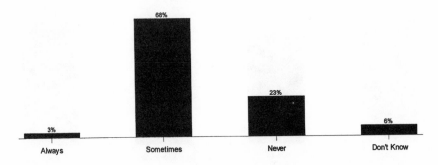

Figure 5.9. "Do you feel that taking the law into one's own hands, often called vigilantism, is justified by circumstances?" *Source*: Gallup Poll, 1985 (see Appendix D).

question asked by Gallup in March 1985 for *Newsweek* produced the answers profiled in Figure 5.9.

Both Gallup polls were cross-tabulated by region. The February poll showed the South with a slightly larger level of justification (83 percent always or sometimes justified vs. 79 percent for the other regions), while the March poll did not show Southern leadership. Neither survey showed a statistically significant regional pattern.

The final survey question that addresses the vigilante issue comes from a 1991 survey conducted in conjunction with National Crime Victim's Week. As part of a survey instrument devoted to crime victimization and crime policy issues, respondents were asked, "Is vigilantism ever justified?" and 33 percent of the national sample answered yes (see Appendix D). This level of support is higher than other readings of general support but only half the "sometimes justified" support that Gallup obtained with the example of the Goetz case. There was no significant variation by region.

Some Conclusions

The individual survey questions that have asked about vigilante values suffer from a variety of limits. The Gallup poll questions assume that Bernard Goetz was engaged in vigilante conduct, when unprovoked self-defense was a possible interpretation. The two earlier Harris questions associate the vigilante label with highly unpopular groups, and the 1975 question speaks of vigilante groups teaching firearms use without any reference. And the key term "vigilante" is frequently undefined.

But the collective portrait that appears in these six questions provides some important clues to contemporary American attitudes. Between a fifth and a third of respondents provide favorable responses to the term "vigilante," depending on the groups or behavior that the surveys associate with vigilantism. When an individual act of shooting a criminal aggressor is the provided example of a vigilante conduct, more than seven out of ten respondents believe such conduct is sometimes justified. Extremist organizations such as the Minutemen and the Ku Klux Klan are disapproved, and association with such groups drives down the approval rating of the vigilante terminology. When the stimulus for a response is self-defense against a particular criminal act, public approval more than doubles.

The South is the region with the highest prevalence of provigilante values wherever there is a pattern by region, but the gap between Southern and non-Southern patterns is significant only for the two Harris questions. While the South does stand out in modern surveys on the vigilante theme, the West as a region does not. The second lowest disapprovals of vigilante groups occur in the Midwest, and the Western region as a whole is slightly lower than other regions in vigilante approval.

A Survey Agenda

The existing survey evidence is quite thin on the issue of vigilante values, but there is much that can be learned from future surveys. Carefully designed questions can explore which aspects of the vigilante tradition appeal to Americans and which aspects provoke disagreement. The same questions can be addressed to foreign and U.S. audiences to test whether the level of U.S. approval for some types of vigilante responses is distinctive. Surveys can ask directly whether citizens think of executions as a governmental or a community response to crime, and the research can explore whether those who believe it to be communal are more likely to support executions and less likely to express distrust of government in their attitudes about executions. The regional patterns of belief in execution as communal or governmental can be compared with expressed trust or distrust in government and with support for execution. Survey research has substantial potential to increase knowledge in a relatively short time.

Behavioral Measures of Vigilante Values

A second obvious way of measuring the contemporary strength of a vigilante tradition in the United States is to search for types of policy or behavior that provide a reliable index of support for a vigilante tradition and to compare the way such behaviors are distributed with patterns of executions. But the first step in that scenario—finding measurable behavior closely linked to a vigilante tradition—is a difficult task. The vigilante content of policies or behavior is a matter of interpretation, and such interpretations can always be contested. In that important sense, vigilantism, like beauty, is always in the eye of the beholder.

Concealed Weapons Laws

The first candidate as an index of the strength of vigilante sentiments is the prevalence of laws that allow citizens to carry concealed weapons on their persons as a potential defense against crime. Almost all the states in the United States have laws that require special permits for citizens to carry concealed weapons. In many states, the local authorities can and do require that applicants for permits-to-carry licenses show a special need to carry a gun and may also require some more evidence of reliability than is required of ordinary gun owners. In those states, the permit to carry a concealed handgun in public is a special privilege.

As a reaction against special requirements for carrying concealed deadly weapons, many states have passed laws requiring that officials "shall issue" a permit to carry a concealed weapon if the applicant is qualified to own guns. These laws remove a frequently major barrier to obtaining such a license and are regarded as an encouragement for citizens to carry concealed weapons (Lott 1998; Zimring and Hawkins 1997). States that pass these laws would seem much more hospitable to the values associated with a vigilante tradition, but they may also be a product of pro–gun ownership and pro–gun owner sentiments that do not link directly to encouraging the use of guns in self-defense.

Nevertheless, of all the gun laws in the United States, this legislation is most closely associated with approval of citizen self-defensive use of deadly force in public places. The stated purpose of such legislation is encouraging citizen use of guns as a crime-control device.

Figure 5.10 shows the prevalence of "shall issue" laws by region in the United States as of 1998. I use the thirty-one states classified as "non-discretionary" by John Lott, Jr., in *More Guns, Less Crime* (1998) as my measure of states approving of widespread citizen carrying of concealed deadly weapons. By Lott's calculations, more than six of every ten U.S. states support this policy. This includes one state (Vermont) with no legislation on the subject, but the "non-discretionary classification" is the most accurate measure of lenient state-level policy on concealed weapons.

The regional concentration of laws encouraging carrying concealed weapons is clear-cut. All but two of the sixteen Southern states have non-discretionary laws, a prevalence of almost 90 percent. The next highest region is the West with 69 percent, followed by the Northeast and Midwest. If these laws are a good measure of positive attitudes toward violent self-help against crime by citizens, this distribution shows that deadly self-

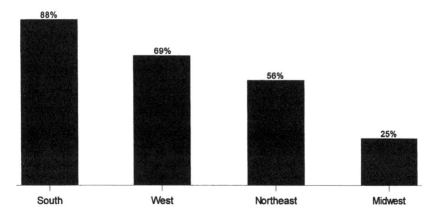

Figure 5.10. Prevalence of "non-discretionary" permit-to-carry laws by region. *Source*: Lott 1998 (Table 4.12, pp. 87–99).

defense is very popular throughout the United States but has particular power in the South and the West.

There are obvious limits to concealed weapons laws as an index of vigilante values. The use of deadly weapons in self-defense is only one form of community crime control, and the approval of carrying concealed weapons certainly does not imply a blanket approval of other forms of nongovernmental crime controls. Further, there are other dimensions of political differences between states and regions that might influence the rate at which lenient permit-to-carry laws are passed, such as the strength of organizations of gun owners in a state and all the cultural and demographic factors that influence the power of gun groups. Recent surveys suggest that handgun ownership is about one-third higher in the South and West than in the Midwest, so this higher intensity of ownership might also predict the greater popularity of shall-issue laws (Smith 2000). But the ownership rate is just as high in the West as in the South, so that the Southern lead in "shall issue" legislation must have other causes. Further, higher handgun ownership itself may be an outcome of larger enthusiasm for private use of force. If any current law could serve as an index of the power of vigilante sentiments and conditions, the permit-to-carry legislation would seem the strongest candidate, and the pattern by region is clear.

Rates of Self-Defense Killings

A second way to test the extent to which the vigilante tradition might be an influence on contemporary behavior is to study the rates of lethal self-defense against crime by private citizens. One strong measure of the extent to which people believe that self-defense is justified is the extent to which it is employed. There is no available statistic that totals the number of citizens fighting off criminal attacks, but cases where police believe that private citizens killed in justifiable self-defense are maintained and reported by the Uniform Crime Report section of the FBI. These most extreme cases of justified self-defense are one index of the general level of self-defense activity and a particularly good measure of whether citizens are willing to go to extreme lengths in defense of their property or persons.

Figure 5.11 shows a regional breakdown of the rate of killings in justified self-defense per 100,000 residents for the four years 1995–98. The figure reports the number of fatal incidents rather than the total death toll, so that each incident that results in a killing is counted only once. Figure 5.11 shows the four-year total of fatal incidents by region, so the rate per 100,000 is on average four times what would be produced within any single year. A multiple-year figure was compiled to provide more stable estimates of this infrequent behavior.

In the years reported in Figure 5.11, the West reported just over five cases per million citizens, the South just over four. The West and the South have reported rates of justifiable fatal incidents that are about two times the rate of the other two regions.

While attitudes toward use of violence in self-defense against crime are one determinant of rates of fatal self-defense against crime, many other factors influence the extent to which different areas have different rates of such killings. Obviously, places with higher levels of violent crime will experience higher levels of attempts to defend against such acts. So the gross level of lethal self-defense by civilians may not be the most sensitive measure available of favorable attitudes toward violent self-defense.

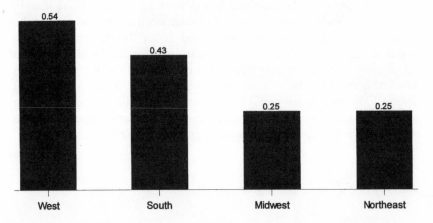

Figure 5.11. Justifiable killing incidents by citizens, by region, 1995–1998 (per 100,000 1997 population). *Source*: FBI Uniform Crime Reports (see Appendix E).

One strategy to control for environmental factors that provoke different levels of self-defensive violence is to compare the extent of citizen killing in defense against crime with the level of justified killings of suspects by police. The theory is that the extent to which the actions of citizens exceed or fall below lethal police self-defense is a more appropriate measure of the level of citizen emphasis on lethal self-defense. Figure 5.12 compares rates of police and citizen justifiable homicide by region for the same four-year period covered in the previous figure.

Using the level of police killings as a control variable shifts the Western region from the top of the citizen self-defense pantheon to the bottom because of the very high rate of police killings in the region. The South is the only region where citizens account for a larger number of lethal incidents than police, followed by the Midwest, the Northeast, and the West.

The major problem with *this* interpretation is that variations in police killings will reflect differences in policy and style as well as environmental conditions. If general support for violent defense against crime leads to higher rates of police shooting suspects, then the level of police killing becomes a measure not only of variations in criminal provocation but also of the community's encouragement of violent self-help by both citizens and law enforcement. So whether the unadjusted rate of citizen killings in Figure 5.11 is a better measure than the adjusted rate in Figure 5.12 is hard to guess, but little of importance in the interpretation of these data is lost by the inability to pick a single best measure.

The United States is the only nation where the police agency publishes rates of civilian lethal force against crime, and it is almost certain that the U.S. rate of these incidents is many times higher than in other developed

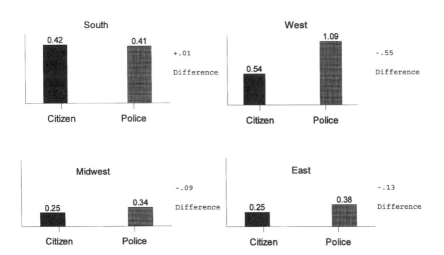

Figure 5.12. Comparing police and citizen justifiable killings by region, 1995–1998. *Source*: FBI Uniform Crime Reports (see Appendix E).

nations. Within the United States, the South and the West are the two regions with the highest levels of civilian killings of criminal suspects. The South is the only region where the rate of civilian killings is as high as the rate of police killings, but the rate of civilian killings per 100,000 is slightly higher in the West.

The Limits of Behavioral Indices

These rates of civilian use of lethal force are important data about American social conditions, but they are incomplete and potentially misleading readings on vigilante traditions. Self-defense statistics usually document individual actions rather than group behavior, and the justification is to prevent or terminate a criminal threat rather than punish the transgressor. While the line between prevention and punishment may often blur, and while areas with high rates of killing in defense against crime may have many more cases within those statistics of private punishment, this cannot be measured in the available data. The broad patterns of use of deadly weapons as instruments of responding to criminal threats are powerfully suggestive of high respect for many aspects of the vigilante tradition. Whether more detailed statistics on citizen use of lethal force are a sensitive measure of the variations in vigilante sentiments is far less certain.

But shall-issue laws and self-defense killings are not direct evidence of why citizens in some regions are less worried about state killings than in other regions. The reason why we are examining shall-issue laws or rates of citizen killings, for example, is that vigilante values may be important as a stimulus to attitudes of acceptance of the death penalty, but there is no clear way to correlate patterns of legislation and shootings with actual underlying sentiments on executions.

While it is easy to imagine a survey research program that will increase our knowledge of the contemporary significance of vigilante sentiments, it is not easy to find other plausible behavioral indicators of vigilante sentiments that can be collected and analyzed. So my guess is that surveys will prove a more valuable path to future knowledge than statistical studies of policy and behaviors that are indices of vigilante values.

The Anatomy of Conflict

One useful way to see the contemporary unrest about the death penalty in the United States is as a conflict between two traditions, each with deep roots in American history and culture. The first tradition is that of fear of government power that produces a high concern for legality. In this account, the due process tradition is based on fear of a government without limits, on the terrible power of the state to compel citizens to do its bidding.

For this reason, the expensive and seemingly interminable processes of state and federal judicial review of death cases profiled in the last chapter are a natural outgrowth of a fundamental strain in American values. Distrust of government and enforcement of limits on government power are widely shared sentiments in every region of the United States. The due process tradition of individual rights against government is as long and as strong in the United States as anywhere.

The second tradition at the center of the contemporary crisis of capital punishment is the vigilante tradition, where groups of citizens regard the punishment of criminal threats to the community as the privilege and responsibility of dominant social groups. For those who are within a dominant group, there is no need to worry about legal limits on the power of government, because community leaders are in charge of identifying targets and choosing sanctions. In the vigilante world view, the need for a fact-finding process may be displaced by personal knowledge and community agreement. The same citizens who might distrust punishment power in the hands of a distant governmental authority trust themselves and their neighbors. And the vigilante tradition gives positive sanction to communal violence if the cause is a just one.

The conflict between vigilante and legality traditions on the question of capital punishment often plays out as a competition between two competing images of the death penalty. Those who oppose the capital sanction stress that the penalty is after all the administration of state power and seek to invoke due process standards and concern about fact finding and discrimination. The image is one of government as powerful strangers.

Those who favor execution try to bring the whole death penalty process within the tradition of community control. The death penalty is in this view protecting victims and potential victims from predators who threaten the community; the vigilante spirit regards community rather than state as the real party of interest in executions. As Chapter 3 established, much of the ceremony and symbolism of modern capital punishment tries to stress the personal interests of individuals—from "victim impact" statements at trial to the closed-circuit telecasts for victims' families of the execution of Oklahoma City bomber Timothy McVeigh. These images of execution as personal justice link the American death penalty to the earlier history of vigilante justice.

Both the due process and vigilante traditions are authentic and important components of American history and culture. The consequence of two strong traditions with contradictory implications for executions is that public attitudes toward capital punishment can be ambivalent and volatile. The dynamics of this conflict are the focus of the next chapter.

While all regions of the United States have some elements of a vigilante tradition, that tradition is not spread evenly throughout the nation. The

South, where the Civil War itself might be characterized as the revolt of a society against its national government, is the modern as well as longtime capital of the vigilante tradition, and those areas in the Southwestern and Western states still closely associated with the frontier tradition may also be more attached to vigilante values than other regions.

There is, of course, no reason to assume that high levels of vigilante behavior and values in the past must persist in the political culture of a place a century later. Where the values and conduct of a previous regime have been squarely rejected, past conduct may have little bearing on current values. As Chapter 2 reported, this effort to break with the past has been a dramatic part of the history of capital punishment in Germany and Italy after World War II, in South Africa after apartheid, and in post-Soviet Central Europe. In the United States, much of the population living in the Western region of the United States, particularly on the Pacific Coast, has attenuated links with the region's history and historical identity. The San Francisco of the mid-nineteenth century that produced organized vigilante conduct is not an important element of the culture of San Francisco in 2003 (Brown 1969, pp. 50–52).

But there is no evidence of this type of contemporary rejection of the vigilante tradition in the American South and Southwest at the turn of the twenty-first century. The race codes and racism of the late nineteenth and twentieth century have been for the most part rejected by citizens in the South. But the romance of popular justice when dealing with crime and criminals has not been clearly rejected in the American South and Southwest. Instead, the Confederate flag and the history and legacy of rebellion have positive sentimental values in the South. The vigilante tradition and values as a popular response to murders and rapes that escape state punishment have never been disavowed in the same way as racial supremacy and the racist terrorism of the Ku Klux Klan. And most lynchings were labeled as crime control even in the deepest South. The majority of all lynching events that are recorded in the Tuskegee figures presented earlier in this chapter were reported to have been organized as responses to homicide, rape, and assault (see Appendix A). That these events almost always involved African American targets certainly complicates the self-serving crime control rationale found in historical accounts. Without doubt, lynch mobs were all too ready to assume that all the African American targets of their rage were terrible criminals. This would make any capacity that modern citizens feel to identify with the fears and tactics of any earlier age rather frightening.

So there is reason to believe that a strong vigilante tradition might be reflected in contemporary patterns of capital punishment. But why would the lynching patterns of a century ago be a *better* predictor of current levels of official execution than the patterns of official execution during the lynching period? Some help on this question might come from the theory that trends in capital punishment over time are determined by the contest between principles of legality and the vigilante tradition. At the turn of the twentieth century, rates of state execution were higher all throughout the United States, so that even regions with lesser commitments to vigilante values such as the Northeast would have sufficient levels of popular support to generate fairly high levels of state execution even if lynchings were not frequent (as in the Northeast) or moderately frequent (as in the Midwest). As general levels of capital punishment have declined, however, it might take a much stronger tradition of pro–capital punishment values to support high levels of execution. As the general environment turned against executions, lower levels of vigilante traditions would result only in a trickle of actual executions in regions such as the Northeast. Only in those places where the balance had always been more favorable to vigilante tradition could the less favorable general climate for support of executions still produce relatively large levels of state execution. This would produce a stronger link between lynchings and modern executions than between traditional and modern rates of execution.

Explaining the Suspension of Distrust

Attributing relatively high levels of current executions to relatively high levels of allegiance and respect for vigilante traditions can also help to explain a number of peculiar aspects of current attitudes toward the death penalty in the United States. One major puzzle discussed in Chapter 3 is the absence of distrust of government power as an argument against executions in the United States, and particularly in those Southern states where 80 percent of all executions take place. If citizens are suspicious of big government in Texas and Virginia and Alabama, why isn't this reflected in suspicion of the processes that select criminal defendants for execution?

The vigilante tradition is a good fit with finding support for the executioner without worry about governmental overreaching. The vigilante is by definition suspicious of his government, and that is one reason why vigilantes are willing to arrogate the power to punish crime to community groups. As long as this tradition is the animating symbolism of the death penalty, the executioner is imagined as an agent of the community rather than of the government. And this mythology of local control can also create hostility to courts and judicial review, which can be seen as government restraint on the local power to punish. After all, if the hangman is a friend of the family, judicial controls are both unnecessary and counterproductive. In this view, the law is getting in the way of the community's efforts to defend itself from violence. The process of "degovernmentizing" the image of the death penalty that Chapter 3 documented continues a tradition of capital punishment as community rather than governmental action.

Executions and Taxes

One easy-to-measure indicator of the extent to which citizens trust state and local governments is the amount of taxes that they pay. The theory is that higher levels of state and local tax are an indication of larger citizen trust in government, since the institutions that determine tax rates are democratically controlled. Where citizens have lower trust in government, they will tolerate only lower tax rates. While this type of measure is not as sensitive as survey questions that might directly ask about trust in state government, it has the advantage of being easy to measure at the individual state level. If taxation is a valid measure of citizen trust, the high-execution states in the United States cluster near the bottom in the degree to which state and local governments are trusted. Table 5.2 provides the ranking in per capita state taxes (from the census) and taxes as a percentage of personal income (from a private tax group) for the ten populous states with the highest rates of execution in Figure 4.3's analysis of execution rates (see p. 75).

The average high-execution state is in the bottom quarter of the per capita tax rankings and the bottom third of state and local taxes as a percentage of personal income. Only one high-execution state is in the top half of the U.S. states in per capita taxes (North Carolina), and none of the ten high-execution states ranks higher than 22 in the percentage of personal income that is collected in taxes. And this is not merely a by-product of Southern states having lower taxes. The three non-Southern states in the table average fortieth out of fifty in state and local taxes per capita. To

Table 5.2.

Rankings of High-Execution States in Taxes per Capita and
State and Local Taxes as a Percentage of Income

Execution Rank	State	Per Capita Taxes Rank	Percentage of Income to State and Local Taxes Rank
1	Texas	49	45
2	Virginia	29	38
3	Missouri	44	32
4	Louisiana	45	22
5	Alabama	46	44
6	Arizona	41	40
7	Florida	43	34
8	Georgia	38	37
9	North Carolina	20	28
10	Indiana	36	25
		Mean: 39.1	Mean: 34.5

Sources: Execution rate: per capita state tax: census; percentage of personal income in state and local tax: Tax Foundation (http://www.taxfoundation.org).

the extent that toleration of taxes is a good measure of trust in government, the states that execute the most are substantially less likely than average to trust the very levels of government that conduct executions. What may bridge that gap between distrust of government and acceptance of execution is the feeling among the populace that executions are a community rather than government function.

Perception and Reality

One major problem that arises when executions are justified by a vigilante tradition of community control is the empirical falsity of imagining that execution is anything other than a government act. The government of Texas may be closer to its citizens than the government in Washington, D.C., but it is a large, formal, and bureaucratic entity nonetheless. With more than 20 million citizens, the population of Texas is larger than the national population of Australia. How can the actions of such an enterprise be disguised as nongovernmental?

In part, of course, attributing governmental action to popular will is an ideological artifact of democracy, where all governmental conduct is imagined as the outcome of popular will. And surely, a better case can be made that the criminal punishments imposed in Texas are the will of its citizens than could be said for executions in Romania and Poland while they were Soviet satellite states.

But the vast majority of governments that have abolished capital punishment have been democracies, and there is no easy separation of the distance between citizen and government in places such as France, England, Australia, and Canada, and the relation between citizen and government in Texas and Florida.

A belief that government in punishing is carrying out the popular will may be separate from historical background or current conditions of punishment, an image not necessarily connected to the structure of government. But we still must struggle to understand why this identification with the executioner as an extension of community will is maintained for the most part in Southern states and not in Northern states, and why some groups are more easily persuaded by it than others. What the tie between lynching and current execution at both extremes may suggest is that a history of vigilante behavior might reduce current concerns about government killing. What the historical data do not explain is why the vigilante tradition is so strong in the South and why the conduct of a century earlier still exerts such powerful influence on the values and behavior in the twenty-first century.

The Many Meanings of Southernness: Alternative Explanations

There are alternative explanations for the patterns we have observed, but the statistical patterns developed in the first sections of this chapter seem to me a much better fit with the vigilante tradition explanation than any of the alternative explanations one hears when discussing this data. The first alternative explanation to an inference about vigilante values from the regional data on lynchings and modern execution is that the strong linkage between lynchings and executions might well be an artifact of both historical lynchings and modern executions being concentrated in the South. This does not mean, a critic might argue, that there is any causal link between lynchings then or the values associated with them and executions now. Perhaps both behaviors are strongly linked to the South as a region but not to each other.

It has already been noted that this criticism would have two flaws as an explanation of the statistical patterns presented earlier in the chapter. First, it explains only the high extreme findings on lynchings and execution, but does not address the fact that the lowest regional and individual state lynching histories are clearly linked to nonexecution and non–death penalty states in the late twentieth century. So more than a Southern phenomenon is involved in the data presented in the chapter. The substantive importance of finding that those American states at the low end of the lynching experience are much less likely to be executing after 1977 is that it produces a direct link between lynching and modern execution policy that has nothing to do with the South. The lowest lynching states are different as well from other American states outside the South (see Fig. 5.5). More than half of all the non-Southern states in the United States *other than the low lynching groups* have had executions, but more than three-quarters of the lowest executing states have had no executions.

Because the low extreme in lynching history is associated with abnormal death penalty behavior outside the South, a causal role for lynching history seems more likely in the South as well. The data on the South have shown that places extensively exposed to lynching are oriented toward conducting executions. The low-lynching history experience shows that the states with the lowest exposure to vigilante violence also have a lower propensity toward modern state execution. To use a tempting metaphor: Those areas not exposed to the vigilante virus have the lowest rates of all U.S. states of contemporary involvement in executions. If the association of lynchings and later executions in the South were not causal, we would not expect a noticeable relationship between a lack of lynching and uncharacteristically low rates of execution in the United States.

A second difficulty with alleging that something other than a vigilante tradition in the South explains its late-twentieth century status as the home of 80 percent of U.S. executions is the need for another aspect of Southern history or current condition that might explain its recent executions. If not a vigilante tradition, what else generates in the South an execution rate almost 200 times that found in the Northeast?

Four possible Southern differences come to mind as explanations of execution propensity that might be independent of a vigilante tradition. The first, already mentioned, is a tradition of official execution in the region that continues into the modern era. There was some support for this theory: The South executed twice as often as the Northeast early in the twentieth century while executing fewer people per million population than the West. But the history of twice as many executed in the South around 1900 is awkward as the only explanation for current differences of 188 to 1 between the South and the Northeast. And merely citing a history of execution begs the question: What feature of Southern culture or government was the cause of the earlier execution propensity?

A second possible explanation is that the South is more violence-prone than other regions, and this tradition of violence might create a higher execution propensity. There is ample support for the thesis that the American South has a larger history of violence and higher current rates of lethal violence than other regions. The higher rate of violence in the South has been well documented by Sheldon Hackney and others, while a lively controversy has emerged around theories to explain Southern violence. But the regional differences are less than 2 to 1 in homicide by region in recent years, again far short of the huge gap in executions. Controlling for different rates of homicide, there would still be an almost 100-to-1 difference in regional execution rates unexplained during the first quarter-century of executions after *Gregg v. Georgia*. Also, the gap between Southern violence and rates of violence in urban Northern states that have Southern postwar migrations has been closing, while the gap between Southern and Northern execution rates has been getting wider (see Fig. 5.4).

A third candidate to share credit for the heavy concentration of executions in the American South is the strength of the political right in Southern states together with the larger support for the death penalty associated with conservative politics in the United States and abroad. It is indisputable that at any given time, citizens with strong right-of-center political orientations are much more likely to support a death penalty (and other harsh penal measures) than citizens with left-of-center political orientations. It is also true that many urban states in the Northeast and Midwest have larger concentrations of liberal voters than most Southern states. Yet many Northern states with solid conservative orientations, such as New Hampshire, Nebraska, Kansas, North Dakota, and Ohio, have much less conspicuous pressure for executions than most Southern states. And the relative strength of right-wing political sentiments in the South is not vastly greater than right-wing political strength elsewhere. There may be particular religions or philosophical orientations that distinguish the right wing in Nebraska from that in Alabama, but making that sort of distinction already takes the discussion out of the usual left-right political context. One ends up again trying to explain vast differences in execution behavior with small differences in general political orientation.

Indeed, it might be more plausible to see support for execution as one element of the political right that makes conservative politics attractive to blue-collar male voters in the South. Instead of a more pronounced conservative political orientation making executions more attractive to Southern voters, it may be that the traditional support of conservatives for the death penalty is one factor that makes conservative politics more inviting for Southerners already more disposed to support executions. Political conservatism is just as likely as an effect of voters supporting a death penalty as it is a cause of support for the death penalty in the South. But this pattern would, of course, not be a cause of the preference for executions.

The Culture of Punishment?

But what of the fourth policy, the straightforward theory that the South leads in execution simply because there is more support for serious punishment of criminals of all sorts? After all, rates of imprisonment are also higher in Southern states and relatively low in the Northeast (Zimring and Hawkins 1991, chap. 6). And this general punitiveness is also a good explanation for traditionally higher execution rates. Instead of a "culture of violence," why not focus on the South as a "culture of punishment"? And what would be more natural than finding the region that leads the rest of the nation in rates of incarceration leading also in executions?

I would not reject explanations of Southern execution dominance based on the South's "culture of punishment," but the Southern inclination toward high levels of punishment cannot be separated from the vigilante tradition itself. Rather than two separate traditions, the values and practices associated with extensive uses of the plantation prison, high levels of corporal and capital punishment, and those associated with lynching and vigilante nostalgia overlap extensively with each other and with racial repression. Racism, vigilantism, and high levels of punishment were concurrent conditions in the South when high levels of punishment came to characterize the region. Rather than posing a discrete alternative to the vigilante explanation, the reference to a broader tendency toward punitiveness in the South reminds us that the values of importance in explaining the origins of the propensity toward execution in the South may be linked to other aspects of cultural values that influence rates of punishment. With the prison farm and the chain gang, as well as with executions, a strong private tradition of using force may reduce the natural suspicion of governmental power when it comes to questions of punishment that is otherwise pronounced throughout the agrarian South.

It is likely that the long tradition of viewing punishment as a community rather than state institution and the coercive white supremacist context in which such punishments took place were defining elements of the Southern propensity to punish rather than separate processes from it. The larger willingness to punish was a function of the particular targets and the particular context of punishment, so that what I have been calling vigilante values are not only a cause of willingness to execute but may also be a contributing cause also of the broader enthusiasm for harsh treatment of offenders in the South.

Limits of Evidence

There are two limits on the power of the arguments presented in this chapter that deserve some concluding emphasis. The first is that the data presented amount to a circumstantial case that vigilante sentiments facilitate executions at the turn of the twenty-first century and that the absence of any substantial history of extreme vigilante behavior in states seems to restrain modern executions. Even a perfect association of century-ago lynchings with current executions would not be proof of the vigilante connection, and the state-level association observed is far from uniform. Delaware has much more execution in its recent history than its lack of lynching would predict, and Mississippi and Tennessee have fewer executions than one would expect.

The second limit of the current analysis is that it provides no clear evidence of how significant as a distinguishing value the modern version of a vigilante tradition might be. There is no direct measure of how intensely citizens in states with a tradition of vigilante behavior believe in equating governmental punishment with community action. There is no indication that what I have called a vigilante tradition is one of ten most important values in anybody's portfolio, or even one of the top twenty. Even if these traditions distinguish some Southern states in ways that predict different execution policies, this does not mean that vigilante instincts are anything other than minor elements of personal identity in states with significant vigilante traditions. Such traditions may influence institutional behavior much more than the personal outlook of most citizens, and these traditions may not be a central element even in the modern governments that have become the American execution belt. Indeed, even where executions are quite common in 2003, we do not know how important they are to the government and culture where they are practiced.

Conclusion

This chapter has presented a series of four new interpretations of American experience that are supported by evidence of widely varying strength. The first assumption on which this chapter is based is that the large variations between the states and regions of the United States are an important source of data about what elements in American history and culture have produced different policies toward capital punishment than are found in other Western nations. This conclusion is strongly supported by available evidence. There is a larger difference between Minnesota and Oklahoma on issues of capital punishment than between Minnesota and Australia.

A second interpretation is that historically high rates of institutionalized vigilante behavior are associated with high current rates of execution in the United States, while historically low rates of vigilante violence are associated with low levels of current capital punishment. The circumstantial case for this association is strong, but causal inferences are always a problem with circumstantial evidence. The lynch mob and the lethal injection are found in the same American neighborhoods. Where a lynching history is absent, there is a lower-than-average chance that executions take place. The causes of this pattern require much further investigation.

A third interpretation made in this chapter is that the sentiments and values associated with a vigilante past are linked to current regional differences in attitudes and conduct in the United States. The survey and behavioral evidence available on this question is much thinner than that on the association between executions and lynching, but there are indications that some of the features that distinguish Southern attitudes and behavior are linked to positive attitudes toward vigilante action. Careful survey research can quickly test for the current significance of such values in the United States as a whole and in areas with high current rates of execution.

The fourth interpretation that has been suggested in these pages is a theory of how citizen identification with a vigilante tradition produces tolerance for execution behavior by inhibiting distrust of government as a motive for being afraid of or ambivalent about executions. The interpretation is plausible, but the available evidence to support it is modest at best. Here again, the lack of firm evidence on the dynamics of public attitudes is a deficiency that can be quickly addressed by the survey sociologist.

The ambition of this chapter was more than to outline a theory of American difference, but much less than to implicate vigilante values as the proven cause of variations in execution among the regions and states. The hope was to provide a plausible theory of how vigilante traditions might influence contemporary attitudes, to survey available evidence on the theory presented, and to suggest the further tests that can draw us closer to understanding the link between one of the most troubling chapters of the American past and the controversial and distinctive circumstances of execution in the American present.

6

The Consequences of Contradictory Values

THE UNITED STATES is the world capital of mixed feelings about the death penalty. When executions are delayed, citizens get angry. But when short-cuts are used to accelerate executions, many of the same citizens worry about potential injustice. Why is this?

The continuing controversy about capital punishment is the result of a clash of two inconsistent value traditions that cannot coexist. Conducting executions is inconsistent with one fundamental tenet of American culture. But stopping executions violates a second cultural tradition with deep roots in our history. There is no low-conflict path out of the chronic clash of cultures. And any significant shift from the impossible status quo will require a change in long-standing cultural traditions.

Values in Conflict

The two sets of attitudes that animate current conflicts about capital punishment can be conveniently labeled vigilante values and due process values. They are attitudes about the dangers that face individuals and communities rather than comprehensive theories of government or law. The vigilante mindset is one in which the citizen assumes that criminals are clearly identified enemies of the community rather than members of it. The community has the right to defend itself against these alien enemies, and any legal prerequisites to punishment are resented as unnecessary and potentially disabling. Lynching a century ago was used in the last chapter as both a pure example of extreme vigilante behavior and an index of which states and regions in the United States had the highest level of vigilante values in an earlier time period.

My use of prior lynching behavior as an index of vigilante values does not mean that all citizens who hold vigilante sentiments would ever have supported the lynching conduct that occurred in America's ugly past, or now sympathize with any conceivable mob usurping of law enforcement in the twenty-first century. Instead, lynching is a good index of the strength of such values in a community because it was always such an extreme example of the vigilante tradition. Of course, most of the modern citizens who harbor strong vigilante sentiments in the current day nonetheless abhor the lynchings that grew out of such sentiments in earlier times. For the same reason, areas that never generated lynchings may still have strong identification with vigilante values that are reflected in less extreme conduct. The citizens of Wisconsin may never have supported lynchings, but they may still believe that members of the community have the right to take action against criminals when government efforts fail. What the absence of a lynching history shows is lower levels of support for extreme forms of vigilante violence.

Attitudes that support some types of vigilante conduct exist all over the United States, with stronger support usually found in the South. Lynching has been discredited, but less drastic behaviors that reflect vigilante values include belief in the use of deadly force by private citizens against criminal intruders and support for citizens carrying concealed weapons in public to defend against criminal attack. These more modest examples of citizen justice are live issues in many states today, and the support for this type of self-defense is much higher in the United States than in most other developed nations.

As Chapter 4 showed, the higher levels of vigilante sentiments in the United States are encouraged and reinforced by state rather than national control of punishment policy. The fact that the executioner is a product of state rather than national government seems to reinforce the sentiment that execution is a community activity. There is no other developed country where citizens believe that official punishments are an extension of the community rather than a function of the government. The substantial investment that U.S. citizens have in viewing criminal punishment as an extension of community action is not only found in the South and West but is quite widely present in the United States. This pattern raises the question of why Pennsylvania, Ohio, and California do not have levels of execution to rival those of Texas and Virginia.

The answer may be that very substantial commitments to vigilante values are necessary to produce regular executions in current conditions, because the death penalty has become an extreme measure in the United

States at the turn of the twenty-first century. Sustaining the types of limits on appeals and tolerance of errors in capital trials that are now necessary to produce regular executions may also require a large dose of antilegal sentiments.

The reason why the rate of executions is high only in areas with extraordinary vigilante traditions is that most Americans also hold due process values in high regard, in Texas as well as in Vermont. In most states with death penalties, the legal processes that due process concerns generate bring the capital punishment system to a near stalemate. Even when executions occur with regularity and the legal system accommodates the machinery of assembly-line lethal injections, there is substantial discomfort with the ways in which due process values must be compromised to facilitate executions. A conflict-in-values explanation of execution in the United States need not suggest that legality values are high only in New York and not in Texas and Oklahoma. Instead, it is likely that the values of due process and fear of government are strongly held in all parts of the United States but lose out in an uncomfortable competition with death penalty claims only where vigilante sentiments have strong support. Public opinion all over the United States is pro–death penalty, but worries about abuse and injustice are more easily overcome in places with strong support for vigilante values.

A value conflict explanation of the American pattern does not blame the modern death penalty on the absence of a tradition of legality or on the absence of any set of values that has elsewhere been associated with the end of the death penalty. Instead, it is the additional presence of a strong set of countervailing values that generates pressure for executions in the states. It is what we have, not what we lack, in American political culture that has produced the singular death penalty policies of the current era.

There is no strong vigilante tradition to press for execution as an expression of community will in the more than 100 nations where executions have disappeared. The conflict in the United States is unique not because of what is missing in our political culture, but because of what is present: two distinct contradictory sets of traditions. In this regard, the United States stands alone.

Two elements of vigilante attitudes deserve special mention. The first is that the celebration of private and community use of force usually implies some distrust of government. The enthusiastic vigilante distrusts either the government's intentions or its capacity to keep the peace, or both. The vigilante tradition is one that values the community's interests and those of the individual more highly than it values the prerogatives of government. The self-styled right-wing militias of the current era are another extreme example of vigilante priorities.

The second distinctive feature of vigilante attitudes is that they assume away the need for the investigation of crime and the proof of guilt. The threat to the community that animates the vigilante mindset is presented as a known enemy, so police work and proof of guilt are not necessary. As soon as identification and proof are unnecessary, the processes that require them become costly and time-consuming enemies of justice. As long as the vigilante assumes the enemy is known, he is hostile to the formal apparatus of a legal system—the system is all cost and no benefit from the vigilante perspective. For this reason, the vigilante point of view might inform a theory of criminal justice (by demanding minimal procedure), but it can never amount to a theory or model of the criminal process. Investigation and trial are simply not important in the world that the vigilante assumes he inhabits.

Due Process and Fear of Government

While the vigilante attitude distrusts government as too weak to protect the citizenry, those who hold due process attitudes worry instead about a government that is too powerful, one that might exercise that power against its citizens in an arbitrary manner. The due process mindset holds that power to inflict punishment is prone to be abused in many ways. Government can falsely accuse citizens and wrongly punish them for crimes they did not commit. Government can also make mistakes in determining how much punishment guilty offenders deserve. Due process values place deliberate obstacles in the path of government when it seeks to punish those accused of crime. The due process adherent believes that misuse of government power is at least as great a potential problem as crime. Every May 1st, the Law Day speeches proclaim, "It is better that ten guilty men go free than that one innocent man be falsely convicted."

The contrasts between the vigilante and due process attitudes are obviously great: One can imagine the reaction of those who hold vigilante values to the prospect that ten guilty men go free under any circumstances! Yet the contradiction evident between the two attitudes may rest as much in the contrasting factual assumptions behind these two views of punishment as on the different value judgments they express. The vigilante mindset assumes that the offender can be identified without legal procedures, while the due process mindset assumes there is substantial difficulty in sorting out the guilty from the innocent. Behind that contrast lies another: The criminal offender is an outsider in the vigilante imagination, not a genuine member of the community. No wonder he is so easy to identify.

The criminal defendant imagined by the due process attitude is viewed as a member of the community and a citizen. Because the accused is "one of us" rather than an easily identified alien, there may be reason to doubt the capacity of the government to identify criminal offenders correctly in every case. It is not that the vigilante has a more positive view of the capacity of the government to solve crimes; instead, the assumption is that criminal offenders are not difficult to identify. So the task is too easy even for the police to screw up. All the nightmare scenarios of false accusation and wrongful punishment in the due process imagination are not plausible in the world that vigilante values assume, a world where guilt is known.

One implication of very different conditions assumed by the vigilante and due process world views is that the same people might hold both attitudes, depending on the factual assumptions they make in a particular setting. If unconcerned about proof of guilt because the accused seems obviously guilty, the citizen might espouse vigilante sentiments. But where the citizen feels some doubt about guilt, due process values and attitudes may dominate judgments about a particular case.

There is one respect in which the due process and vigilante traditions are similar: Each has an impeccable historic pedigree in the United States. The fear of government power informed both the American Revolution and the structure of the American Constitution. Most of the Bill of Rights is comprehensible only as an embodiment of due process qualifications of government power. Due process sentiments are as important to American political culture as to any political culture on earth, and the tradition of due process concern extends as far back in American national experience as anywhere else. But the vigilante tradition is also deeply imbedded in the culture and experience of the United States. From citizens' committees in the nineteenth century to the Dirty Harry movie character in the 1980s, the individual and group as bulwark against evil is a recurrently honored legend in the culture. So each tradition is as American as apple pie.

If citizens can hold both vigilante and due process attitudes, the rhetorical task of the advocates on either side of the death penalty debate is to activate the sentiments most friendly to that advocate's view of the death penalty. One reason for the wildly inconsistent thrusts in capital punishment policy in recent years is the tug-of-war between due process and vigilante assumptions about the death penalty system.

The Conflict over Capital Punishment

The due process and vigilante mindsets generate direct conflict over how capital punishment systems should be administered. The vigilante assumption is that punishment should be inflicted at the first opportunity, the more severe the better. Criminals are known to the community, and once a criminal, always a criminal. Legalities and appellate review are unnecessary frustrations of justice for victims and communities in this world view. The criminal offender is an enemy soldier who becomes a battlefield casualty in the war on crime, but a much more deserving target than the casualties of other battles. All of these attitudes are consistent with support of death as a consequence of criminal conduct.

From a due process perspective, the death penalty is a particular night-mare because it involves an ultimate and irrevocable punishment. The due process mindset rejects the arrogance of presuming that the state can take life without risk of mistake, and this has made a priority concern about capital punishment a natural extension of the expanded scope of constitu-tional constraints in the criminal process. Moreover, the claim of govern-ment to kill for its own purposes excites the suspicions of the due process adherent. It is not simply the killing of a factually innocent citizen that invites concern, but the killing of citizens who stand in opposition to the state that worries the due process adherent.

Two Models of Criminal Justice?

Students of the criminal process may hear echoes in my discussion of vigi-lante and due process attitudes. In his celebrated article, "Two Models of the Criminal Process," Herbert Packer posited two conflicting models for organizing a criminal justice system. A due process model advanced by Packer established a set of obstacles to state punishment because of dis-trust of state power without limit and because of fear of the punishment of the innocent. Packer's due process category is very close to the due process tradition just outlined. He summarizes the due process view of state power to punish:

> Power is always subject to abuse, sometimes subtle, other times, as in the criminal process, open and ugly. Precisely because of its potency in sub-jecting the individual to the coercive power of the state, the criminal pro-cess must, on this model, be subjected to controls and safeguards that prevent it from operating with maximal efficiency. According to this ide-ology, maximal efficiency means maximal tyranny. And, while no one would assert that minimal efficiency means minimal tyranny, the proponents of the Due Process Model would accept with considerable equanimity a sub-stantial diminution in the efficiency with which the criminal process oper-ates in the interest of preventing official oppression of the individual. (Packer 1964, p. 16)

This summary is a powerful evocation of the assumptions behind oppo-sition to the death penalty at the turn of the twenty-first century. But what about Packer's contrasting model?

> The value system that underlies the Crime Control Model is based on the proposition that the repression of criminal conduct is by far the most im-portant function to be performed by the criminal process. The failure of law enforcement to bring criminal conduct under tight control is viewed as

leading to the breakdown of public order and thence to the disappearance of an important condition of human freedom. . . . The claim ultimately is that the criminal process is a positive guarantor of social freedom. In order to achieve this high purpose, the Crime Control Model requires that primary attention be paid to the efficiency with which the criminal process operates to screen suspects, determine guilt, and secure appropriate dispositions of persons convicted of crime. (Packer 1964, pp. 9–10)

There are obvious parallels between the vigilante versus due process and crime control versus due process models. But there are also two important differences between the Packer models and the conflicting stances in the struggle between vigilante and due process attitudes. First, in his discussion of crime control, Packer was constructing views about law and legal procedure rather than discussing the more general attitudes that lay behind them. Thus, his crime control model of criminal procedure is sharply different from what I have been calling a vigilante tradition.

Packer's model was of a government function, while vigilante values concern the role of citizens and nongovernmental groups. Certainly, assumptions that criminals are a known external enemy are more likely to produce crime control than due process priorities in criminal justice. But vigilante attitudes and assumptions would approve much more radical outcomes than the efficiency-oriented legalities of a crime control model.

This observation links to the second significant difference between the vigilante value systems examined here and the criminal justice models examined by Herbert Packer. Both of Packer's models of criminal justice are constrained by and subscribe to constitutional limits and constitutional values. Therefore, principles of legality unite his two theories of criminal justice, but these principles do not constrain the sentiments of vigilantism. Indeed, Professor Packer spends three pages discussing the common boundaries of commitment to legality and constitutional limits on power that constrain both of his models of criminal justice. But these commitments to the rule of law cannot be assumed in the modern holder of vigilante values. This may be one reason why attempts to create larger numbers of executions frequently involve limiting the scope and stringency of appellate review (Zimring 1999). The crime control model of Herbert Packer is more restrained and vastly more respectful of government than are vigilante values.

To the extent that Professor Packer's crime control model was ever meant to serve as the authoritarian outer boundary of American values, it may be faulted for wishful thinking and lack of detailed historical analysis. While the contrasts between Packer's two models are instructive, they fail to exhaust the possibilities to be found in current culture or American historical experience. And it is probable that many modern proponents of streamlined execution systems are prone to push much further than Packer's crime control model would allow.

The Case for American Particularity

Both the due process and vigilante orientations reflect sentiments that are also found in many nations at many times. But in tying modern executions to the persistence of a vigilante tradition, Chapter 5 was using that tradition to explain historical developments in the United States that have not happened elsewhere. The implicit argument is that vigilante values and traditions are much stronger in parts of the United States at the turn of the twenty-first century than in other developed nations. If not, why are they not executing criminals in Australia, with an extensive frontier tradition, or in Canada or Mexico? The greater force of the American vigilante tradition and the greater expression of these values generated in the American federal system are the most likely cause of America's persistence as an executor.

I think that what I have described as vigilante values are more prevalent in the United States than in any other Western developed nation, and, furthermore, that the tradition is particularly strong in those regions and states where executions are frequent. Chapter 5 discussed modern concealed weapons laws and firearms self-defense practices that set the United States apart from other Western developed nations. Comparative survey research is not available to confirm stronger support in the United States for such values than on the Continent. To that extent, the model that follows is based on assumptions.

The data presented in Chapter 5 on lynching present a case for a history of collective violence in the name of crime control in the United States that should also be distinguished from episodes of ethnic violence where identity alone determines the targets of lethal violence. There is in such cases no patina of law enforcement to justify the modern versions of tribal war that bedevil societies in the Balkans and Central Africa. The systematic killings of the Nazi period lacked both the communal structure and the anticrime rationale. What I have called the vigilante tradition may be no more defensible than "ethnic cleansing" morally, but it is a distinct set of behaviors and attitudes, a theory of crime and social response to criminals rather than naked intergroup conflict.

Three Consequences of Value Conflict

If the foregoing explanation of value conflict is correct, it suggests three developments in the future of the death penalty in the United States. First, the debate about executions will remain more important in America than it was or will be in other nations, particularly for those citizens who wish to retain capital punishment. Second, chronically high levels of conflict and dissatisfaction are a structural feature of the contradictory values at war in the United States. There may be no built-in momentum in the United States toward a settlement or easing of tensions. A third implication of this value conflict explanation is that no truly definitive end to the conflict about the death penalty can be put in place without a change in one element of our political culture. No matter which side wins, when the chronic conflicts about executions end in the United States, the cessation of conflict will mean we are living in a different country.

The Ideological Importance of Capital Punishment

One of the remarkable features of the politics of abolition of the death penalty in Europe and the Commonwealth nations has been the short duration of resistance and societal conflict when executions stop. Chapter 2 showed that the standard pattern in Western democracies is for executions to end even though substantial majorities in public opinion polls still support the death penalty for murder. Yet the opposition to ending of the death penalty expressed in public opinion polls has not reversed abolition in any Western nation after 1960, nor has abolition produced protracted efforts to bring back the death penalty. Gestures of support for possible reintroduction of the death penalty were made by Margaret Thatcher in Britain in 1983 (Wicker 1983), and a free vote was permitted in Canada by a conservative government somewhat earlier (Witt 1987), but these efforts did not produce either success in reversing policy or the persistence of a political movement to restore the death penalty. Opposition to abolition, while broad, has been short-lived and ineffectual.

Part of the reason that public sentiments to retain capital punishment do not get mobilized into persistent political action to bring it back is that the death penalty is not of enduring political significance to those groups who favor it. In any debate about capital punishment, conservative factions will favor the penalty and liberal factions will oppose it. But beyond the predictable divisions between wets and drys, there are no political constituencies in most developed nations for whom capital punishment has a special and enduring salience.

But the United States may be different from its developed peers in the sustained political importance of capital punishment. The two larger concerns implicated by the death penalty—federalism and the symbolic importance of the vigilante tradition—make the death penalty a more important political issue. Each of these emotionally resonant values gives citizens a separate reason to care about the death penalty and to worry should the state's capacity to execute be removed. So the prospect of abolition creates the potential for opposition from citizens who are politically conservative or authoritarian in their orientation, who place high values on community punishment in the vigilante tradition or who revere the claim of states' rights in a federalist system.

The multiple meanings of capital punishment to Americans have a potential impact on both the breadth of support for the death penalty (the proportion who favor the penalty) and the depth of support for death (the intensity of support for capital punishment), but the more important element added by the vigilante and federalist agendas is intensity of support. Adding up all three pro–death penalty constituencies does not add much to the proportion of death penalty support because of the strong overlap between conservative, vigilante, and federalist values. Most of those who care deeply for states' rights and vigilante traditions are squarely in the conservative political tradition that is also warmly disposed toward capital punishment. This overlap means the multiple dimensions of meaning do not expand significantly the proportion of the population that supports the penalty. But many of the supporters of capital punishment in the United States care more deeply about the death penalty because of all the related symbols and may persist in supporting it for much longer than in typical abolition scenarios.

The current level of support for capital punishment in the United States is in the same range as was found in Great Britain, Germany, and Canada just prior to abolition of the death penalty (Hood 1996, chap. 7). What is harder to measure is the intensity of support in the United States. Supporters of capital punishment in the United States may care more deeply about the death penalty and may persist in its support for longer than in typical abolition scenarios.

Three-quarters of those who say they support the death penalty in the University of Michigan's national election survey of 1996 express strong support for the penalty, while fewer than half of the persons who oppose capital punishment in that survey express strong opposition (see Appendix D). In the South, the ratio of strong to weak support for capital punishment is 4.5 to 1. Comparable data for other Western nations on the intensity of support for the death penalty apparently does not exist, so that the uniqueness of the U.S. pattern of announced strong support is a matter of conjecture.

There have already been some indications that an effort to remove death penalties, particularly in federal courts, would meet with sustained opposition in current conditions. Chapter 4 mentioned the swift relegislation of death penalties in states where *Furman v. Georgia* struck down previous laws. While the intensity of feeling behind that earlier resistance was not measured, the legislation in thirty-five states was a larger-scale concrete counterreaction to abolition than had been noted in any Western nation in the past half-century. More recent episodes in critical Southern states suggest that even an icon as purely symbolic as the Confederate flag stirs up strong positive support in states such as South Carolina (where the issue was the flag on a monument in the state capital) and Mississippi (where the voters rejected removing the Confederate flag design from the state flag) ("A Mississippi Stuck in the Past" 2001; Burritt 2000; Copeland 2001). There is reason to believe that the opponents of American abolition will be more deeply committed to their cause and more mobilized in its defense than the quickly compliant opponents of abolition on the continent and in the British Commonwealth, but how much greater the resistance would be is a critical unanswered question.

The Continuing Conflict

One of the puzzles surrounding recent developments in the debate about the death penalty in the United States has been the continual conflict and dissatisfaction about executions and the absence of any sign that accommodations and adjustments in American law and culture are under way. As the next chapter shows, the level of hostility and discontent generated by the death penalty dispute increased rather than decreased throughout the 1990s. The heat generated by the issue on both sides shows no signs of cooling down.

A value conflict theory of American capital punishment policy provides an explanation for the chronic dissatisfaction and also for the trend toward legal reforms at cross-purposes. If any level of execution offends due process values, then even minimal numbers of executions will create the distrust and anxiety about injustice that the execution process triggers. At the same time, if community expectations for fast executions are as high as vigilante values would suggest, the same low level of executions that still provokes distrust about due process may also generate anger about delay and the system's dishonesty. Moving up or down the scale of execution policy will not solve the problem, because each step toward reducing one set of concerns will increase the tensions created by the contrasting expectations. Fewer executions means more anger about punishment avoided. More executions means larger anxieties about injustice and arbitrariness.

Only those parts of the United States without any executions and with very low levels of vigilante tradition can escape from the dilemma of a head-on clash of conflicting expectations. Where there is no strong pressure for execution as community justice, there is no fundamental conflict associated with the death penalty. Everywhere else, the competing and inconsistent demands of due process and vigilante justice make capital punishment policy a no-win exercise. There is simply no comfort zone capable of accommodating the conflicting demands. Discord about capital punishment is inevitable because it is a natural consequence of the structure of inconsistent American values.

Change or Stalemate?

This inherent conflict leads to the final prediction from a value contradiction theory of the capital punishment debate: No stable and long-term solution to the death penalty conflict seems likely without reducing the power of one of the two traditions that stand behind the dispute. Without a major change in our ideals about due process and legal representation, the processes that produce executions in the United States must remain profoundly disquieting. Without a change in pressures for unlimited punitive response, any suspension of executions will generate more sustained pressure for reinstatement than other developed nations have experienced, and the most sustained resistance and hostility will be concentrated in those states with strong traditions of vigilante values and large numbers of modern executions.

CONTRADICTION AND CONFLICT

In theory, it should be possible to construct a system with high-quality legal services, meticulous due process, and the generation of regular executions. In American practice, however, once there is strict enforcement of a detailed set of legal requirements put in place to govern the administration of a death penalty, a good lawyer becomes a long-term life insurance policy for a capital defendant. There turns out to be no such thing as an error-free capital trial, and the concept of a legal error being provably "harmless" when a defendant has been sentenced to death presents both logical and rhetorical problems. A high volume of executions anywhere in the United States depends on limiting the access of capital defendants to good lawyers and cutting off the tools that good lawyers can use to obtain reversals and delays. The next chapter provides examples of such cut-back strategies while reviewing the death penalty's recent legal history.

The real world necessity for those wishing to protect a capital punishment system from threats to its existence is to lower the expectations of the public and the government for legal system review in capital cases. As long as strong due process values are part of the culture, the way in which a death penalty system must operate will fall far short of the standards citizens will hold for the most drastic of criminal punishments. So public values about the requirements of legality in all cases must shift for citizens to have any level of comfort with the rules necessary to produce regular executions.

The very high standards for due process that many citizens view as necessary are in large measure a reflection of the severity of the penalty and the ambivalence of citizens about whether it is really necessary. With the stakes so high, the demands that many would wish to impose on the criminal justice system may not be achievable for a substantial number of cases.

The consequences for the United States of the contradictory values that lie beneath disputes about the death penalty are disquieting. The chronic conflict and dissatisfaction with current conditions are a structural outcome of a clash of two strong but inconsistent traditions. If all that changes is the number of executions or procedures in death cases, the conflict will continue—and citizens will not adjust over time to new policy with equanimity. Abolish executions without diminishing a strong vigilante tradition, and the demand to execute will crop up more persistently than in any other nation that has abolished the death penalty. Restrain appeals and restrict legal services without removing the American cultural commitment to due process, and the discomfort with the system will only grow. There are deep inconsistencies in American culture that destabilize efforts to resolve our capital punishment conflicts. No observer wants the hypocrisy, inefficiency, and arbitrariness of current conditions. But change in the rate of capital punishment must be associated with one of two shifts in culture to put the conflict to rest.

A competition between vigilante and due process traditions is in many ways a war between the best and the worst of the values of American culture. The rule of law and its opposite have coexisted in the culture for centuries, the kind of dualism that delights postmodern literary critics. This discussion assumes that the long romance with our vigilante tradition is an important part of the appetite for violent punishment and a powerful restraint on citizens worrying about executions as a government excess. But no matter the energy and authenticity of a vigilante tradition, it is now and always was a very dangerous idea for a plural and democratic government. The values of due process function to protect us from government excess. The value of the rule of law must protect us from both citizen excess and government excess.

Is This Conflict Truly Fundamental?

Two legal conflicts during the second half of the twentieth century provide some guidance when considering the type of public concern and the level of hostility that will be generated by disputes about the death penalty in the near future. At the high extreme in social discord was the fundamental conflict in American values that was the central issue in the major school desegregation case, *Brown v. Board of Education*, decided by the U.S. Supreme Court in 1954 and implemented in a massive number of subsequent cases over the next generation. The legal and social life in much of the United States paid lip service to the principle of equal opportunity and the related provision in the Fourteenth Amendment to the U.S. Constitution of equal protection of the laws, but state and society were also organized around a racially segregated set of institutions that was racially discriminatory at its core.

The U.S. Supreme Court's effort to deny this contradiction by its creation of a doctrine of "separate but equal" in *Plessy v. Ferguson* in 1896 is a moving testament to the power of psychological denial to neutralize the critical powers of Supreme Court justices under stress. Separate but equal was an oxymoronic concept the moment it was coined—there could be no justification for enforced separation of the races without a theory of racial difference that at no point in human history has been other than invidious. No matter the history of some peculiar arguments attendant to its legislative enactment, racial segregation in education, voting, and other conditions of government was a gross violation of any concept of equal protection of the law directed at racial discrimination. But racial segregation of education, employment, political access, and governmental benefits was also the order of government and society in a great many American states up to the minute *Brown v. Board of Education* was decided and for many years thereafter. In deciding that case, the U.S. Supreme Court forcefully attacked the legitimacy of the organizing principle of government in many states in the United States.

This particular fundamental conflict is the largest example of chronic and unresolvable hostility to the ruling of a court where two irreconcilably inconsistent principles are in conflict, and each commands the loyalty of an important constituent group. What made the desegregation issue an ultra-high conflict contest was the central importance of racial separation and of its overthrow to the lives of about 40 percent of all American citizens. Here was a matter of principle that could not be finessed or avoided, which was of defining importance to the lives of tens of millions of citizens. It was also a zero-sum status competition between segregationists and African American claimants in which one side had to be right and the other fundamentally wrong.

The fundamental value conflict thesis outlined earlier predicts that the outcome in an issue of this sort will be rejected by the losers and regarded by them as illegitimate as long as the rejected principle in the case remained an approved part of the culture. From this perspective, the "Impeach Earl Warren" billboards that dotted the roadways of the South and Southwest in the 1950s and 1960s should have come as no surprise. Indeed, the real surprise about the war over school and public accommodation desegregation in the United States was the relatively swift victory of the principle of racial equality in the United States, and the lack of any real damage to the prestige and legitimacy of the U.S. Supreme Court from *Brown v. Board*. In terms of the frontal challenge the Court issued to other political institutions and the extent of the Court's efforts to delegitimize folkways of long standing, the desegregation opinions make the Court's work in constitutional criminal procedure and even in *Roe v. Wade* look like modest incursions in the American order. Why did the Court's position prevail in relatively short order (see Kluger 1977; but see Rosenberg 1991)?

It helped that the Supreme Court itself was unanimous and decided the question of principle in broad strokes. *Brown v. Board of Education* is a great opinion because it lacks legalisms. But consider the arrogance of a nonrepresentative branch of national government overturning a longstanding way of life for tens of millions of Americans in more than twenty states. Why did this not provoke much more resistance, particularly among better educated younger Southerners and among Southern elites?

In retrospect, what may have doomed segregation and swiftly reorganized the American legal community around a nondiscrimination principle was the widespread feeling even in the South of the wrongfulness of the invidious racial judgments that a segregationist schema must express. Loyalty and nostalgia for tradition were strong throughout the South, with powerful pecuniary interests tied to segregated state ways, but there was by the 1950s no moral high ground in the United States for segregation based on race. The contradictions of equal protection and legally coerced racial separation were evident, at some important level, to many who were powerful participants in segregation as a way of life. The scriptural arguments for racial segregation were not supported by neutral theological authorities or persuasive moral reasoning. There could be in mid-twentieth century America no moral passion for racial segregation. There was a deep attachment to traditions that depended on segregation but no belief in the moral superiority of racism itself. This phenomenon is what Dillard University President Alfred Dent was referring to when he spoke of Southern whites being themselves emancipated by the legal rejection of segregation, because "they may at last put down the spiritual burden that comes with being on the wrong side of a moral issue" (Ashmore 1957, p. 20).

So when the U.S. Supreme Court took its moral stand in *Brown*, the other side ultimately could not answer in kind. And that was an important part of the death sentence for white racial superiority as an official American value. The battle took a generation to conclude, but the assault on invidious racial distinction was resolved by the defeat of white supremacy as a core component of American cultural values.

The Death Penalty Analogy

The dispute over the death penalty is a low-stakes matter when compared with the epic struggle between nondiscrimination and race segregation. Race-based rules were a defining element in the ways that tens of millions of people lived. By 1954, either the dominant method of social organization for almost 40 percent of the country would be rejected as un-American or

African Americans would be denied full citizenship in the nation of their birth as a matter of principle.

By comparison, the death penalty is important to many citizens as a symbol of the capacity of their community to control its enemies, but nobody's definition of self, no person's livelihood or basic citizenship is at stake when executions are present or absent in state government, except, of course, the condemned. Capital punishment in the United States is not a way of life.

The symbolic values at stake in the United States include both states' rights and the image of community capacity to punish that is linked to the vigilante tradition. But the death penalty is small beer next to the defining historic importance of racial classification as a method of organizing government.

The death penalty is by itself also much less practically important to citizens than American cultural traditions that are of middle-range significance. The social inertia of tens of millions of guns owned by citizens makes any major shift in the criteria for legal gun ownership a larger attempt at using law as an instrument of social change than abolishing a rare state-run event such as execution would be. Very few Americans have direct and significant ties to the practice of state execution. Ending executions entails no house-to-house searches. Execution is a highly visible act of government that can be extinguished without required changes in citizen behavior.

Yet the symbolic baggage of the American vigilante tradition and of state prerogatives as a proxy for community punishment power also distinguishes the dispute over the death penalty in the United States from the pattern of abolition observed in the long list of developed nations that abolished capital punishment in the decades after the end of the Second World War. So the second important comparison with the current circumstances of American capital punishment is the transition from retention of a death penalty to its abolition in Western European and Commonwealth nations. Putting aside those instances where an abrupt shift in regime produced a swift abolition of the death penalty—Italy, Portugal, Spain, Romania, Czechoslovakia—the general pattern was for executions to decline to zero, and periods of de facto abolition then to be followed by abolition of the death penalty for civil or "ordinary" crimes. The pace of abolition de jure was typically quite leisurely. While the final governmental push toward abolition came when the left-of-center party was in power, the process of abolition was gradual, its significance in domestic politics was never great, and the aftermath of abolition did not witness a bitter struggle to return the penalty.

In the postwar abolitions, high levels of public support for the death penalty for murder never produced a protracted, partisan political struggle, and there was only one reinstatement of an abolished death penalty after a postwar abolition—in New Zealand—where the death penalty was quickly and finally abolished again (Zimring and Hawkins 1986, chap. 1).

The business-as-usual process that led to abolition of the death penalty in Britain, France, Canada, and Australia was neither an important political innovation in its own right nor an integral part of a larger political shift. The abolition of the death penalty in Canada, for example, was by the time it took place a minor change in the political landscape. It happened almost a decade after the last execution, and the political structure of Canadian government was very much the same after abolition as before. From the data, Gordon Hawkins and I argued that in most Western nations that abolish the death penalty,

> [t]he benefits that occur should be viewed as negative, symbolic, and representative. They will be negative in that removing this excrescence from the body politic is analogous to the removal of a wart from the human body. (Zimring and Hawkins 1986, p. 164)

And again,

> The abolition of capital punishment should not be seen as an instrument for the achievement of social progress in the form of wider recognition of a broader human rights agenda. Rather than facilitating further reform, usually the abolition of the death penalty *represents* progress that has [already] been achieved. (Zimring and Hawkins 1986, p. 165; emphasis in original)

That sort of end to the death penalty is a low-conflict political event, one that does not energize citizens to rebel even when upward of two-thirds of the population expresses some support for the penal practice that is being abolished. Thus, in Europe and the Commonwealth, the process of abolition was essentially uneventful. The documents and pronouncements associated with domestic abolition—from the Royal Commission to proposed suspensions of the death penalty—were infused with neither passion nor intensity. The abolition of capital punishment went forward as a quiet and diplomatic exercise. Abolishing the death penalty in places such as Britain and France appeared to be the most banal of government reforms.

The key difference between any plausible scenario for the end of the death penalty in the United States and the end of the death penalty in other developed nations is that other values and traditions might have to change in the United States before a peaceful adjustment to government without executions can be completed. In other developed democracies, there were no collateral changes necessary to the end of executions. To be sure, conservative and authoritarian constituencies were offended in Britain, Germany, and New Zealand, and public opinion registered support for the death penalty (Zimring and Hawkins 1986, chap. 1). But there was no linkage of executions to a cultural value system where the execution process was of special significance. The death penalty could be removed without leaving a hole in the culture.

Even in Japan, the only other developed democracy that still executes, the end of capital punishment can be achieved without surgery on deeply held community cultural traditions. Public opinion in Japan generally supports a death penalty for murder at approximately 80 percent (Watts 2000). But transition to an execution-free nation would not change the core content of Japanese culture. Capital punishment in Japan is a matter only of government policy. Any transition to abolition in Japan, where executions are in secret and at the convenience of the Ministry of Justice, would probably not generate fundamental conflict with any cultural traditions. After all, if government authorities suspend executions, the same support for authority that produces high approval for a death penalty would assure a respectful reception when the authorities decide to end the practice.

A Precedent for America?

Just as an analogy with antisegregation litigation would overstate the importance of the conflict over capital punishment to American political order, the example of other nations' paths to abolition seems to understate both the level of commitment to the death penalty that exists in the United States and the intensity of the assault on the penalty that will be necessary to end it. What distinguishes the United States from Britain, France, and Canada is not the percentage of the population that expresses support for a death penalty but the intensity of some elements of that support and the distinctive political structure that exists to translate sentiment into political action at the state level. Federalism, sectionalism, and an ideology of deference to state government amplify the conflicts behind the capital punishment question. The vigilante tradition has an American constituency. Zimring and Hawkins to the contrary notwithstanding, putting the death penalty to rest in the United States will be much more than the removal of a superfluous wart on the body politic. It will require greater effort (and achieve more good) than the standard abolition in a Western developed nation.

Part of the problem is states' rights. There is more than a little irony in the fact that the ideology of states' rights was sustained over much of the twentieth century to justify regimes of segregation, but that states' rights ideology has survived long after the moral and political death of racial segregation itself.

Yet the substantive core of the support for death as a penalty seems to be an ideology of capital punishment as community justice that appears most intensely today in these areas where extreme forms of vigilante justice thrived in earlier times. This vigilante tradition imagines the power behind punishment to be citizens acting collectively. This image reduces the fear of capital punishment as government power by denying that the power is really governmental. It creates an image of the citizen as more powerful than the criminal, and in this sense one can imagine the vigilante's hanging tree as an early American version of victims' rights. But the linkage of execution to the interests and power of private citizens has also characterized the most remarkable remaking of the image of the death penalty in the last two decades of the twentieth century. Dealing with this legacy will be an important task in the early years of the twenty-first century for those in search of abolition in the United States.

The most important unknown quantity in the American capital punishment conflict is the contemporary strength of commitment to the communal justice/vigilante tradition. The due process branch of the value conflict has its own pressure group (the legal profession) and strong institutional structure in all levels of American government. Due process is a fundamental value in American political culture.

The commitment to a vigilante tradition has not been tested in any sustained conflict over the last half-century on the death penalty. There is no good test of the current power of vigilante sentiments. The swift passage of new statutes after *Furman v. Georgia* was not a pitched battle where anti–death penalty forces put up a fight in most states. There is a strong public sentiment in favor of punishment at all levels of government in the United States (and in most democracies), but these sentiments are not necessarily linked in strong support of capital punishment. Robbers are just as unpopular in Wisconsin and Michigan as in Missouri and Oklahoma.

The evolution of a communal imagery for execution in the 1980s and 1990s shows the natural affinity of vigilante traditions to support of executions, but this does not mean that the vigilante tradition itself has a powerful emotional hold on most citizens even in high-execution environments.

Because we do not know the contemporary power of vigilante nostalgia, it is hard to judge how fundamental the conflict is between such values and the contradictory due process tradition. If the loyalty to vigilante values and imagery turns out to be a paper tiger, the transition away from executions in the United States would be easier to achieve and will be emotionally resolved in a relatively short time after executions end. Even in this best case, the hangover to be expected from abolition in the United States will be more substantial than it has been in other Western nations. The larger the current commitment to vigilante ideology, the more intense will be the resistance to ending executions. But the real test of the power of this strain of values will begin as the campaign to end executions acquires momentum. To the extent that one can only guess about the current power of vigilante values, it will be necessary to plan and conduct a campaign to end executions in the United States without any clear sense of the strength of commitment to capital punishment.

The American Prospect

The path toward ending a death penalty in the United States will be vastly easier to follow than the agonies of earlier years about race and legal equality but much more difficult than the abolition of the death penalty in the developed Western nations. The structural complications and the vigilante tradition make the capital punishment dispute in America a value conflict of middle-range intensity. Because there are no widespread social or economic institutions based on execution, abolition will not provoke as much resistance as trying to change popular habits such as driving cars or owning guns. But to the extent that the conflict is between two important and inconsistent values with public support, the affection of American culture for vigilante justice will have to be neutralized before the absence of executions can be fully accepted by the population in areas where an execution tradition is present.

The value conflict behind the death penalty debate in the United States has two implications for efforts to use the courts and the political process to end executions. First, the question of capital punishment is more important in and to the political culture of the United States than it was to most nations where the executioner has been gently retired. The vigilante ideology is a dangerous and seductive doctrine. When states disguise the use of extreme governmental power as instead neutral public service, that misrepresentation is a worthy enemy for all who would wish to render the United States an execution-free zone.

So the United States is not one of those nations where abolition of the death penalty is like removing an extraneous wart that is no longer closely connected to the rest of the body politic. Putting capital punishment to rest in the United States will require resolving a long-standing conflict between claims of community power beyond the law and the principle of legality. And the triumph of legality over the ghosts of vigilante violence will be a cultural improvement of no small moment for the United States.

So the good news is that writing the last chapter to capital punishment in America will be a more important and more socially necessary task here than in most other nations. The bad news is that abolition may be much harder to achieve in the proximate future in the United States than in almost any other advanced nation.

That introduces the second implication of the American setting for the future of the death penalty debate. The type of campaign to bring an end both to executions and to the culture that values them should differ from abolition campaigns in other nations not only in degree but in *kind*. The distinguishing feature of the death penalty in the United States is not the prevalence of citizen support. The death penalty may be more important to its supporters in the United States, and it is imbedded in the political institutions of some states and linked to a powerful sentimental attachment to vigilante values.

Under such circumstances, a low-visibility campaign to influence quietly the opinion of legal elites, to tiptoe toward abolition in the standard pattern of abolition in the postwar years, may not be enough. A campaign of higher salience, one that has many different targets in the culture of support for American capital punishment, will be necessary to create the circumstances where legal and political elites will feel both the capacity to act and the motivation to do so. The mechanics of abolition in the United States may look unremarkably similar to the gradualism and procedural tentativeness of the usual pattern, but the program to produce these results must be more intense and multifaceted than the traditional prelude to abolition. And the moral and cultural campaign against capital punishment in the United States must continue long after executions stop. As long as the vigilante image of execution has substantial public acceptance, the aftermath of abolition in the United States will be anger and the urge to reverse policy. The struggle to secure the future of abolition in the United States may go on for many years after the last execution. The ultimate goal of abolitionists is to change not merely American policy but American culture.

III

CAPITAL PUNISHMENT
IN THE AMERICAN FUTURE

THE LAST TWO CHAPTERS of this book use the value conflict described in Chapter 6 as a foundation for explaining the recent history of capital punishment in American law and politics and for predicting the future course of the death penalty in the United States. Chapter 7 treats the cross-currents of policy reforms in the 1990s as a case history of conflict between inconsistent value traditions. The two major policy crusades of the 1990s were the attempt to speed up the path to execution and the effort to discover innocent defendants on death row and deliver them from wrongful execution. But steps taken to achieve each of these goals can work only to defeat the other objective. No wonder there was more controversy about the death penalty in the 1990s than ever before in American history.

Chapter 8 projects the future course of events in the conflict over capital punishment. My focus is developments in national politics and in the judiciary in the next fifteen to twenty years and the impact of these changes on the death penalty system and efforts to stop executions. I argue that the end game for American capital punishment has already begun but that the struggle will be intense. Different strategies are required for the pursuit of abolition when there is strong support in the culture for capital punishment than the quiet and polite path to abolition in Western Europe. Some of the specific objectives of an American abolitionist campaign are outlined. The effort required to end executions in the United States will be greater, but the benefits to the society and culture of exorcizing the vigilante spirit is well worth the additional work. The United States will not be at peace with the absence of capital punishment until it has become a better nation.

7

The No-Win 1990s

THE 1990s should have been the decade when the death penalty was restored as a normal part of the criminal justice process. The decade began in the fifteenth year after the Supreme Court of the United States had authorized a resumption of executions in its 1976 decisions. All the major systemic constitutional challenges to the death penalty had been rejected by 1988, and a steady stream of death sentences since the 1970s had built up a backlog of more than 2000 prisoners awaiting execution. By 1990, thirty-seven states had recent death penalty legislation, and thirty-four of those states had prisoners on death row. Yet only thirteen of the thirty-seven death penalty states had conducted an execution by the end of 1989. It appeared that a determined U.S. Supreme Court and strong pro–death penalty public opinion would end this log jam in the 1990s.

The 1990s also should have been the decade when the huge regional and state-to-state differences in execution rates evened out. Up through 1989, nine of the first thirteen states to conduct executions had been Southern, but the large number of condemned prisoners in many Northern and border metropolitan states provided powerful evidence by the start of the 1990s that executions would soon be spread more evenly over the three-quarters of American states that had reaffirmed their support for executions. Was this the decade when execution became business as usual for criminal justice?

What happened, instead, in the 1990s was a peculiar mix of expected developments and policy surprises, a pattern that has not been easy for observers to explain. The number of executions in the United States climbed almost fivefold during the 1990s, and the number of states conducting executions at some point during the decade also more than doubled, from thirteen in the 1980s to twenty-nine in the 1990s. Yet Southern states continued to account for three-quarters of all executions. And even though the number of executions increased, the death row population continued to grow from more than 2000 in 1990 to 3500 in 2000.

The major surprise about capital punishment in the 1990s was that anger, distrust, and dissatisfaction grew rather than diminished throughout the decade. The death penalty system that was operating in the 1990s had no friends and no defenders. Execution increased, but law and order partisans were enraged by the delay and uncertainty that took the bite out of death sentences while they meandered through more than a decade of state and federal appellate review before execution became a realistic prospect. The law-and-order lobby led a crusade to put sharp limits on appeals in death penalty cases. Opponents of the death penalty were alarmed by the grossly inadequate resources and legal representation that were universal in states that produced high rates of executed death sentences. Death penalty opponents and due process activists led a crusade to stop executions in several states while the error-prone machinery of justice was subjected to sustained scrutiny. By the end of the 1990s it was all but impossible to find an informed observer who was content with the system that had evolved to administer and review death sentences in the United States.

This chapter shows that the dissatisfaction with the death penalty that proliferated in the 1990s was a classic result of two contradictory value traditions driving policy in two inconsistent directions. The enemies of delay in executions went to war against the power of federal courts to examine the merits of death penalty appeals. This movement was a protest against constitutional standards being enforced in death penalty cases. In the U.S. Supreme Court and in the Congress, a series of obstacles to reviewing state death sentences were deliberately put in place to smooth the path to executions. Yet a series of innocent defendants had been delivered from execution by the same cumbersome judicial process and delays that were the subject of the full scale law-and-order assault.

Widespread among the public during the 1990s were both anger at execution delays and concern that the system risked executing innocent people, a situation guaranteeing that there was no level of appellate review and no volume of execution that would be acceptable to public opinion. Further, as the number of executions increased during the decade, the level of discomfort with the execution system increased as well. At the end of the decade, the conflict over capital punishment in the United States was at its highest point in a generation, and no clear path out of the turmoil was evident. The angry 1990s were no accident. The contradictory impulses of that decade were a reflection of the contradictions of capital punishment in the United States.

The War on Appellate Review

The major objective of death penalty supporters in the 1990s was to cut down the delay between death sentences and execution. The story of this crusade is an important chapter in American constitutional history. The 200 death sentences a year are an impossibly tiny fraction of the multitude of felony convictions recorded each year in the United States, and the 3700 prisoners on death row in 2002 are less than one-tenth of 1 percent of sentenced felony offenders. But death penalty cases are unique in American criminal justice and have provoked a sustained attack on judicial principles and processes over the last twenty years that carries important consequences throughout the criminal justice system. This section describes the special features of death cases that incite the hostility of prosecutors and Supreme Court justices and shows how these frustrations have produced multiple limits on the ability of condemned defendants to seek the review of federal courts.

How Death Penalties Are Different

The most serious criminal punishment available for the vast majority of felons is imprisonment, confinement in coercively controlled institutions for a duration that can range from a few months' time to the remainder of an offender's life. The ordinary legal process after a defendant is convicted and sentenced to prison is that confinement to prison begins during any appeals the defendant might wish to pursue. Even when the defendant can stay out of prison during a first appeal, the prison sentence will start prior to any processes of collateral attack such as habeas corpus, the postconviction reexaminations that may take years to resolve. In these circumstances, the appellate process might seem a nuisance to the prosecutor and does carry some risk of frustrating the prosecutor's objectives if the defendant should win a reversal of his conviction, but the judicial review itself does not stop the state from imposing the prison sentence. The punishment itself is not postponed by the process of appeal.

Prosecutors seek death penalties when they believe imprisonment alone is insufficient punishment for a particular offender. But there is no way that a death sentence can be carried out while any significant question remains about its legal propriety. So the state's special penal purpose in death cases—the execution of the offender—must be postponed until all appeals are finished.

For defendants who wish to avoid or postpone execution, the best method to stave off the executioner is to keep the process of appeal going forever. The fact that all state court remedies must be exhausted prior to the start of the all-important federal court review process plays into this strategy quite nicely. The defense attorney's duty in cases where his or her client wishes to avoid execution is to manipulate the system by all lawful means to postpone execution.

For a prosecutor who is intent on seeing the death penalty consummated, the lengthy appellate process becomes a major frustration and the object of resentment, because as long as the defendant's appeals continue, the state's penal objective cannot be achieved. In these circumstances, state lawyers will see any delay of execution as a victory for the prisoner and a defeat for the prosecution. The power of judges to prolong the process during the multiple appeals throughout the state and federal courts is resented in death cases because it cheats the state of its penal objective. When this happens, the legal system itself becomes an enemy of the state's lawyers, and the appeals process becomes a target of attempts to minimize the power of appellate tribunals, to speed the path through appeals, and to reduce the power of judges to review issues that could have been raised and considered at some earlier point in the process. Prosecutors grow angry at the courts and conclude that federal judges and capital defendants are making common cause of putting off executions.

What is singular in this conflict is that the appellate process itself becomes the state's enemy, and judges and legal standards can provoke high levels of anger and hostility. In this conflict, it is the agents of the state punishment authority, not least the state's lawyers, who see vindication in the execution process. They are in pursuit of their own version of closure by lethal injection, and they are often furious when judicial delay postpones the meaningful victory that execution represents. With this mindset, lawyers in public employment can become distrustful of the judicial process and cease to identify with the objectives of legal appeals.

This systematic tendency for delay to make prosecuting attorneys into enemies of the appellate process goes far beyond the usual tensions that adversary competition generates in litigation. The need to win in criminal trials may foster a resentful zero-sum game between prosecuting and defending lawyers in the adversary system, but this usually does not make the officers of the judiciary or the legal process itself into enemies of criminal prosecution. Other criminal appeals generate adversarial tension between prosecutors and defense lawyers; the death penalty generates special adversarial tensions between prosecutors and the appellate process. The state's lawyers view the judicial process as their enemy.

Judicial Hatred of "Last-Minute Litigation"

A further frustration of the death penalty system is the pressure that last-minute litigation puts on appellate court judges. Judges, particularly judges in courts of last resort, are not fond of being the target of criminal appeals that are only moments removed from a scheduled execution. Many justices on the U.S. Supreme Court developed a particular distaste for the eleventh-hour filing of legal motions that are quickly appealed to the federal circuit courts and on to the Supreme Court as the only hope of securing a delay of execution. This practice, which a committee headed by Justice Powell disdainfully called "last-minute litigation" was a major source of discomfort for justices, who were put on the spot by having to rule on motions made in the time just prior to an execution.

For a Supreme Court justice, last-minute death penalty litigation is a public relations disaster. If the last-minute motion is rejected by the U.S. Supreme Court, the judges become the last step before the execution and its apparent cause. (The headline reads, "Smith Executed after Supreme Court Rejects His Appeal.") If a delay of execution is granted, then the highest federal court can be blamed for frustrating the punishment process ("Last-Minute Stay Halts Execution"). So there is either blood on the hands of justices when they refuse to act or blame for the frustration of state criminal punishment if the justices decide to order further legal reviews.

One natural reaction to the discomfort of this dilemma is resentment of those prisoners and lawyers who put the justices on this hot seat. Judges and committees speak of the abusive or manipulative use of federal courts with the clear implication that such last-minute writs should not be filed. But the problem here is that a conscientious lawyer will always file a writ if there is nothing else that presents any hope for the condemned client. When a lawyer has an honest belief that an execution will be unlawful, only a constipated conception of legal ethics would argue against a last-minute appeal that has any chance of putting off an execution. Thus, the only hope for protecting judicial image and avoiding the pressure of eleventh-hour writs by deterring any last-minute appeals is to make such appeals literally hopeless, to structure a set of legal rules that cannot produce a remedy, no matter what the claim.

The Allure of Iron Rules

What the judges who hate "last-minute litigation" need to find is a set of legal rules that removes all judicial power to enquire about a condemned prisoner's claim. Only when the law is clear that justices cannot act can the judge claim he is not responsible for an execution that follows. The best and only insurance policies against a judge having moral responsibility for an execution are mechanical rules without exceptions. And the most reliable mechanical rules available to close the doors to courts of justice and lock them shut are procedural requirements that trigger defaults when they are violated.

The creation of sharp restrictions on the time and manner of raising objections to the legality of state death penalty procedures became the main weapon of those who wished to pave the way to quicker executions. The strategy was to restrict the types of objections that condemned prisoners could raise on appeal and to provide ironclad legal reasons for rejecting any last-minute appeals as the time for execution draws near. Many states have rules that require objecting to constitutional errors at trial or forfeiting the right to seek appellate relief because of such errors at a later date. Other state systems impose short time limits on notice of appeal. The U.S. Supreme Court has fashioned a series of restrictions on what types of constitutional errors can be the basis for relief in federal courts (see *Teague v. Lane* [1989]; *Wainwright v. Sykes* [1977]; *Brecht v. Abrahamson* [1993]), and has also held that almost all constitutional objections to a state death penalty provision must be presented in the prisoner's first federal habeas corpus or be lost (*McKleskey v. Zant* [1991]). In 1996, the federal Congress added strict time limits on any delay between the end of a condemned defendant's state court proceedings and the filing of a federal habeas corpus petition in capital cases. The intention of these rules was not hard to intuit from the title of the legislation: Anti-Terrorism and Effective Death Penalty Act of 1996.

But refusing to hear constitutional claims all but guarantees unjust outcomes in death penalty cases. The primary effect of strict procedural rules that trigger defaults in death cases is to put a premium on the sophistication, the skill, and the careful attention to detail of those lawyers who represent death penalty defendants at trial and early in the appellate process. Defendants with good lawyers will have their objections to trial procedures carefully raised at trial and preserved for appeals. Time deadlines will be noted and followed. Usually, the technical content of complicated procedures will be skillfully mastered and probably used to the client's advantage. Good lawyers thrive on appellate procedural complexity. But the innocent or less-skilled attorney will make mistakes that literally become a matter of life and death for the defendant. The larger and the more complex the layer of procedural rules, the greater the gap between good lawyers and bad. The client pays the penalty for his lawyer's mistakes, and often that penalty is death.

The second problem with rationing access to careful review in death penalty cases by using procedural rules and defaults is that whether deadlines and requirements of timely objections have been met has little to do with the degree of unfairness in a defendant's capital trial. Indeed, the defendants with the less skillful lawyers may be more likely to have been unjustly convicted or condemned than those with good legal representation. In most death cases, the state has more influence over who will serve as a defendant's lawyer and with what resources than does the defendant. The less skilled the attorney, the more likely the defendant will have been unjustly convicted of a capital crime. So the same bad lawyering and low level of resources for the defense that prejudice the client's trial chances will cost the defendant the chance to appeal when procedural defaults govern access to the courts. Complicated procedures and short deadlines will not favor those defendants who were the victims of unfair hardships at trial; indeed, the most disadvantaged defendants at trial face a form of double jeopardy because bad lawyering handicaps the defendant at trial and prejudices his chances of having the merits of his appeal ever examined.

Execute the Innocent? Procedural Default and the Constitution

Two cases decided by the U.S. Supreme Court in the 1990s illuminated the clash between procedural defaults and the claims for substantive justice in death penalty litigation. The first of these head-on collisions was *Coleman v. Thompson*, decided by the U.S. Supreme Court in 1991. Coleman had been convicted of the rape and murder of his sister-in-law and sentenced to death. He claimed innocence. The state of Virginia required specific identification of grounds for appeal to be provided within thirty days of the entry of the final verdict in a posttrial state habeas corpus proceeding. Coleman's lawyers filed his notice of appeal thirty-three days after the verdict had become final, three days after the deadline imposed by Virginia. Rather than waive the three-day violation, the Virginia Supreme Court refused to examine the substantive basis for the defendant's claim that his death sentence was improper. Coleman's failure to meet the thirty-day state deadline was the Virginia Supreme Court's only basis for refusing to address the merits of whether the death penalty had been imposed in conformity with constitutional requirements.

When Coleman turned to the federal courts by filing a writ of habeas corpus, the federal District Court ruled that the failure to meet the thirty-day deadline in the earlier state proceeding was an "independent state ground" that cut off the power of federal courts to inquire about whether the defendant's federal constitutional rights had been violated at his trial. The Supreme Court of the United States upheld this result in an opinion written by Justice Sandra Day O'Connor. The record in this case does not indicate whether disciplinary action was taken against the attorneys responsible for the three-day delay. Mr. Coleman, however, was put to death by the state of Virginia without any federal court ever considering the merits of his claims of constitutional error at his trial.

The majority opinion in the U.S. Supreme Court's decision puts heavy emphasis on procedural analysis and the interests of federalism. The defendant's argument that his claim of ineffective assistance of counsel in the state court habeas proceeding should require a federal habeas corpus inquiry was rejected by Justice O'Connor for the majority on the following grounds:

Given that a criminal defendant has no right to counsel beyond his first appearance in pursuing state discretionary or collateral review, it would defy logic for us to hold that Coleman has a right to counsel to appeal a state collateral determination of his claims of trial error.

Because Coleman had no right to counsel to pursue his appeals in state habeas, any attorney error that led to the default of Coleman's claims in state court cannot constitute cause to excuse the default in federal habeas. (501 U.S. at 756–57)

Justice Blackmun, in dissent, is quick to point to the mechanical logic of the majority analysis:

... [T]he Court today continues its crusade to erect petty procedural barriers in the path of any state prisoner seeking review of his federal constitutional claims. Because I believe that the Court is creating a Byzantine morass of arbitrary, unnecessary and unjustifiable impediments to the vindication of federal rights, I dissent. (501 U.S. at 758–59)

The motive behind the majority's rule in *Coleman* is not hard to find. The felt necessity for ironclad procedural barriers to review of a condemned defendant's claims is the fear of endless delay and last-minute litigation. But how can the morality of this type of procedural foreclosure be justified by the judges who use such doctrines? What sorts of assumptions about condemned defendants can permit judges to lock the door to further judicial review and continue to sleep at night?

The easiest way to relax about attaching life-or-death consequences to procedural mistakes is to assume that all the condemned who pursue appeals are guilty of the charges against them and were also rightfully convicted of those charges. The death penalty appeals process can then be imagined as a game designed by the defendant to delay execution rather than an important forum for enforcing federal constitutional standards in state capital trials.

But what if a truly wrongful conviction has occurred? How can the federal courts preserve the power to cut through the technicalities when monumental problems make the original trial suspect? For the first round of federal habeas corpus litigation, the Supreme Court has tempered parts of its procedural requirements with exceptions where gross injustice would result if a procedural default were enforced. Justice O'Connor uses this exception to reclaim moral high ground in her *Coleman v. Thompson* opinion for the court: "As Coleman does not argue in this Court that federal review of his claims is necessary to prevent a fundamental miscarriage of justice, he is barred from bringing these claims in federal habeas" (501 U.S. at 755).

This "fundamental miscarriage of justice" exception provides something of a safety valve for federal courts as well as a basis for justifying rigid rules in the nonmiscarriage cases. If a defendant can show strong evidence of a fundamental miscarriage of justice, the failure to observe a state procedural requirement will not keep the defendant from getting a hearing in federal court. But shouldn't any prejudicial error in a death penalty case be fundamental enough to counter a notice of appeal that was only three days late? The Court's answer to that question has been "No," and the circumstances deemed fundamental for the purposes of this rule have been quite restricted. The defendant wishing to persuade the courts that enforcing a procedural default would risk a fundamental miscarriage of justice is best advised to present strong evidence that he is not guilty of the capital crime (see Hertz and Liebman 2001, pp. 1227–1240).

And there are a number of reasons why this approach is of limited benefit to condemned prisoners. First, there is no such "fundamental miscarriage of justice" exception when the defendant fails to meet many procedural hurdles provided by federal law. We will observe the impact of this when discussing our second case study from the 1990s, *Herrera v. Collins* (1993). Second, the defendant has the burden of establishing the miscarriage of justice condition, and this will be a particular problem for prisoners without adequate (or any) appellate lawyers. So even the small safety valve provided in cases such as *Coleman* benefits only the lucky prisoners and has relatively small impact in states where the resources available to the condemned are quite limited.

But the doctrinal safety valve available in state procedural default cases is of great importance to judges who would otherwise worry about the morality of enforcing procedural defaults in death penalty litigation. That is why the case of *Herrera v. Collins*, decided by the Supreme Court in 1993, presented a particularly discomforting challenge to the jurisprudence of procedural defaults in death cases. Convicted of a police murder in Texas, Herrera had exhausted his state appeals and completed a federal habeas corpus proceeding without presenting any evidence that the shooting of the police officer was committed not by him but by his brother.

Shortly before his scheduled execution, however, Herrera filed a second federal writ of habeas corpus alleging that he was not guilty of the crime and outlining the evidence of innocence he was prepared to present in federal court. Prior to this case, the Supreme Court had ruled that a defendant in this position had waived the opportunity to raise any issue that had not been presented in the first habeas corpus, an important procedural barrier if last minute-litigation in federal courts was to be avoided in death cases.

But Herrera argued that the execution by a state of an innocent person would itself be a new violation of the defendant's constitutional rights so that a habeas corpus hearing to determine whether he was innocent should be required even when a former habeas corpus opportunity had been provided. A more direct conflict between the requirements of substantive justice and the need for procedural finality would be hard to imagine than the question presented by this case. Open up the courthouse doors—even a crack—by requiring a new hearing on evidence that the defendant did not commit the murder, or that somebody else did, and an avalanche of allegations to that effect could be expected as execution dates approached. On the other hand, what greater catastrophe for a legal system could be imagined than the execution of an innocent defendant who offered evidence to that effect that the legal system refused to hear?

The Herrera case produced not one but three noteworthy judicial opinions, including an opinion for the Court by Chief Justice Rehnquist that should be read by all students of American law. How does a constitutional Court balance a procedural violation against the claim that an innocent defendant will be killed by the state if the Court will not allow a hearing?

The Rehnquist opinion does not provide an explicit answer to the question of whether the execution of a defendant who was actually innocent of the capital crime would be a constitutional violation, nor does the Chief Justice flatly exclude a provably innocent defendant from access to further habeas corpus even if he had already used up his one allotted shot at federal postconviction review. The bulk of Rehnquist's opinion seems to prepare the ground for this sort of rejection by rehearsing arguments for finality in criminal cases and suggesting that executive clemency by state governors would be available for the truly innocent even if no federal court could intervene to halt the execution of an innocent.

But having tiptoed up to the edge of rejecting even the constitutional claim of an innocent defendant at death's door, Rehnquist instead refuses to answer the question Herrera posed for the Court. Instead, the Chief Justice tells us:

> *We may assume, for the sake of argument in deciding this case, that in a capital case a truly persuasive demonstration of "actual innocence" made after trial would render the execution of a defendant unconstitutional, and warrant federal habeas relief if there were no state avenue open to process such a claim.* But because of the very disruptive effect that entertaining claims of actual innocence would have on the need for finality in capital cases, and the enormous burden that having to retry cases based on often stale evidence would place on the States, the threshold showing for such an assumed right would necessarily be extraordinarily high. The showing made by petitioner in this case falls far short of any such threshold. *Herrera v. Collins*, 506 U.S. 390, 416 (1991) (emphasis added)

While the decision to reject Herrera's appeal is supported by six justices, only two (Justices Scalia and Thomas) support the view put forward in Scalia's concurring opinion that the imminent execution of a demonstrably innocent defendant would not for that reason be a violation of the cruel and unusual punishment clause of the Bill of Rights. Justice O'Connor, by contrast, begins her long concurring opinion by expressly supporting "the fundamental legal principle that executing the innocent is inconsistent with the Constitution." After an extensive review of the evidence against petitioner Herrera and a discussion of the difficulty of framing a precise test for the extent of exonerative new evidence necessary to trigger a federal hearing, Justice O'Connor returns in her last paragraph to adamant disavowal of any suggestion that execution of the innocent could ever be constitutionally sanctioned: "Ultimately, two things about this case are clear. First is what the Court does *not* hold. Nowhere does the Court state that the Constitution permits the execution of an actually innocent person" (506 U.S. at 426) (emphasis in the original).

Justice Kennedy joins the O'Connor opinion, and Justice White adds his own reassurance that "in voting to affirm, I assume that a persuasive showing of 'actual innocence' made after trial, even though made after the expiration of the time provided by law for the presentation of newly discovered evidence, would render unconstitutional the execution of the prisoner in this case" (506 U.S. at 429). With the three dissenting justices, a total of six of the nine judges then on the Court recognize a constitutional violation in the execution of the innocent. Add to that the fact that even Justice Rehnquist, famously, is willing to assume this "for the sake of argument." To be sure, the late Mr. Herrera did not benefit from this support of the constitutional principle, but why are the opinions in *Herrera* not a victory for capital defendants with claims of innocence?

The problem with the theoretical right to federal review espoused by Justices O'Connor, Kennedy, and White is that it requires very persuasive evidence of exoneration to win even a preliminary hearing in federal court. The practical aspect of this was noted by Justice Scalia, who would worry about the possibility that claims of "actual innocence" might become an accepted basis for federal courts postponing executions but takes comfort from the standard proposed by O'Connor and White for demonstrating a claim:

> With any luck, we shall avoid ever having to face this embarrassing question again, since it is improbable that evidence of innocence as convincing as today's opinion requires would fail to produce an executive pardon. (506 U.S. at 428)

If Scalia is correct that the defendant must prove innocence beyond the shadow of a doubt to open the courthouse door, why the heavy emphasis from half the judges who support Herrera's execution on the existence of a federal claim in cases of actual innocence? It is not because they anticipate any regular hearings in federal district courts relitigating guilt—O'Connor and White have fashioned tests that come close to inverting the standard of proof beyond a reasonable doubt and require powerful evidence of innocence to secure a federal hearing for the defendant. Very few cases could qualify. Why all the fuss about a tiny loophole? And what, to use Scalia's term, is so "embarrassing" about the question presented in *Herrera*?

What is important to Justices O'Connor, Kennedy, and White is the legitimacy of the entire apparatus they enforce against capital defendants. The rules enforced in cases such as *Coleman v. Thompson* make moral sense to judges such as Sandra Day O'Connor only if it is assumed that all who suffer deadly consequences because of their lawyer's mistakes deserve to die in any event. The notion that an innocent defendant could be helpless either in the labyrinth of procedural traps erected by states such as Virginia or in the procedural default rules of federal habeas corpus would render the whole process illegitimate to many of the judges who have supported the creation of the system. What is "embarrassing" about the question posed by *Herrera* is that procedural rules that risk the execution of the innocent would not merely lead to a bad result but would undermine the moral justification for an entire system of procedural defaults. The attack on appeals that played such an important role in the 1990s would then become an assault against fundamental American values of fairness. So that reacting to the problem posed by *Herrera* is a test of enthusiasm for ironclad rules that divides the pro–capital punishment judges on the U.S. Supreme Court into two opposing sides.

Of course the creation of a review that is available only to those able to prove their innocence persuasively would be a hollow hope for most defendants even if they are innocent. Those who lack good lawyers, DNA exclusions, or exceptional good luck could never meet the strict proof of innocence requirement of judges such as O'Connor, Kennedy, and White. The ambition in cases such as *Coleman* and *Herrera* seems to have been to create a costless constitutional comfort for those who administer the system without adding to the delays in the death penalty process. In reality, the rule they support can generate grave risks of executing those innocent defendants who would not be able to demonstrate more than substantial doubts about their guilt at the beginning of a habeas corpus proceeding.

It is a tribute to the moral sense of judges such as Kennedy and O'Connor that they cannot endorse the mechanical logic of procedural default without discomfort. But the empty promise of the current rules provides no real quality control in those cases where the legal and investigative resources available to contest a capital charge have been minimal. It is likely that those who subscribe to the O'Connor/Kennedy/White position in *Herrera* are fooling themselves that the process they administer reserves its arbitrary results for the actually guilty. But the recognized possibility that the apparatus of death penalty efficiency might prejudice the innocent is a potential fault line in the Supreme Court's campaign against delay.

The larger the number of procedural default cases that lead to execution, the higher the risk of catastrophic injustice. If there are fifteen or twenty such cases turned down because more than substantial doubt must be shown to get a hearing, one or two or three innocent defendants among the fifteen or twenty substantial doubt cases will be put to death. Because the inquiry was not launched, we may never know which, if any, of the defendants in such cases were actually innocent. But the risk of wrongful execution will be no less real because the specific victims are not identifiable. As we see below, one thing that separates the early 1990s from later in the decade was that the reality of such risks was widely recognized in the United States by the close of the 1990s.

Executions, Innocence, and Legitimacy

If the major problem of speeding up the path to execution was always the risk of killing the innocent, the events of the late 1990s underscored how real that risk had become. The criminal punishment of those who are innocent is always a tragedy, but when the punishment wrongfully imposed is death, the mistake is a disaster that undermines the legitimacy of the death penalty as a criminal punishment. When innocent defendants are found in our prisons, the mistake provides a motive to investigate the functions of police, prosecutors, and courts in an effort to reduce the margin of error that has produced the mistaken punishment. But we do not use the discovery of this type of mistake as a foundation for questioning whether imprisonment should continue to be a criminal punishment. By contrast, it is argued that the extremity and irreversibility of capital punishment means that the danger of mistaken execution becomes a basis for questioning the legitimacy of death as a punishment. A mistaken imprisonment is a criticism of the police and the courts; a mistaken execution is an indictment of the institution of capital punishment.

But why the distinction between these two forms of mistake and their implications? There are three overlapping explanations for the special significance of wrongful executions in the twenty-first century. First, it can be argued that death is irreversible in a qualitatively different way so that a significant possibility of error undermines the legitimacy of the practice in a way that does not apply to punishments such as imprisonment. That theory has some plausibility. Yet it is hard to imagine that the deprivations of imprisonment are in any important sense reversible simply because the subject of the imprisonment survives the experience physiologically and can receive monetary compensation. Much of the pain of unjust incarceration cannot be undone, so prison too is irreversible in its damage to the innocent.

A second way of distinguishing the death penalty from other punishments that can be mistakenly applied is to argue that the absolute claim of the state to use all of the condemned prisoner's life as an instrument of government policy is inconsistent with a substantial possibility of error. It is the clash between the arrogance of the claim to kill and the error-prone reality of the process that leaves the death penalty especially vulnerable; the hubris that is the foundation for the claim to kill is inconsistent with the potential for erroneous application. In this account, mistaken death sentences and executions reveal that state confidence in its processes of guilt determination is a form of false advertising. But why is that observation not equally true with mistaken imprisonments? What is the greater hubris of execution? The usual answer to that question is to emphasize the irreversibility of execution, which returns us to the analysis of the pains of imprisonment just concluded.

A third possibility is that the institution of imprisonment is not questioned when innocent people are punished because the prison is regarded as a socially necessary form of punishment and control, while the additional deprivation imposed by execution is not regarded as clearly necessary. If the additional deprivation of execution as a punishment is regarded as possibly gratuitous, then the obvious remedy when the death sentence is wrongful is to cut back the degree of punishment to that which is strictly necessary, that is, to imprisonment. In this view, the special arrogance of executions is the embrace of an awesomely severe punishment that is not strictly necessary.

This third approach to the link between mistaken execution and undermining the legitimacy of the death penalty is plausible in both its substance and the historical timing of the 1990s concerns about innocence. The stories of the falsely hanged have always been compelling, but they function as an argument against death as a penalty when there is no longer a strong social consensus on the strict necessity of the penalty. In this sense, the legitimacy of executions must already be in question before arguments about the risk of execution of the innocent become a significant part of the critique of the legitimacy of the death penalty.

This emphasis on death as an already suspect punishment not only distinguishes between imprisonment and execution in contemporary U.S. experience, but it explains why the arguments about the execution of the innocent had their largest impact in the United States at the very end of the twentieth century. Nobody argues that the risk of false execution in the United States was lower in earlier years of the twentieth century, an era of almost nonexistent federal court review of state punishments, of Jim Crow jurisprudence, and of primitive or nonexistent legal services for capital defendants. As bad as things are in Alabama in 2003, the era of the Scottsboro boys makes the current system look like a substantial improvement. Why then is the current system more vulnerable to public concern about arguments against execution based on the risk of mistake when that risk must surely be lower now than before?

Perhaps because it is only when the legitimacy of the capital sanction is already open to question that the additional injury of false execution becomes an important argument against state execution. If this is correct, then cases of false convictions in capital cases will more often be the last important events in the path toward abolition of the death penalty rather than an early spur to organize opposition to the penalty where none has been present before.

Innocence and Death Penalty Policy

After a brief introduction to the rhetoric of the innocence debate, this section presents a summary of the events that put special emphasis on the innocence issue in the later years of the 1990s and then discusses the empirical data available on the risk of wrongful death sentences and executions. The third subsection of this analysis examines the range of proposed remedies to wrongful executions. Then the last part of the chapter demonstrates the contradiction of trying to speed up executions and reduce the margin of error for death sentences at the same time.

THE RHETORIC OF INNOCENCE: AN INTRODUCTION

The potential dangers of executing the innocent have always been a part of debates about the death penalty. The twentieth century history of capital punishment is littered with confirmed or contested cases of wrongful execution and a much larger collection of persons revealed to be innocent while under sentence of death. After *Gregg v. Georgia* approved the restarting of executions in 1976, a series of problematic death verdicts received some public attention, and one Texas case where an innocent defendant was sentenced to death was the subject of a much-noticed documentary film, *The Thin Blue Line*.

Earlier in the twentieth century, the issue of erroneous criminal conviction had been major ammunition in the assault by the American legal realists on the formalistic hubris of Anglo-American justice, as when Jerome Frank and his daughter Barbara published *Not Guilty* in 1957 (Frank and Frank 1957). The subject of the realist criticisms was criminal justice in general. The target of the post–*Gregg v. Georgia* campaign, however, was exclusively the death penalty. Hugo Bedau and Michael Radelet, two prominent anti-death penalty scholars, published their compendium of wrongful convictions and executions first as a law review article entitled "Miscarriage of Justice in Potentially Capital Cases" in 1987, and then as a book, *In Spite of Innocence*, published in 1992. Stephen Markman and Paul Cassell, pro–death penalty lawyers, published a response to the Bedau and Radelet law article in 1988.

The thrust and parry in this law journal exchange of the 1980s is in some respects typical of the later and more politically visible debates about innocence. The first of these is that the argument about the risks of false punishment of the innocent is clearly identified by both sides as a proxy war about capital punishment. Bedau and Radelet make no secret of their goal: "Only one further major reform remains available: abolishing the death penalty entirely" (Bedau and Radelet 1987, p. 89). Markman and Cassell declare the question they wish to address is:

> Whether the risk of error in administering the death penalty is sufficiently high both to outweigh the potential benefits of capital punishment and to offend the moral sensibilities that must support a free society's criminal justice system. (Markman and Cassell 1988, p. 121)

So this is a debate not about criminal procedure but about capital punishment.

The second typical element of this late 1980s debate about innocence and the death penalty is the centrality of a dispute about the rules of engagement. Bedau and Radelet portray the entire death penalty system as error-prone, and thus use evidence of false convictions at murder trials, and rejection of valid claims in appeals, as indications of the unreliability of the capital punishment system. They identify their subject matter as the totality of capital punishment system failures. Markman and Cassell, by contrast, dismiss false convictions and wrongful rejection by appellate courts as not prejudicial. As long as errors are discovered prior to execution, their implication is that the system is working. On this account, a high rate of reversal in death cases for prejudicial error is evidence of a healthy capital punishment system. Opponents of the death penalty see a high rate of reversals of death trials as evidence that major errors in death cases are routine events that threaten to swamp the system.

This failure of supporters of the system to regard any mistakes short of execution as system failure is curious in two respects. First, it ignores wrongful conviction and mistaken rejection of appeals as risk factors for wrongful execution. Conviction and unsuccessful appeals are, after all, the necessary conditions for wrongful executions. Why not worry about their prevalence? How do we know that later events will rescue the system from disaster? Second, as we see later in the chapter, a focus on discovering the innocent late in the process places tremendous emphasis on late stages not only in the appeal process but also many years after conviction. But these are precisely the time frames and repetitive appeals that "Effective Death Penalty Acts" were attempting to abrogate in the other major pro–death penalty legal campaign of the 1990s. There is danger in putting too much weight on the later stages of capital appeals if careful reexamination during federal habeas corpus is an endangered species.

Innocence in the 1990s

The rhetorical flourishes and arguments about Joe Hill in the law review debates of the late 1980s seem almost quaint fifteen years later, and the early debate provided little advance warning of the explosive prominence of wrongful death sentences attained by the late 1990s. This section briefly describes the rise to centrality of questions of conviction of innocent defendants and the risk of wrongful execution.

SCIENCE

The major events that transformed the issue of innocence to center stage in the 1990s were equal parts science, scandal, and politics. The science in the equation was DNA matching, an increasingly sophisticated method of comparing the DNA profile of a criminal suspect with any biological materials left by an offender at a crime scene. When biological residue from an offender is present, DNA matching provides a potentially reliable way of either tying a particular subject to the crime scene or excluding the subject as the person responsible for the material found at the crime scene. Such biological samples are currently available in a large number of sexual assault cases, including many sex murderers and in a minority of other capital murder cases, perhaps 20 percent. The science behind DNA is vastly more powerful and also more reliable than forensic comparisons such as fabric matches or technical comparisons of hair color, texture, and shape. And the capacity for specific pattern identification makes the conclusions from DNA matches much more powerful probabilistic statements. Careful DNA matches with good samples will either implicate the subject of the match or exclude him; there are very few equivocal findings.

By the late 1990s, careful DNA work was acquiring the reputation as a gold standard for establishing guilt or innocence when samples are available, even years after an original trial and in spite of eyewitness or other testimony to the contrary. Barry Scheck and Peter Neufeld identify sixty-five cases of what the title of their book describes as "actual innocence" that have been established through DNA procedures, including *eleven* death sentence cases (Scheck, Neufeld, and Dwyer 2000). But the credibility of DNA matching procedures has two effects on the "innocence debate" that are powerful well beyond these numbers. First, DNA exclusions end the debate about whether a reversal or nonprosecution is really an exoneration. A broad public opinion accepts DNA findings as definitive, so there is no tactical advantage to prosecutors denying definitive DNA results as establishing innocence. Placing the exculpatory impact of such tests beyond the range of prosecutorial rhetoric about proof of innocence is a major step forward from simply undermining trust in the evidence that was offered as proof of a defendant's guilt. DNA became the currency of proof of innocence in a number of cases in the 1990s.

The second impact of the DNA procedure is the undermining with hard science of what Bedau and Radelet called the myth of infallibility. When DNA evidence contradicts eyewitness testimony in a case where biological samples were available, it weakens the trust that can be placed in eyewitness testimony even where biological evidence is not available. By undermining the certainty attached to testimonial evidence that is contradicted by DNA, the DNA procedure casts a much wider shadow of doubt over conventional testimony of guilt than just in cases of available biological contradiction.

SCANDAL

The scandals of the late 1990s involved increasing numbers of cases where apparently innocent suspects had been condemned by patterns of improper prosecutorial and prosecution expert witness conduct, as well as clusters of troublesome outcomes suggesting that entire systems were misfunctioning. The most famous cluster of falsely condemned prisoners was found in Illinois, a major industrial state with a death row population of 155 at the beginning of 1995 (Snell, Bureau of Justice Statistics 1996). Illinois conducted a total of twelve executions between 1990 and 1998, more than any state north of Missouri. No fewer than thirteen defendants on death row in Illinois were exonerated after convictions and death sentences, and ten of these cases were discovered after the beginning of 1995. The pivotal event in the discovery of most of this cluster of cases was not the state or federal appellate review process, but a research project in a journalism course taught by Northwestern University professor Larry Marshall. One of those rescued, Anthony Porter, survived only because litigation about his mental retardation had postponed an execution that would otherwise have been the end of the case. As the two *Chicago Tribune* reporters who investigated the Illinois cluster put it, "Tack 20 more points onto Anthony Porter's I.Q. and you put him in his grave, one more of the more than 700 people executed in the United States in the past quarter-century" (Armstrong and Mills 2002b). Some of the prosecutorial behavior that had contributed to the epidemic of false convictions in Illinois was well beyond careless: Nondisclosure of potentially exonerating weaknesses in one case led to the criminal indictment of prosecutors (they were acquitted at trial in 2001). In January 2000, the Republican governor of Illinois, George Ryan, a previous supporter of the death penalty, announced a moratorium on all executions and appointed a special commission to investigate. Here is Governor Ryan on the suspension of executions in Illinois: "Until I can be sure that everyone sentenced to death in Illinois is truly guilty, until I can be sure with moral certainty that no innocent man or woman is facing a lethal injection no one will meet that fate" (Armstrong and Mills 2002b, p. 215).

The cluster of Illinois cases was large but the phenomenon of discovered innocence on death row has been nationwide. According to the anti–capital punishment Death Penalty Information Center, the number of condemned prisoners exonerated after time on death row was ninety-eight between 1973 and the close of 2001. Illinois, with its thirteen cases, was second in the nation in that category to Florida's twenty-one. A total of thirty-nine exonerations were recorded after the beginning of 1995, or 40 percent of the total since 1973 (Dieter 2002).

One reason for the larger number of exonerations in recent years is the increasing use of DNA matching tests. DNA is listed as playing a substantial role in only eleven of the ninety-eight listed cases, but all of its impact was recent. DNA evidence did not have any credited role in the first fifty reported exonerations but was listed as a "substantial factor" in ten of the thirty-eight cases since 1995. The importance of DNA in a quarter of the recent exoneration cases not only increases the reliability of the conclusion that a defendant was wrongfully convicted, it also seems to have increased the volume of exonerations by providing a new category of exculpatory evidence that has been used in the process. DNA evidence is available in substantial proportions of rape/murder cases where the close physical contact and retrievability of the offender's seminal fluids from the victim helps determine identifications. Similar evidence is not available in most other cases.

The Illinois exonerations have provoked sympathetic responses in other states where there is conflict about the legitimacy and reliability of the capital punishment system. Moratorium bills were passed in two states—New Hampshire and Nebraska—only to be vetoed by unsympathetic governors (Armstrong and Mills 2002a), and moratorium legislation had been introduced in a wide variety of other death row states by the end of 2001, including Texas (Mills 2001). And the governor of Maryland announced a moratorium there in May 2002.

THE SAGA OF JOYCE GILCHRIST

A second major scandal involving death penalty trials has produced much less official rethinking about the reliability of the system. In Oklahoma, a police laboratory technician named Joyce Gilchrist was a frequent and apparently well-qualified expert witness who was employed by the Oklahoma City police crime lab and presented trial testimony invariably favorable to the prosecution in a host of criminal cases. Among the cases where Gilchrist's testimony was presented were eleven capital cases that resulted in executions. A host of discovered problems with the factual basis for Gilchrist's testimony have so far failed to shake the faith of Oklahoma officials in their death penalty system.

The crime lab chemist's testimony is frequently the only expert testimony of its kind produced in a capital trial because defendants are not given the resources to hire independent forensic experts. While a certain amount of antidefendant bias can be expected in cases where the only forensic evidence comes from a branch of local law enforcement, the professional standards of the technicians are supposed to compensate for the lack of defense experts to test the physical data that are the basis of expert opinions in hair matching, blood groupings, or semen matching.

But professional standards were not prominently in evidence in the recent career of Joyce Gilchrist. Two federal courts concluded she gave false testimony in a 1992 rape/murder trial and reversed the death sentence in that case. The FBI reviewed Gilchrist's analyses in eight cases and "concluded she had misidentified evidence or made other serious mistakes in six of them" (Hastings 2001). A police laboratory reanalysis of slides that were used to place a defendant at a rape/murder scene because the semen stains on the victim's pillow matched his blood type found that no semen stains were present in those slides (Hastings 2001). The defendant in that apparently false testimony case had been executed a year before the reanalysis, but public officials in Oklahoma from the governor down to the spokesperson for the local district attorney were unconcerned. Their faith in the guilt of this particular defendant was stronger than doubts about the misrepresented physical evidence. Indeed, authorities have already announced that in all eleven cases where Gilchrist's testimony was followed by an execution "based on a preliminary review, authorities previously said there was no taint . . ." (Hastings 2001).

It is, of course, understandable that those who prosecuted and sentenced defendants to death might be inclined to persevere in the belief that the executed defendant was guilty as long as they could, but the capacity of public officials to shrug off false scientific evidence as a cause of injustice speaks volumes about how hard it would be to convince an unwilling judge or prosecutor that questionable eyewitness evidence or prosecutorial misconduct should produce doubt about the guilt of a defendant he or she has convicted. All the more so when that defendant has been executed.

One wonders whether the Gilchrist affair would have produced a different official and public response in a Northern death penalty state such as Illinois or Ohio. If so, there is irony in the fact that the flow of executions is largest in precisely those places where the resistance to examining the system is the strongest. Oklahoma had more executions in year 2000 than Illinois had experienced in the twenty-five years after *Gregg v. Georgia*. It appears that the larger the level of execution in a state, the harder it will be to have the dangers of false conviction and mistaken execution accepted.

THE POLITICS OF INNOCENCE

One measure of the sudden importance of disputes about mistakes related to the death penalty is the role the question played in presidential politics during the campaign in 2000. Just as Bill Clinton had become the Democratic presidential candidate in 1992 after being governor of a state that conducted executions, George W. Bush became the Republican candidate for president after serving five and a half years as the governor of Texas, the state with the highest total of executions in the United States. One aftermath of the scandal in Illinois was substantial interest in whether the Texas justice system was as error-prone as the Illinois system and also whether any execution during Governor Bush's administration might have involved an innocent defendant. The journalistic investigation during the presidential campaign turned up evidence that Texas capital justice was a far from perfect system, with unreliable defense counsel, a Court of Criminal Appeals where judges ran for election on promises to get tough on crime, and seven cases where apparently innocent defendants had been rescued from Texas death sentences (Armstrong and Mills 2000a,b).

When questioned on such matters, Governor Bush's position was that exonerations that take place prior to execution were evidence that the system was working and that there was no proof that an execution of an innocent defendant had happened on George W. Bush's gubernatorial watch. While candidate Bush did not support either moratoria on executions or any other specific reforms in death penalty cases, his position on the legitimacy of executions might still provide some comfort to moratorium forces because there was no rhetoric of acceptable risk in candidate Bush's position on execution of the innocent. Implicit in Governor Bush's optimism on the accuracy of the Texas system was that only a zero-risk system should be regarded as acceptable.

Have We Executed Innocent Defendants?

Despite Governor Bush's rhetoric of zero risk in Texas, there is some indication that the majority of American citizens are less confident than their political leadership about the capacity of a death penalty system to operate error-free. When public opinion polls ask citizens about the probability that innocent defendants have been executed, the majority of respondents believe that such miscarriages of justice have happened, and many citizens think that falsely convicted persons have been executed with some regularity. These opinions persist despite the fact that there is no single defendant who has been executed in the modern era who has had his innocence so persuasively established that death penalty advocates such as Markman and

Cassell would concede the issue. Then why do so many people who support the death penalty nonetheless believe that false execution is a recurrent event in modern criminal justice? Have the respondents in public opinion polls watched too much television drama? Are they mixing fictional "Movie of the Week" plots into their perceptions of the less dramatic reality of street-level criminal justice?

A more likely reason why the average citizen believes in the recurrent risk of execution of the innocent is the statistical probability that such cases happen. Taking what I shall call an actuarial approach to the known facts about system performance in death cases makes the execution of the innocent seem all but inevitable, even when particular cases of false execution cannot be identified. If the American tolerance for deadly error is relatively low, only the absence of clearly identified cases is saving the system from major embarrassments. The analogy here might be to an Asian or African nation that wishes to deny a high prevalence of AIDS among its population and therefore does not test large samples of its population; thus the true rate of infection cannot be known. This type of ignorance will provide comfort to those who cannot distinguish between bad information and good public health. Both good health and bad data will generate a zero rate of known HIV infection, but only one is associated with low levels of true public danger.

AN ACTUARIAL APPROACH

On July 2, 2001, Justice Sandra Day O'Connor gave a speech to a group of women lawyers in Minnesota that bluntly announced, "If statistics are any indication, the system may well be allowing some innocent defendants to be executed" (Bakst 2001). The approach that Justice O'Connor was using would not satisfy critics who demand that those who worry about innocent defendants facing death should name names and be prepared to prove innocence beyond doubt in those cases. An extension of this type of approach could begin with the population of cases where we know an innocent person was rescued from a death sentence and use knowledge about how the late stages of death penalty cases are processed to make estimates about how many other innocent defendants may have slipped through the system to their deaths. This type of analysis can help identify the weaknesses in the current system and also reveals some surprising things about the historical role of delay and redundant appeals in reducing the number of wrongful executions.

We can launch a statistical estimate of the incidence of false executions by trying to create an estimate of the margin of error of capital trials. A natural starting point is with the number of discovered errors in cases where death penalties had been assigned. If the ninety-eight exonerations claimed by the Death Penalty Information Center are divided into the population of death sentences produced during 1970–2000—about 7,000—that provides a discovered error estimate of about one death verdict in seventy, which is demonstrably false on the historic record. The next key questions are, How many other death verdicts generated by the system are also mistaken, and what proportion of those undiscovered false verdicts may have produced executions?

WHAT CAUSES TRIAL ERROR?

Most of the estimates of importance in making a good guess about false executions concern the efficiency and bias in judicial appeals and habeas corpus proceedings in death cases. But it might be helpful at the outset to consider the error risk of the death penalty trial itself. Given a standard of proof beyond a reasonable doubt, how can as many as one in seventy death sentences be false on the discovered numbers? Is there a natural limit on error rates that is not much higher than one in seventy because of the reliable nature of evidence of guilt in the capital trial process?

While the standard of proof in criminal trials is quite high, the nature of the evidence used to prove guilt has a substantial margin of error in many if not most capital cases. Not all killings are potentially capital murders, and the way the statutes are drafted makes killings where victims and offender are not acquainted more likely to be punishable by death than deaths that involve family members and close acquaintances. A majority of all cases that generate death sentences in the United States involve strangers—usually robberies—and identifying offenders in stranger cases can be hazardous. For all the credibility of a person remembering that she saw the defendant commit the crime, eyewitness identification by crime victims turns out to generate a wide margin of error. Academic psychologists have demonstrated substantial levels of false positive identification (see Loftus 1996). The testimony of others accused of complicity in the same crime on issues where they are seeking to displace blame is problematic, and the testimony of "jailhouse informants" who claim to have heard incriminating evidence while sharing jail space is reputed to be the least reliable evidence of guilt presented in America's criminal courts (Illinois Governor's Commission on Capital Punishment 2002). Further, as the story of Joyce Gilchrist suggested, while some types of biological evidence are quite powerful, other types of physical evidence from the crime lab carry potential for abuse.

Then there are the inferences to be drawn from the prior record of the suspect on trial. In the case of Malcolm Rent Johnson, one of the eleven Oklahomans executed after Joyce Gilchrist testified for the prosecution, the state attorney general's office was not concerned that false testimony of Joyce Gilchrist may have produced the execution of an innocent defendant. One reason provided for this confidence was the defendant's previous record of two rape convictions that made him a suspect in the rape/murder that sent him to his death. But the problem with inferring guilt from previous record in this fashion is that the prior record was a basis for selecting the defendant as a suspect. When dealing with suspects who have been selected for scrutiny because of their prior criminal records, it may be particularly hard to separate the issue of prior record and current guilt, but the "round up the usual suspects" strategy of law enforcement leaves an uncomfortable margin of error. The risk here is the false conviction of innocent defendants with criminal records.

When estimating the odds that innocent persons have been executed, there is one further bias in how cases are selected for death sentences and execution that may put the innocent at risk. There is a correlation between a low quality of legal representation in both trials and appeals and a high rate of execution. The concentration of executions in Southern states with low defense resources is much more pronounced than the concentration of death sentences, as Chapter 4 established. Bad lawyering at trial renders even a meritorious defense and appeal vulnerable to technical defaults. Bad lawyering at trial also leaves critical facts undiscovered in the defendant's case and weaknesses in the state's evidence that are unknown. And it is the states that most enthusiastically slam the door on cases of procedural default that exhibit high rates of execution. The natural tendency is for this to increase the expected proportion of erroneous executions of all kinds, including the execution of the innocent.

POSTTRIAL PROCESSES AND WRONGFUL EXECUTION

A good actuarial approach to wrongful execution would make two estimates prior to producing an assessment of the magnitude of false executions in the United States. The first is the extent to which current posttrial legal processes can successfully identify cases of innocent defendants. The second is to factor in the risk of execution for all persons under sentence.

One key point to consider when trying to guess the significance of the ninety-eight exonerations between 1970 and 2001 is the effectiveness of the appellate process in identifying cases of true innocence in the population of death penalty appeals. If we were confident the system could locate all cases of innocence through the normal appeal and habeas process, our residual estimate of innocence cases eligible for execution would be zero. If we thought that the system correctly identified as false half its falsely convicted defendants in the appellate and federal review process, then ninety-eight further undiscovered cases would remain in the system at risk of execution after appellate screening. If the screening estimate was that two-thirds of all false conviction cases were not identified as false convictions, then the best guess would be closer to 200 cases of false conviction expected to survive the review process not identified as such.

The evidence on the quality and quantity of screening is mixed. There is no good reason to believe that current judicial review is particularly sensitive to mistaken eyewitness identifications, to prosecutorial withholding of exculpatory statements (unless this has been somehow discovered), to truth-telling alibi witnesses ignored by convicting juries, or to factually true "somebody else did it" defenses rejected by juries. These issues of fact are quite difficult to relitigate under the current system, and that means the system will typically not reopen such cases to discover errors.

Where biological samples are available at crime scenes, the new science of DNA testing does create a capacity to pick up errors that did not exist before quite recently. At present, such evidence is available in a small fraction of capital murder cases—perhaps one case in fifteen. Better evidence collection and advances in analysis procedures can expand that total in the future. But the expanding capacity of DNA is a double-edged sword on the issue of execution of the innocent. Recall that none of the fifty-two defendants exonerated prior to 1993 had DNA evidence as a basis for their release, while eleven of the forty-six released prisoners had DNA evidence after 1993. The increasing rate of exoneration and the sudden impact of the new technology on 24 percent of recent exonerations suggest that some defendants who would have been exonerated with the newer technology were put to death under the older system. No conviction in the United States prior to 1979 generated any DNA exclusion, while the number of 1980s convictions reversed by DNA totaled seven. Did the chances of convicting the innocent suddenly increase in the 1980s, or did misidentifications slip through the cracks before then? Where are the six or so defendants not freed by DNA after 1970s convictions to match the seven defendants from the 1980s?

The Arithmetic of Wrongful Executions

There is one element of arithmetic of great importance in comprehending the conflict between efficiency and fairness in death penalty systems. Given the unselective nature of appeals processes and the accidents of fate that were necessary to deliver many of the ninety-eight exonerated defendants from the death chamber, it would not be unreasonable to estimate that another one-seventieth of the death sentences in the United States over the period 1970-2000 involve innocent defendants. Since all nonexecution cases where a jury later acquits are counted as false convictions, this would suggest that another one-seventieth of all capital cases would produce acquittals if retried. There is no exact science behind that guess, but it is as plausible as many other estimates and far more likely than the zero additional error estimates that some supporters of the system assume.

If we adopt that provisional estimate of wrongful death sentences—another ninety-eight in thirty years—would that mean an estimate that ninety-eight innocent persons have been executed in the United States? Certainly not, and the reason for this is that the death penalty system we have has executed only about one in every ten persons sentenced to death. Assuming that the delays, reversals for other reasons, and geographically determined different rates of execution are spread evenly over the innocent and the guilty alike, the chronically low rate of execution in the United States will have rescued nine out of ten falsely convicted prisoners from death. But here would lie both a great irony and a fundamental conflict. The irony is that the system would be rescued from a bloodbath of the innocent by its own inefficiency. The fundamental conflict is that any reforms that speed up the appeal and execution process would also increase both the odds that innocent defendants are executed and the volume of such wrongful executions.

SOME QUALITATIVE GUESSES

Rather than simply guess about the total population of falsely executed persons by using estimates of the undiscovered innocent, it is also possible to use some of the data that have been collected on patterns of exoneration to make guesses about the volume of cases and their origins and causes. If I had to guess about the number of false executions since *Gregg v. Georgia*, my aggregate guess would be about five. One or two of those would be the DNA cases from the 1970s that did not happen because there were no DNA screenings for the cases in that era. At least one case would come from the state of Virginia, where, as Chapter 4 showed, in the 1990s death sentences lead to the execution chamber more quickly than anywhere else in the United States. Even though Virginia has the second-highest total of executions to date in the United States, only one falsely convicted prisoner has been exonerated from its death row. Regarding the fourth and fifth projected execution of an innocent: it could be anywhere the executioner does business. The risks would be greatest in those states with high volumes of execution. And of course the estimate is a very soft number. But is a better estimate zero?

IDENTIFYING AN INDIVIDUAL VICTIM

Whatever the statistical likelihood of wrongful execution in the United States, there is no single consensus candidate among the executed as a clear case of the wrong man being put to death. The absence of such a poster child actually executed is a puzzle if not an embarrassment to the critics of the death penalty system. Moreover, the absence of an unambiguously innocent defendant who has been executed might be regarded as a challenge to those who believe on actuarial grounds that innocent defendants are missed by the current system. If so many defendants are wrongfully convicted, why do we not later hear of these cases as well as the cases where the defendant was still on death row when the error was discovered? Could five or seven or ten innocent defendants be executed and disappear without any notice in the United States?

A thorough answer to this question requires an excursion into the arithmetic of American capital punishment as well as an understanding of the limited communication channels from death row and execution chambers back into the American social mainstream.

The arithmetic we have just reviewed suggests that fewer than one in every ten death sentences issued since 1970 has yet resulted in an execution. So even if the ninety-eight known innocent prisoners had been joined by another ninety-eight whose innocence could not be established, fewer than ten executions would have resulted. The system may be very inefficient at sorting out cases of innocence, but the overall inefficiency of the death penalty has so far limited the damage of false execution.

But why would five or seven wrongful executions not have produced at least one case where the defendant's innocence would be known now with certainty? One should begin to think about this problem with a clear understanding of the obscurity and isolation of most condemned American prisoners. For every Sam Sheppard case or celebrity like Mumia Abu-Jamal on death row, there are 500 obscure prisoners with no economic resources and very few social contacts who can provoke an official or media inquiry. For most death row defendants, the only connection with the resources and communication channels that can draw attention to a claim of innocence is the lawyer who represents them in the appellate process. But among the powerful pressures that operate to consider a case closed when a defendant is executed is the end of the publicly funded lawyer-client relationship (if it lasted that long). Whatever constituency a defendant might have had to establish his innocence does not typically survive his execution.

When lawyers do persist in efforts to vindicate an executed client, the system is resistive. A rare illustration of systemic resistance surfaced in 2001, when lawyers representing a foundation and four newspapers sued in Virginia to permit biological materials available at a California crime laboratory to be preserved there and tested to determine whether more sophisticated procedures now available could link this sample taken from the victim to Roger Coleman, the Virginia prisoner executed in 1992 for rape and murder after the Supreme Court of the United States had turned back his effort to reopen his case in *Coleman v. Thompson*. The state of Virginia resisted this request, arguing that "continual reexamination of concluded cases brings about perpetual uncertainty . . . and disparages the entire criminal justice system" (Masters 2001). In June 2001, Virginia

Circuit Judge Keary Williams ordered the sample removed from a California crime lab and returned to the state of Virginia, having concluded that there would be "no benefit" to society in using DNA tests to assess whether innocent persons had been executed. "How can investigation of the death penalty as it was implemented in 1992 be beneficial in scrutinizing the death penalty as it is carried out in 2001 when the processes are so different?" (Farrell 2001). The impact of this approach to reopening cases of contested propriety is clear. In three other cases where lawsuits sought biological evidence after execution, the prosecutors successfully resisted. In only one reported case was the sample provided, and that testing was inconclusive.

By far the most important element of the adversary system that makes innocence cases harder to identify after execution is the absence of a definitive legal proceeding to resolve conflicts in evidence and inference. The majority of the ninety-eight identified wrongful death sentence cases have the validity of that label certified by the defendant's later acquittal at trial or the choice of a prosecutor not to press charges when a decision on reprosecution must be made. Because there is no procedural necessity of further action by prosecutors and juries, the claims of the already executed are never tested. In the records of cases that led to execution, there are a fair number of evidence conflicts about eyewitnesses, alibis, and reported confessions of others, but there is no way to overcome the legal conclusion from the original conviction or to resolve the doubts and conflicts that emerge from later discovered evidence. Cases such as that of Gary Graham and David Spence in Texas or Leo Jones in Florida can never be rehabilitated from limbo by legal processes. For those wishing to take comfort from the official version in any evidentiary conflict, the finality of that legal process is irrefutable.

But it was probably inevitable that the state of Virginia would fear a case such as *Coleman* might happen. Science may provide the critics of capital punishment with an opportunity to contradict official versions of capital crimes with more persuasive data than alibi witnesses or the reported confessions of others. In the minority of cases where biological evidence is available, the credibility of that evidence will create overwhelming pressure to allow access and testing. Efforts to destroy evidence to avoid such results are unlikely to strike a responsive chord with public opinion. So for one narrow category of cases, tests of validity after execution are possible.

Remedies

Three different types of remedy have been mentioned in discourse about the problem of mistake in administration of a death penalty: (1) making

DNA matching resources available to all death row defendants where the tests are relevant; (2) making substantial improvements in the minimum standards for lawyers in capital trial and appeal; and (3) maintaining a moratorium on executions until a study of the system reveals the causes of mistaken death verdicts and the system has been fixed.

The special role of DNA evidence in several exonerations in sex felony murder cases has produced support for making the resources of reliable DNA investigation available wherever it is relevant in a capital case. Making such resources available is an obviously good idea and may in fact be constitutionally required under some extension of the arguments about execution of the innocent aired in *Herrera v. Collins*. But if currently known cases of apparent false conviction are the guide, DNA matches have played a key role in discovering less than one in every eight false conviction episodes. So finding an optimal solution to the DNA matching issue would still leave seven-eighths of the known false conviction problem unaddressed. So more than DNA reforms must be undertaken if the larger issue of false convictions is a substantial concern.

When she suggested in her speech in Minneapolis that "[p]erhaps it is time to look at minimum standards for appointed counsel in death cases and adequate compensation . . . when they are used" (Bakst 2001), Justice O'Connor identified both the key stage in the system where reforms would be necessary and the current weak links in the system. Because the problems that can produce wrongful convictions are so various, quality control across the spectrum of capital trials would be required to identify problems and preserve objections for appeal. What defendants need at trial are competent and experienced lawyers with adequate support services. On appeal, lawyers who are skilled in investigation and knowledgeable in the substance and procedure of death penalty law are needed. If the sort of reforms Justice O'Connor put forward had real substance and were enforced, it would revolutionize capital trial and appellate practice in almost every state in the United States that has experienced more than a few executions.

But a tremendous shift in resources and priorities would be required. At the outset, to give retroactive effect to such minimum standards would require the reversal not of hundreds of death sentences in the United States but of thousands. And to fail to give retroactive effect to such standards would leave the risk of false execution undisturbed in thousands of cases.

Thus, while there may be an important distinction in principle between tough new standards for trial and appellate counsel and a moratorium on executions, the practical impact of these two approaches would be similar for a long time if they were implemented with serious resolve. Putting a new minimum standard on the quality of the defense would block the execution of those who had lawyers below the new standard. If the standard is set high enough to reduce substantially the chances of false execution, it would require the retrial of very high proportions of all death row cases in the South and Southwestern United States.

Further, providing good trial and appellate lawyers to all capital defendants in high-execution states will slow down the process, virtually end procedural defaults, and put tremendous stress on the trial resources of high–death penalty prosecutors' offices. So if the direct impact of upgrading minimum standards for counsel in capital cases does not halt the death penalty process, then the indirect impact of a flood of better defense counsel might finish the job.

Would the improvement in lawyering resolve the problem of false convictions? There are two ways that better legal representation would reduce the odds of false conviction and execution. First, a much larger proportion of mistakes and dishonesty would be discovered at trial and preserved for appellate litigation. Second, the reforms would slow down the system and all but halt executions. As recently mentioned, even an indiscriminate decrease in executions would reduce the chances of erroneous execution.

But there is no guarantee of zero risk in any level of real-world lawyer competency standards. Better lawyers could reduce risks substantially. But no death penalty can function where there is zero tolerance for a risk of false execution.

MORATORIUM AND ABOLITION

The most frequently proposed remedy for many procedural defects in the death penalty system is a suspension of execution either for a period of years or until specific reforms have been identified and implemented. The suspension strategy, usually called a moratorium on executions, attracted support from a wide variety of different groups over the last years of the 1990s, and it was implemented in Illinois and Maryland as a specific response to the epidemic of mistaken death sentences. A committee of the American Bar Association has also urged a moratorium as a recognition of the procedural injustices of the current death penalty process, and left-of-center justice system critics have introduced moratorium proposals in twenty states (American Bar Association 1997).

As a response to the problem of executing the innocent, a general moratorium strategy is in one respect overbroad. By no means do all condemned prisoners contest their guilt, so why should the guilty be spared from lethal injections while the system is reformed in the way it responds to the possibly innocent? This has not been extensively discussed in places such as Illinois, but it may be that the execution of the innocent is regarded as only one of the risks run by the current system, with concern also that poor lawyering costs many defendants a chance at lesser punishments. To the extent that the entire system is suspect, the proponent of a moratorium would wish to have all executions suspended.

But then what? Those who support the moratorium on executions as a next step in death penalty policy may have two sharply different conceptions of what they might expect to happen after the suspension period is over. For many, a moratorium is a useful prelude to abolition of capital punishment, a suspension for a period of years while the public gets used to life without the executioner. After a long period of inactivity, it is hoped that the period of de facto abolition during a moratorium will put the political burden on proponents of a death penalty and thus ease the transition to de jure abolition of capital punishment. That kind of transitional suspension of executions was frequent in other developed nations (Zimring and Hawkins 1986, chap. 1). During this kind of moratorium, there are no frantic efforts to fashion reformed methods of providing legal services. The reform the system is moving toward will not need any new procedures for capital trials because there will not be any.

But those who support a moratorium as a prelude to a reformed death penalty are hoping for a much more activist, indeed, revolutionary transition in the organization and funding of legal services in capital cases than has ever happened previously. And no matter how effective the new regime might prove to be, the nasty residue of thousands of death penalties rendered under the old system would have to be set aside. Could such a reformed system proceed without the arbitrariness, the selection of killers of white victims for death, the huge geographic variations, and the chance of wrongful executions? The only prior moratorium period in U.S. history, the ten years without execution from 1967 to 1977, is no precedent for testing effort at systemic reform. All the states did after *Furman v. Georgia* was to refashion the legal definition of capital murder, a cosmetic legislative change that had no great ambitions, no costs, and produced no measurable progress toward just results in death cases.

The careful and pragmatic report issued in 2002 by the blue ribbon commission on Illinois capital punishment illustrates the radical nature of the reforms necessary to improve death penalty systems as well as the difficulty of achieving most of the necessary changes. The panel was composed of thirteen persons, nine of whom had some background as state or federal prosecutors, so this was not a sellout to the abolitionist cause or a group of advocates with little real-world experience. By the end of its two-year study, the panel reported that a slight majority of its members favored the end of the death penalty. Short of that, the panel made eighty-five separate recommendations that would narrow the number of murders eligible for death, drastically improve defense counsel and the resources put at their disposal, forbid conviction for a capital crime solely on uncorroborated jailhouse snitch testimony, videotape police interrogations and train judges (Illinois Governor's Commission on Capital Punishment 2002). Despite all of the above, the commission was sure that the system would still be error-prone. No recommendation was made by the commission on what steps the governor should take with all the condemned defendants put on death row by the discredited prior system, but the huge gap between the old and the recommended systems put pressure on the governor to mandate clemency for those condemned by the old regime.

The price for making these improvements in Illinois would be very high. The benefit would be a reduced but still significant risk of false conviction in capital murder trials. The key question is not whether these reforms are worth the effort and treasure they would require. Instead, the real question is whether the death penalty itself is worth the enormous effort that would be required to make it less of an outrage to justice.

Of course, even the best and most expensive efforts at reforming death penalty systems may be doomed to disappointment by the historical context of executions in the twenty-first century. If nothing short of a system with zero risk of false execution will prove acceptable, the game is over before it has started. If the death penalty itself does not have the status of perceived necessity that will generate public tolerance of some margin of error, then the intolerance of mistake in death cases is a symptom of vulnerability that is really based on a perception that the executioner is no longer necessary to the maintenance of public order and safety. If it is doubts that the executioner is truly needed that will render his mistakes intolerable, no moratorium devoted to reforms can put Humpty Dumpty together again. Since nothing available to reformers can make a criminal justice system infallible in its administration of the death penalty, an unwillingness to risk false execution that is nested in the perception that execution is no longer a necessary technique of public safety inevitably points to the end of death as punishment.

The Contradiction in 1990s Reforms

More than any other period in the history of the United States, the 1990s were an era when the contradictions of capital punishment were on public display. It is difficult to conceive of two more contradictory reform trends than finding ways to remove the obstacles to executions by strict enforcement of procedural defaults and scrutiny of capital convictions for the wrongfully condemned. As we have seen, procedural defaults do not discriminate between weak and strong cases; they punish defendants with less skilled lawyers. For those innocent defendants who have been lucky enough to get exonerated, the combination of the attention of sympathetic outsiders and time to investigate or merely to wait for exculpatory happenstance have been critical. Figure 7.1 shows the time between year of death sentence and year of exoneration for the ninety-eight formerly condemned prisoners listed as exonerated on the Death Penalty Information web site as of December 2001. These data on timing come from the web site.

The average delay between a death sentence and an exoneration is eight years, and only one-third of the cases of established innocence occur within

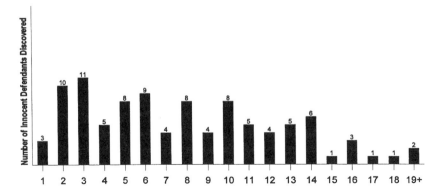

Figure 7.1. Cases of discovered innocence by number of years after verdict until discovery of innocence. *Source*: Data drawn from Death Penalty Information Center's list of innocent inmates released from death row, as of the end of 2001. Available at http://www.deathpenaltyinfo.org/Innocentlist.html.

five years of a death sentence. Instead, the outstanding characteristic of the time distribution of discovered innocence is the gentle downward slope of the curve. After modest concentrations of exonerations two and three years after verdict, there is very little drop off in the frequency of discovered innocence cases each year as time from death sentence increases. In twenty-five of the ninety-eight cases, the innocence of the accused was discovered between four and seven years after the death sentence was passed, but twenty more exonerations—80 percent of the annual rate in years four through seven—occurred in the four years between eleven and fourteen years after the original verdict. Since many of the ways in which exonerations happen are not connected to the lawyer work associated with the direct appeal and standard habeas corpus process, there is no evidence that speeding up habeas corpus deadlines will make any of the factual discoveries that fuel the exoneration process happen any faster.

To determine whether those eventually exonerated had been relieved of the threat of a death sentence much earlier than the final date published, we searched the web site records on twenty consecutive "recent cases." A chronology of dates was available for fourteen of these cases. The median time to removal of a death sentence was 9.5 years for this group, compared with a 10.5-year median time to complete exoneration. The death sentence was reversed much earlier than final acquittal in only one of the fourteen cases we checked, and the removal of the death sentence was within two years of final exoneration in eleven of the fourteen cases. Most of the delays noted in Figure 7.1 are time spent under sentence of death (Dieter 2002, cases 53-69) (see Appendix F).

What mechanical deadlines will do is to execute defendants prior to the establishment of their wrongful convictions. Since a condemned defendant has no obvious incentive to slow down the process of establishing inno-cence, it is hard to accuse the ninety-eight defendants in Figure 7.1 of intentional delay in establishing their innocence. A strict limit of nine years after death verdict for the delay of execution would have presumptively removed thirty-five of the ninety-eight cases, or 36 percent of this exon-eration sample, from the ranks of those rescued from wrongful execution. The gentle downward slope over time of any curve based on the data in Figure 7.1 means that each year after verdict through the fourteenth year is associated with a significant volume of exonerations.

Unless the nature of legal representation and postconviction review in the United States changes fundamentally, there seems to be a zero-sum relationship between speeding up the trip to the death chamber and find-ing and exonerating wrongfully convicted defendants. In the system we have, quick is the natural enemy of careful. Yet public pressure in the 1990s was asking the system to be both speedy and careful.

If the zero-sum nature of the contest between efficiency and fairness con-tinues, the public's expectations from the capital punishment system are bound to be disappointed. Public opinion favors reducing delay to execution. Pub-lic opinion also favors not only extreme care to avoid execution of the inno-cent but, increasingly, a moratorium on executions until system reliability can be established. What the public demands is both efficiency and fairness. The same citizen can find himself angry in his support for the swift execu-tion of those he is certain are guilty (where the appellate process will seem a waste of time) and ready to stop the entire enterprise of state execution when he suspects that innocent people are at risk.

What we saw in the angry and volatile 1990s were the contradictions in capital punishment policy becoming more permanent and more problem-atic parts of the public life of the United States. The angry war on appeals described in this chapter takes its emotional energy from the same assump-tions of guilt that provide moral justification for the American vigilante tradition. The same assumption of guilt that provided a moral excuse for lynching and now leaves us comfortable with a "shoot first" policy in armed citizen defense makes judicial review and delay appear to be the enemies of the people's justice. Indeed, the assumption of guilt seems also to provide a rationale for the moral permissibility of procedural default in a case such as *Coleman v. Thompson.* Chapter 3 showed how this has been helped along by the campaign to reimagine state capital punishment as private and com-munity justice in the age of victim impact statements and psychological closure by execution.

At the same time, the contradiction of jury verdicts in death cases by incontrovertible DNA exonerations and the scandals of prosecutorial mis-conduct in a wide range of death penalty cases have created a constitu-ency for halting the entire operation of a death penalty system pending major reforms. The movement to promote a moratorium in executions has one public relations advantage in this highly conflicted environment:

ambiguity about the eventual impact of suspending executions on the death penalty itself. In the short run, a moratorium strategy may provide a way for conflicted citizens to have their cake and eat it too: to stop executions but maintain the symbolic presence of capital punishment as a future policy. In this sense, the moratorium strategy in the current United States is spectacularly suited to American ambivalence about executions. But at the end of any blue ribbon committee study period, the contradictory impulses in American culture will force a choice between conflicting value traditions. The machinery of execution must be either disassembled or redesigned and restarted. Either choice will provoke anger and dissatisfaction.

The Legacies of the 1990s

What permanent impact did the 1990s have on the death penalty in America? Without doubt, the issue of capital punishment is more important in the United States in the first years of the twenty-first century than a decade before. Uncertainty, conflict, and dissatisfaction are the predominant emotions associated with death penalty questions. When compared with the expectations many people had entering the 1990s, the big news to emerge about the death penalty in this singular decade was that nothing was resolved. Execution rates increased, but this was associated with higher rather than lower levels of conflict. The push to speed up executions produced a backlash from the organized bar and in the politics of the death penalty. A higher rate of execution amplified conflict and dissatisfaction.

In retrospect, the failure to resolve the conflicts associated with the death penalty in the 1990s was inevitable because of the clash of two inconsistent value systems that produces the peculiar American attitudes toward the death penalty. The attack on appeals did not put doubts about the death penalty to rest, because it conflicted with due process values that still hold sway with most citizens. The scandals in Illinois and Oklahoma did not cut away much public support for execution in the high-execution states because of the continued viability of vigilante values, at least when there is little public doubt about the guilt of the condemned. At the end of this remarkable decade, we had learned that the ambivalence and conflict associated with capital punishment are not transitional phenomena but enduring features of American attitudes and values.

Of all the public figures who have played a role in discourse about capital punishment in recent years, Justice Sandra Day O'Connor seems most captured by the conflicts of the current era. A political conservative from the capital punishment state of Arizona, Justice O'Connor wrote the majority opinion that approved state procedural defaults as a way of limiting the arguments that condemned prisoners could make in federal habeas corpus in 1991. The next year she joined in the majority in the Herrera case but was adamant that procedural rules should not punish the truly innocent. By 2001, she was publicly acknowledging the chances that the current system had led to the execution of the innocent and supporting reforms to reduce the incidence of these disasters. In her 2001 speech to an organization of women lawyers in Minnesota, Justice O'Connor provided an epitaph to the high-conflict 1990s. Noting that Minnesota does not have a death penalty, Justice O'Connor remarked, "You must breathe a sigh of relief every day" (Bakst 2001).

8

The Beginning of the End

THE LAST CHAPTER of any book about the death penalty in America must, of course, be about the future. The level of activity and controversy about capital punishment has never been greater in any era of American history, and the issue has never been of greater public importance. Major changes have occurred in the level of executing, the issues in controversy, and the meanings of execution in culture and law over the last fifteen years. The contradictory crusades of the 1990s warn us of both the velocity of change and the difficulty of predicting even tomorrow's trends in American capital punishment. What happens next? How long will it take for a significant change in capital punishment policies? What are some of the leading indicators of change in American attitude and conduct? How can citizens act to influence the American future?

To answer these questions with authority, we need a crystal ball; lacking that, this chapter uses the findings of this study to provide a new framework for thinking about the future of capital punishment in the United States. The tug-of-war between vigilante and due process values and the structural predictions about the impact of such conflict provide a somewhat more disciplined way of thinking about the future of the death penalty in the United States than would unmitigated speculation.

What are the likely developments over the next fifteen years in institutions that will host the climactic battles about the death penalty in America: the federal courts, governments in capital punishment states, and the national government's executive and legislative branches? What should be the distinct objectives of a campaign to end the death penalty in the United States? What new initiatives are necessary to create an effective abolitionist movement?

For middle-aged Americans who want to live to see their nation kick the execution habit, more than regular exercise and good eating habits will be necessary. In addition to the pragmatic and incremental campaigns of recent years, the value conflict context of the capital punishment debate suggests that morally centered objections to execution and morally committed activism will be needed to create an atmosphere where change can be facilitated. The campaign to abolish the death penalty in the United States will not succeed by stealth. Abolitionists must instead demand attention to benefit from the growing sense among citizens—including many of those who support the penalty—that state execution does not command the moral high ground in the American future. The end game against execution will require passion as well as reason, to the extent that a deeply held affection for vigilante values must give way.

Environments and Institutions

A necessary prelude to discussion of a program to abolish the death penalty in the United States is a survey of how the key environments and institutions that will influence the future of death penalty policy in the United States are likely to develop in the middle-range future. What will be the major cultural and political influences on the institutions and decision makers who have the power to make death penalty policy? My short list of the key institutional settings for analysis is as follows: (1) the capital punishment policy and attitudes of other developed nations, (2) the orientation of the United States Supreme Court, (3) the number and distribution of executions, and (4) the orientation of the executive and legislative branches of the national government.

Developed Nation Policy Toward Capital Punishment

The first key environment in my list that has the power to influence death penalty policy is also the least obvious of the major influences on future American policy. The United States has unabashedly ignored the example of foreign national policy on the death penalty in political debates and even in litigation in the Supreme Court about contemporary standards of decency under the Eighth Amendment's prohibition of cruel and unusual punishment (see, e.g., *Atkins v. Virginia* 2002; *Stanford v. Kentucky* 1989). Why should foreign practice be considered a critical issue during the future American struggle?

As Chapter 2 established, the current aggressive and orthodox view in Europe that all civilized nations must refrain from execution is a new development, nascent in the 1980s and fully developed only in the 1990s. This new platform for anti–death penalty activism is very different from a difference in domestic death penalty policy between other developed nations and the United States that does not get projected into international debate. The United States and Europe are now farther divided on the question of capital punishment than on any other morally significant question of government policy. This is not just another policy difference but the most extreme current conflict in the developed West.

This gap between the United States and the rest of the developed West, along with the willingness of foreign leaders to criticize and stigmatize American practice, is a brand new factor in the American discourse on capital punishment. To be sure, there are limits. Europe has not used its economic power to coerce change in U.S. policy in the carrot-and-stick pattern that speeded abolition in places such as Poland, Latvia, and Lithuania. But uniform and aggressive judgments that American practices are morally deficient are not without powerful impact on U.S. elites. Despite American pride and willingness to stand alone, the moral and intellectual challenge on the death penalty has already cast some shadows on the American consensus. If the campaign persists, it will certainly become a more important part of American debate in the ever-smaller developed world of the early twenty-first century.

But will this aggressive and unanimous orthodoxy continue in Europe and in the developed Commonwealth nations? Might not the recurrent cycles of leftward then rightward political drift create governments of the right in one or more major European nations who might withdraw from the anti–death penalty consensus?

A change in execution policy is highly unlikely among any of the nations of Western Europe. Indeed, the degree to which the consensus against capital punishment has been insulated from any vulnerability to governments of the mainstream right in Europe is one indication of how far most of the developed nations have come—and how fast—since the early 1980s. Early "free votes" about capital punishment in England and Canada shortly after abolition were evidence that the issue was then regarded as one of domestic politics as recently as the early 1980s. But any attempt to revive a capital sanction in any nation in Western Europe of the current era would be seen as secession from the broader European community, a move well beyond the ambitions of the mainstream right in any Western European power. Further, since nostalgia for executions has not played an important role in any appeals of even the far right in Europe, policy on capital punishment now seems an unlikely wedge issue even for profascist parties trying to break up Europe.

It is mainly the transformation of the death penalty from a criminal justice issue to a constitutional limit on government power in Western Europe that provides protection from serious discussion of reintroduction of a death penalty in political discourse. Crime fears are an important issue in contemporary Europe, and there is evidence that political trends favor expansion of punishment (see Garland 2001, pp. 9–10). But the death penalty has been removed from the field of choice in penal policy: It is no longer regarded as a question of punishment policy. And there is no indication that the pressures that provoke greater imprisonment have any potential to spill over to the death penalty in Western Europe.

The reclassification of capital punishment may be relatively new in European history, but it appears to be rock-solid, even when political pressure from the right is significant. France, for example, was widely expected not to sign a protocol extending the European ban on the death penalty to acts during war but did so just two days before the President of France was pitted against a far-right candidate in a run-off election. The French Ambassador to the Council of Europe observed, "In the current context of the rise of forces of backwardness and narrowmindedness, this signature underscores the continuity of policy in our country, a country of human rights" ("European States Drop Wartime Exception to Ban on Death Penalty" 2002).

But might not the intensity of Europe's commitment to abolition in America wane if governments of the right show much less enthusiasm for American capital punishment bashing? This development is a much larger possibility than any European retreat on the death penalty itself and not without importance for U.S. policy. A substantial reduction in the intensity of European condemnation of executions in the United States would have palpable impact on the level of discomfort that American elites feel from European scorn, now and in the future. The European left would of course maintain *its* high-intensity campaign against the death penalty, but such criticism will be less effective if it is left-sectarian rather than supported on a nonpartisan basis in Europe and the Commonwealth.

Thus, one significant constituency in Europe to watch for the level of its anti–death penalty rhetoric is the mainstream right, that is, the British Conservative Party, the German Christian Democrats, and parallel right-of-center French and Italian parties. Participation from the center-right in the pressure campaign against American capital punishment will strengthen the impact of foreign critiques on American elites. The battle for center-right support in Britain and Europe will thus be one central aspect of the future politics "for export" of capital punishment in the developed West that may have a significant effect in the United States. The death penalty question has zero importance in the domestic penal policies of European nations, but if the center-right participates in the push for transnational abolition, capital punishment will become a more important foreign policy question.

INFLUENCE ON AMERICA

The critical influence of strong European and Commonwealth opinion on capital punishment is in the personal rather than the political interactions that grow more frequent and more important every year. Businessmen, students, and tourists from the United States may be asked pointed questions by their peers who have been raised on the new moral orthodoxy of capital punishment as governmental primitivism. Foreign visitors will debate and instruct on U.S. campuses. Foreign films, books, and music may raise these issues as well. Government-to-government pressure can include complications in the extradition of suspects from foreign custody to U.S. states (and federal authorities) where a death sentence is possible as well as economic pressure on trade with high-execution U.S. states. The saga of Zacarias Moussaoui discussed in Chapter 3 is in that respect a preview of coming attractions.

But it is the damage that foreign attitudes do to U.S. dignity rather than the financial or law enforcement consequences of U.S. policy that carries the most important potential for the American debate, damage to the American self-concept that the United States is a politically advanced system with high regard for individual liberties. In this self-concept, there is a special vulnerability to any credible changes of primitive or despotic government. The chief impact of strong foreign pressure of this kind would be to create doubt in the minds of youth and adults who spend time interacting with educated citizens from other nations.

The Supreme Court

The U.S. Supreme Court has been and will probably continue to be the most important branch of the national government for influencing state execution rates and policies. As decisions such as *Coleman v. Thompson* (1991) and *Herrera v. Collins* (1993) illustrated, by the 1990s America's leading constitutional court was aggressively disengaging from the supervision of state death penalties. In part, this was a reaction against the constant pressure of death cases for the Court, the no-win dilemma of either frustrating state criminal justice policy with constant delay or appearing to be the proximate cause of executions.

But a large part of the Court's push to loosen controls on state death penalty processes also reflected the tastes of individual judges who had been put on the Court to reverse what the Republican right regarded as a civil rights judicial activism. During the Ronald Reagan and George H. W. Bush presidential terms, there was strong pressure toward result-orientation in Supreme Court judicial selection. While the policy produced some mixed results, it also put two judges on the Court who do not regard the death penalty as in any sense constitutionally special (Justices Antonin Scalia and Clarence Thomas) and who join a chief justice who generally finds that the values that compete against special constitutional concern for death penalty cases are always weightier than any worries about executions. Chief Justice William Rehnquist always seems to have his thumb on the scales in death penalty cases, while Scalia and Thomas do not believe the Court has any responsibility for scrutiny. In the 1990s, at least two other Reagan/Bush justices would usually join in the results preferred by these three most aggressive adherents of deregulating state death penalty processes.

The result has been a set of legal outcomes in the Supreme Court that have been less qualified in their support of deregulating death than most other parts of the mainstream legal establishment. On the death penalty, the U.S. Supreme Court has been far to the right of the American legal establishment for at least a decade. While the American Bar Association recommends a moratorium on all executions (American Bar Association 1997), the Supreme Court considers it a close question whether constitutional standards would be offended by the execution of an innocent defendant. As that gap between the legal establishment and the Supreme Court has widened, judges such as Sandra Day O'Connor have shown signs of discomfort in maintaining positions that fall outside the mainstream of a legal profession that has grown more worried about executions, and more likely to act on such concerns, with each new year. There is some evidence that justices in this very conservative court's middle ranks are more inclined in recent years to impose limits on state death penalties. The Court's recent extension of the Eighth Amendment to prohibit the execution of people with mental retardation has been the most prominent example of this trend (see *Atkins v. Virginia* 2002).

What is likely to happen to the personnel and the orientation of this Supreme Court over the middle-term future? There is a very low probability that the Court can escape from its central importance in setting standards for other federal courts to administer in state death cases, and there also is very little chance that the federal courts will play a less prominent role in the regulation of state death sentences. As weak as the quality controls examined in Chapter 4 might now be, the gaps that would open between South and North and between conscientious and less conscientious Southern state courts without effective federal court case-by-case review would be rather too reminiscent of the Scottsboro boys to expect the organized bar in the North or the national media to tolerate without protest.

And there is also no great chance that the federal rules will get less concerned with quality control of the death penalty process. Only if a majority of the Supreme Court adopted the Scalia-Thomas approach of deconstitutionalizing capital punishment could the pendulum swing much farther to the right in the future than its current setting. Instead, the field of choice in the Supreme Court's midterm future is probably between the current level of disengagement, at one extreme, and a much more active involvement in constitutional control, at the other extreme. The key determinant will be the orientations of the judges that join the Court, although some important shifts can be anticipated also in sitting judges over time.

Trying to predict the ideology of new appointments to the U.S. Supreme Court over a ten- to fifteen-year period is handicapped by lack of information about future presidential elections. Each president's political party and personal preferences are of great importance in the makeup of the Court. The presidential election in 2000, which was too close to call even in retrospect, promises to push new judicial appointments to the right in a continuation of the Republican tendency to appoint to the high court candidates who appear to be on the right-hand edge of the mainstream. Recent Democratic selections have been centrists, in part because of the political risks of making liberal appointments to the Supreme Court during the law-and-order 1990s. This asymmetric pattern is likely to continue. Might that push the Court even further to the right on the death penalty?

It could happen. But there are three countervailing pressures that are likely in death penalty jurisprudence of the midterm future. The first is the tendency for centrist judges to grow impatient with using procedural defaults as a strategy for managing capital cases. The most famous example of this sort of on-the-job training was Justice Harry Blackmun, a mainstream Minnesota Republican who dissented forcefully from the Court's death penalty activism in *Furman v. Georgia*, joined the majority revival of state death penalties in 1976, but ended his judicial career announcing, "I refuse to tinker with the machinery of death" (*Callins v. Collins* 1994). There is certainly no universal gravitational pull in this direction associated with Supreme Court service; Rehnquist, Scalia, and Thomas have been unaffected by fuzzy feelings about the problematics of execution. But justices with less wholehearted ideological credentials tend to grow more skeptical of a laissez-faire approach to state capital punishment. This historical tendency is one reason why Justice O'Connor's remarks in 2001 sowed seeds of hope in anti–death penalty observers. Her credentials as a conservative are impeccable, but her pragmatism and failure to pursue an unvarying party line in the *Roe v. Wade* controversy make some shift in her death penalty propensities possible. Justice O'Connor and Justice Anthony Kennedy were the decisive votes in the *Atkins* decision in 2002 that applied the Eighth Amendment to prohibit execution of people with mental retardation.

A second contemporary trend that might push the Court toward higher levels of concern in death cases is pressure from the negative opinion of foreign elites discussed in the previous section. Here again, it is not so much the official protests from abroad that might provoke judicial second thoughts but the dinner conversations and Salzburg seminar comments that have cumulative influence on high-status American jurists who lack

rock-solid ideologies. This exposure is only one of many ways that a continuing consensus from other developed countries can have a direct influence on trends in the United States, but it could be one of the most
important channels of influence.

The third potential influence on judges is a product of their own commitment to the due process tradition that is in conflict with the operation
of state death penalty machinery in the United States. When any doubts
arise about the validity or reliability of state fact-finding processes, the
belief in the power of federal courts to correct injustices is a prejudice we
would expect to find among many federal appellate judges. Some of the
embarrassment of what Justice Scalia referred to in *Herrera v. Collins* (1993)
as the "embarrassing question" of executing a possibly innocent person is a
natural outgrowth of the appellate judicial temperament: a belief that courts
can and should function to correct potential injustice. The hands-off doctrine of the past two decades was an attempt to relieve the federal courts of
the pressure from last-minute appeals, but this disengagement came at a
price: the inability to intervene to avoid potential miscarriages of justice.
Iron rules of noninvolvement that would keep the Supreme Court from
participating in the execution process can fit with a judicial self-concept as
guardians of justice only as long as a judge is certain that manifest injustice
is not a risk that will be generated by judicial inattention to the particular
merits of a capital appeal. There are signs on the current Supreme Court
that doubts already exist among centrist judges.

For all but ideologues of the hard right, the judicial experience and case
exposure that comes with Supreme Court service push them toward the
exercise of greater judicial scrutiny in death cases. The only clear antidote
to that type of leftward drift is the appointment of judges at the right extreme in the continuum. (These are not likely to be in any sense "nonin-
tervention" judges, as students of the U.S. Supreme Court's work in
Eleventh Amendment cases or indeed in the *Bush v. Gore* preliminary in-
junction in the 2000 presidential election well know.) If a hard-right-lean-
ing Court solidifies in the first years of the twenty-first century, then political
pressures to restrain states' death penalty activities would have to flow
through other channels. With any less sectarian a Supreme Court, the
Court's caseload will remain of central importance to the campaign against
state and federal execution, and increased scrutiny rather than further decreases in federal court supervision is the most likely outcome.

While a rightward-leaning Supreme Court can function as a deterrent
to increasing federal court regulation of death cases for the duration of
its time in the majority, it does not seem likely that the current Court or
its immediate successors will build a set of principled precedents that
would restrain judicial activism in death cases beyond the tenure of the
Court majority that supports restriction. The current accumulated constitutional law on the death penalty is itself a study in contradictions.
The archetype of this structure is *Furman v. Georgia* and *Gregg v. Geor-*

gia, both still good law despite the obvious tensions between them. Most of the cases with large operational impacts in death cases are procedural edicts without significant substantive principles at their core (see *Coleman v. Thompson* [1991]; *Herrera v. Collins* [1993]; *Teague v. Lane* [1989]). There is some legacy of reversal or qualification when close cases have been decided but court personnel change (*Payne v. Tennessee* [1991]; *Tison v. Arizona* [1987]).

So most of the Supreme Court's precedents in death penalty cases govern chiefly by the consent of a current court majority. More than most other areas of constitutional law, death penalty jurisprudence is subject to quick changes as the personnel of the Court or the views of sitting justices change. There is more volatility, and less long-term predictability, in the Court's death penalty work than in almost any other area of its continuing concern. All this may be bad news for those who hope for principle-based jurisprudence from the nation's supreme judicial court, but it also means that radical change might always be just around the corner in the tangled legal pathways of the death penalty.

Variations in Executions and Execution Policy

One major influence on how attitudes toward executions develop in the United States will be the volume of executions in the United States, as well as the scandals and controversy surrounding death sentences and executions yet to be conducted. To what extent will the record of the past twenty years be prologue to the level of executions in the United States, the distribution of executions among the states, and resulting controversies about the justice of particular executions and the processes that produced them? A high volume of executions might produce more public perception that execution is a normal criminal justice process, but it also increases the chances of scandal and a documented deadly mistake.

Two elements of future execution policy beyond the sheer number of executions that are likely to have special influence on public opinion and the politics of capital punishment are: (1) the emergent role of the federal government in conducting executions, and (2) the dilemma of diversification—that any push toward reducing the dominance of the South with more executions in Northern and Eastern states intensifies both controversy and scrutiny.

THE SYMBOLIC FEDERAL ROLE

The operational significance of the federal death penalty in the United States is tiny, but its symbolic importance is much greater. Even though a potentially expansive federal "drug death penalty" was signed into law in 1988, the thirty-one people under sentence of death in the federal and military systems in 2002 make up less than 1 percent of the death row population, and the two federal executions prior to 2002 compare with more than 700 in the states (Death Penalty Information Center 2002). Further, once Timothy McVeigh accelerated his execution, all the remaining federal condemned had been sentenced for crimes that were obscure and of no obvious public importance.

The exemplary symbolic importance of the national government having and using a death penalty was the central motive for a federal death penalty. The participation of the national government in a death penalty is a seal of approval for the enterprise of executing criminal defendants by the states. To the extent that there is a status competition between states who execute and those who do not, the example of a federal death row and federal executions is one way to validate the practice in those states that conduct their own executions. This symbolic approval is an obvious motive for the 1988 and 1994 federal death penalty legislation, because all of the persons under federal sentence of death under those statutes would have also been subject to state death penalties for their crimes.

This limited and redundant, but symbolically important, federal death penalty is also a natural target for efforts by special interests with general positions both pro and con on the death penalty. Cross-currents of pressure can delay the march to exemplary federal executions. Even though the Clinton presidency was supportive of the death penalty as a matter of general policy, the Justice Department of Attorney General Janet Reno was a place where inquiries about death case defendants and about the racial and ethnic patterns of federal capital case processing were taken very seriously. Executive branch inquiries delayed the first federal execution from late in the second Clinton term to early in the Presidency of George W. Bush (Walsh 2000).

No matter who is president, federal death penalty policy has become one of the most important issues for any federal attorney general, and policy toward the federal death penalty will continue to command attention hugely out of proportion to the number of federal condemned prisoners or executions. What happens in the federal system will probably be an early indicator of trends in the state death penalty systems and in the federal court regulation of state cases.

STATE POLICY AND PRACTICE

But the main arena of capital punishment policy will continue to be state government, which has 99 percent of all condemned prisoners and has conducted all but two of the first 750 executions after *Furman v. Georgia.*

Among the most important elements of future state-level execution policy will be the number of executions and the distribution of executions among the thirty-eight states with death penalty legislation. The volume of executions increased by an extraordinary 300 percent during the first eight years of the 1990s but then leveled off at the turn of the new century. The recent number of executions nationwide is as high as at any time in the last half-century, but the fraction of active death sentences early in the twenty-first century that become executions in any given year has never exceeded 3 percent since executions resumed. With 3700 people under death sentence, either the number of executions will expand well beyond any number during the last century (a high of 199 in 1933) or the gap between death sentences and executions will remain vast.

There are a host of important issues that will determine the rate and pattern of state executions in the coming years: What will the aggregate rate of executions be? Will the media and private citizens discover a large number of questionable executions? Will there be extensive investigation about questionable law enforcement and capital trials? Will public levels of discomfort about executions increase or decrease? Will officials in some state governments begin to worry about efforts to speed up executions? All of these variables will depend in large part on the distribution of state executions in the coming years. The more evenly the executions of the future are spread over the thirty-eight death penalty states, the greater the level of controversy and scandal that will result. My label for this phenomenon is "The Dilemma of Diversification," and it is already evident in the location of scandals and moratorium efforts in recent years.

THE DILEMMA OF DIVERSIFICATION

A relatively stable feature of the first twenty-five years of executions in the United States was a significant variation in the risk of execution for individuals on death row depending on their state and region. Chapter 4 provides the basic data: Slightly more than half of all condemned prisoners are from the South, but four out of five executions happen there. At the regional level, Southern defendants are 3.4 times as likely to be executed during this period as non-Southern defendants. At the extremes in state policy, the range in execution risk given a death sentence varies by about 50 to 1 when Northern industrial states such as Ohio, Pennsylvania, and California are compared with the highest-risk Southern jurisdictions such as Virginia, Texas, and Oklahoma.

These huge variations are obvious symptoms of troublesome differences in standards of justice. But any leveling of the huge state-to-state differences in execution risk that would generate higher execution rates in Northern industrial states would also increase both the scrutiny that execution cases receive from the bar and the media, and the likelihood of politically significant death row scandal. It was no accident that Illinois, the Northern state with the highest number of executions in the 1990s, became the state with the largest political conflict about the wrongful conviction of capital defendants. The epidemic of innocence cases in Illinois was a concentration of *discovered* cases. The much smaller impact in Oklahoma of the Joyce Gilchrist scandal (see Chapter 7) is an obvious example of a higher tolerance for misconduct without crisis in high-execution Southern jurisdictions. And it turns out that Florida has actually generated more death row exonerations than Illinois.

The theoretical explanation for why executions create more scrutiny in places where there is greater ambivalence about the death penalty is not rocket science. The more concerned that parts of the population are about the propriety of executions, the greater the chance that problematic actions in the death penalty system will be transformed into visible scandals. It is much more likely that a journalism class in a private university will get concerned about death cases when the political environment is one of manifest ambivalence about executions.

The implication of these patterns is clear: The higher the level of execution in non-Southern states, the larger the political risk to the executing jurisdictions. So a continuation of the extreme concentration of execution risk in a very few states seems objectionable, but any real diversification of executions will increase the vulnerability of death penalty systems to outside scrutiny. So the practical choice for death penalty systems is between gross unevenness in execution risks or increased exposure to scandal and the pressure for reform. In this sense, those Northern states where authorities have slowed down the flow of cases to reduce execution pressure have been protecting their courts from negative publicity. In these states, the true impact of any "effective death penalty" acceleration of executions might be to increase resistance to the functioning of the death penalty system. But, as Chapter 7 showed, keeping the flow of executions slow in large Northern states will also render these systems more vulnerable to the exoneration process because a larger number of innocent defendants will live long enough to be discovered. It is much easier to establish the innocence of a condemned defendant who is still alive.

DNA AND THE ALREADY EXECUTED

One other dimension of execution policy that will have impact on the death penalty debate will be the experience of those jurisdictions that experiment with moratoria on executions or other broad restrictions on death sentences or executions. The political consequences for those states that pursue restraint will be carefully monitored by other politicians in state government. If the moratorium process does not generate widespread discontent where invoked, its political appeal will increase substantially. The Illinois Governor's Commission Report in 2002 is a trial balloon for protracted interruptions in execution if commutations come with the prospective reforms (Illinois Governor's Commission on Capital Punishment 2002). One early reaction to Illinois was the suspension of executions in Maryland.

The continuing politics of capital case innocence will be closely connected to moratorium debates. The claimed death row exoneration total passed 100 in 2002, and the search for evidence of innocence in cases of executed defendants has already resulted in three court cases seeking biological material from state evidence that can be tested using new DNA procedures (see Farrell 2001; Liebman et al. 2002, note 77). As mentioned in Chapter 7, the identification of a DNA-innocent executed defendant would put a human face on the issue of wrongful execution and provide a poster child for moratorium campaigning across the nation, so the states are resisting providing samples in postexecution cases. But as large numbers of states pass DNA access legislation for living defendants, the objection to testing when the defendant has been executed will seem bereft of moral principle. The bumper crop of innocent defendants discovered in Florida (the nation's highest, at twenty-one) included one condemned prisoner who had already died on death row of natural causes. If the scientific credentials of DNA testing remain high, it is unlikely that the states can continue successfully resisting efforts at DNA testing. And deliberately destroying biological evidence will risk public scorn as DNA testing becomes a standard element in the justice system. So the pressure to test biological samples with improving DNA methods should be quite difficult to deflect.

The Presidency and Congress

While most of the operational elements of death penalty policy are clustered in the state level of government in the United States, each of the branches of the national government is of critical significance and influence in the broader conflict over capital punishment. The more salient the question of the death penalty becomes in the nation, the larger will be the influence of leadership in the federal executive and legislative branches to its resolution. The influence of any American president on the death penalty question is enormous. The president proposes both new Supreme Court justices and the federal Attorney General. Most of the time, the president sets the tone and to some extent selects the topics of national dialogue.

Beyond the direct influence a president has on the composition of the Department of Justice and the Supreme Court, there is an indirect impact on two levels of death penalty discourse. First, a president helps classify the death penalty issue—is it a moral or political question, a national or state concern, a question of limits of government or of policy toward criminals. Second, the opinions of an elected president are one powerful influence on which views are considered politically possible at the state level and in Congress. A president willing to take political risks on the death penalty, or to appoint persons with skeptical views, would be a major shift in an American scene that now assumes there is a large political cost to expressing doubts about the death penalty. That theory has not been tested in national politics for a long time.

The influence of the federal Congress is less concentrated but still powerful. A senate majority shares power with the president on judicial nominations—a potentially important counter to the strategy of Republican presidents to push Supreme Court nominations beyond the moderate right. Senate and House committees are important avenues for fact finding and consciousness raising.

In all of these potentially important roles, it is hard to say whether breaks with tradition by presidential or congressional leadership will function as what economists would call a "leading indicator" or as a "lagging indicator" on the death penalty. A leading indicator interpretation imagines that a brave presidential initiative begins to turn the tide in public perceptions— that the shift at the top of the political food chain might be the effective start of the change process. But the lagging indicator interpretation would argue that the reason a bold statement by a president or an attorney general would be significant in predicting further political change is because the political landscape on the issue would have already changed to allow such a presidential initiative to appear as anything but foolhardy.

To the extent that sectional politics would make direct presidential action on capital punishment politically costly, indirect gestures ranging from judicial appointments to blue ribbon commissions to a focus on procedures and discrimination are likely from a national president without a strong sectional identity. In Congress, however, the potential for more direct advocacy is the other side of the coin of sectional divisions. Here the sectional divide on the death penalty can help produce abolition advocacy. Senators from Minnesota, Wisconsin, Michigan, Maine, and Massachusetts have more freedom of action because of state policy. Even Republican congressional representatives from such states might become potential leaders on death penalty issues. High-conflict states such as Illinois, Ohio, and Pennsylvania might provide congressional leadership from left-of-center representatives, particularly if brave state governors in such settings are not punished politically.

In the Western European pattern, the timing of when left- versus right-leaning parties assumed control of national government was a key to the order in which the nations moved to formal abolition after World War II. But abolition was a function of parliamentary majority action in those cases, so that the impact of election was unmediated and relatively immediate. The influence of the president and of an independently determined congressional majority on the timing of abolition in the United States will likely be much less direct, particularly if judicial action is the primary means of halting executions. If acts of Congress are an important aspect of abolition, then presidential leadership would become much more important, and the attitudes and actions of a president would have a more direct impact on whether and when legislation becomes federal law.

The Multiple Objectives of an Abolition Campaign

Three changes will be necessary to create a climate of opinion that will allow if not facilitate the governmental actions that will end capital punishment in the United States. The particular sequence of governmental acts that will end the death penalty is not known, of course, but that is not a serious handicap to a discussion of shaping the debate about capital punishment, because the significant tasks for creating a desirable climate of opinion for abolition are the same whether the level of government is state or federal and whether the branch of government is judicial, legislative, or executive. The elements in any anti–death penalty campaign that support one type of governmental action to restrain executions will help the prospects of all others as well.

The usual way of analyzing public support for the death penalty in the United States is to focus on the percentage of the population that reports supporting the death penalty for murder in public opinion polls. Yet, in other nations, a public support level in the low or middle 60 percent range is not an important barrier to abolition of the death penalty; nor is that level of support an important predictor of execution policy in regions of the United States. Whatever separates the Northeastern states, where executions are quite rare, from the South, where they are quite common, it is not the proportion of citizens in public opinion polls who favor the death penalty for murder. Public support for the death penalty was greater in countries such as Canada, Great Britain, and Germany when the penalty was abolished (and for some years thereafter) than the current 63 percent support in the United States, yet this neither prevented effective abolition of the death penalty nor produced any political backlash or reversal of policy (Zimring and Hawkins 1986, chap. 1). As Chapter 1 also showed, the current level of death penalty support is no higher in the South than in the East and the Midwest, yet the South's rate of execution is more than 100 times that of the Northeast. The link between general levels of death penalty support and death penalty policy is quite tenuous.

This pattern does not mean that public attitudes in the United States are unimportant in explaining the exceptional course of United States policy, but it does mean that the intensities of public feeling, both in support and in opposition to the death penalty, must be more important than just counting hands. Also important is the social reputation of executions in states and regions and the traditions in particular localities. A majority in opposition to capital punishment is neither a sufficient nor a necessary condition to the abolition of the death penalty in the United States.

But there are suggestions in the value conflict character of the death penalty dispute in the United States of several specific strategic objectives that abolitionists should pursue in creating a societal foundation for governmental abolition of the death penalty in the near future. The three strategic objectives of principal importance are: to make the death penalty a major issue in every important part of American public life, to undermine the moral confidence and sense of justice of death penalty supporters, and to create a broad and morally committed community of activist opponents of the death penalty. All three of these objectives tend to weaken the social reputation of capital punishment. If they can be simultaneously pursued, they will produce widespread expectations that policy will soon change. Such expectations can quickly become a self-fulfilling prophecy.

Generating Discourse

One remarkable characteristic of the postwar decades that witnessed the end of the death penalty in Western Europe was the absence of extensive public debate about the death penalty in those nations that were on the threshold of permanently retiring the hangman. Chapter 2 referred to this thirty years in Europe as a period of "change without discourse." At one level, this phenomenon could be explained by the extensive debates that had already taken place in Europe earlier. The Western half of the continent was to some extent talked out by the time that postwar politics permitted the political transition to abolition. But what this explanation also tells us is that the low-visibility efforts that preceded the end of the death penalty probably made tactical sense for those who were pursuing abolition in places such as Britain, France, Canada, and Australia. Gradual abolition was the path of least resistance in Great Britain in the 1950s and 1960s, in France after 1965, and in many other places.

The findings of this study and the "fundamental conflict" characterization of capital punishment in the United States suggest that the quiet abolition of capital punishment is not the path of least resistance in the United States. The essence of the fundamental conflict label is that there is no low-friction path of least resistance in the United States on the death penalty. All roads lead to attention, anger, and dissatisfaction. But the momentum of state executions in the South and West suggests that if death penalty policy is left to the states with little public scrutiny, executions will continue.

Under these circumstances, the more important the death penalty becomes as a public issue in the United States, the better the prospects for motivating policy changes in the direction of abolition. To the extent that this theory is plausible, it counsels a strategy of discourse and protest that is the opposite of the gentle politics of abolition in postwar Western Europe. The tone and activism of present-day European efforts would be better suited to consciousness raising on an American stage than the quiet politics of European abolition after the war.

One irony of the potential role of high public attention as a change agent for the death penalty is that even events that do not have any obvious anti–death penalty spin may function to facilitate potential opposition. Even the Timothy McVeigh execution in 2001 may have been an event where the death penalty had very heavy public support but where the execution did not produce any clear increase in support for capital punishment generally. Over the longer term, if such a high-salience event keeps people concerned about capital punishment, it might weaken support. In this sense, the potential contribution of a wide variety of attention-getting events to public reconsideration of capital punishment recalls the old Hollywood press agent adage that "there is no such thing as bad publicity." There surely are a few themes and media portrayals of the death penalty that would hurt the cause of abolition, but for the most part, greater public attention to capital punishment is good news for abolitionists.

In the United States, the entire spectrum of cultural life and communication can contribute to keeping the question of capital punishment high on the public agenda. News media, blue ribbon committees, public intellectuals, and investigative reporters are important at the top end of the intellectual commons. But movies and the soap-opera television journalism that is closely linked to popular culture are also important in keeping public involvement high. A Geraldo Rivera special report on lethal injections may have substantive and esthetic shortcomings, but it can keep the pot boiling. And just as Susan Hayward's *I Want to Live!* shaped public reaction in the 1960s, the current generation of death penalty films is an important influence on popular understanding of the death penalty (Sarat 2001, chap. 8).

If the objective of a communication campaign is to keep the issue of capital punishment a high visibility public controversy, a broad variety of ways to raise the issue should be encouraged. There is no zero-sum competition among different perspectives on capital punishment, no single "right" approach or theme. Instead, a wide variety of perspectives can contribute to a high level of general interest.

While several core issues are significant to all audiences—the chance of error, the politics of execution as government action, the human rights movement, DNA exonerations, and so on—there are also a wide variety of special perspectives for special audiences. Just as the Pennsylvania case of Mumia Abu-Jamal has special salience to left-of-center African-American organizations, there are as well issues and cases that will resonate with other special constituencies. The American death penalty should become an important branch of feminist studies and critical legal studies, as well as a special interest of families of developmentally delayed adults. The study of the death penalty should attract members of mainstream religious and ethical traditions, and implicated professions such as lawyers and physicians. Once different types of constituency groups start clustering in opposition to some aspects of death penalty policy, the momentum of mainstream groups joining up can increase. This kind of momentum will require that the identified opposition broadens from the reliable but politically marginalized interests that now dominate over execution vigils. An execution without Quaker protest would be unthinkable; an execution vigil where the majority in attendance are Quakers is a sad commentary on American mainstream values. Protests of executions should round up more than the usual suspects.

Weakening the Intensity of Death Penalty Support

If it is the depth rather than the breadth of support for capital punishment that distinguishes the U.S. pattern from other nations that have decisively rejected the death penalty, then one significant task in providing a foundation for abolition is to weaken the intensity of death penalty support among the large groups and opinion leaders where that support is concentrated. The goal of this sort of campaign is not so much to reduce the announced support for a death penalty—the statistical yield for that would be greatest with undecided or current weakly committed voters. The goal, instead, is to soften up the hard-core support for capital punishment, to create doubters instead of converts. The ultimate objective of such softening is to render many supporters of capital punishment more willing to lose gracefully when executions end.

The targets for special efforts of this kind must exclude a fair number of Americans who support the death penalty and are rock-solid in support, that is, the most extreme 20 to 25 percent of the population in death penalty support. Most of them are not susceptible to changing their views until well after changes in policy. It is the next 30 percent of the population that will be critical in the near future: opinion leaders of the right and center who distrust government power but wish to stay very tough on crime, Republican women who are less disposed by gender to believe in execution but tied to pro–death penalty views by family and political loyalties, evangelical Christians of both genders attached to the views of their leadership, and non–right-wing males of the working and middle class who are drawn to the death penalty by the culture of American toughness but not by political party. In those recent polls where gradations of support are tested, almost all of this 30 percent report supporting the death penalty "very strongly" (see National Election Survey 1996, reported in Appendix D).

For all of these groups, appeals based on distrust of government and on government power as a core concern in capital punishment will be important, as will the exonerations of prisoners from death row as a concrete indication of governmental fallibility. For the cosmopolitan right, the critique by foreign observers and the disdain expressed toward the execution process can be an important influence. The fraudulent nature of death penalties as administered will also be of potential importance to right-leaning intellectuals. For the noncosmopolitan right, sowing the seeds of moral doubt will be of critical importance.

Respect for authority is one critical dynamic that makes the non-libertarian political right favor existing death penalties all over the world. But that kind of tie was not strong enough to sustain continuing controversy after abolition or to provoke reversal of policy after left governments had dropped the death penalty when the right returned to power. The very quality of "my government right or wrong" that generates conservative support for existing death penalties also allows for the grudging acceptance when governments choose to limit their punishment powers. Softening up the substantive commitment to capital punishment in the United States to the level found in England and Germany just prior to abolition would be a major achievement for the abolitionist cause. Saying "yes" to a phone interviewer on the question of support for capital punishment (over 65 percent in Germany and Great Britain when the penalty was ended) is not the same as caring deeply. Moving supporters of the penalty that far would permit the end of executions in the United States even if the penalty received majority support. There would still be states' rights opposition, of course, but there is no strong evidence that this principle is important by itself to broad segments of the capital punishment-supporting public. The salience of vigilante values is more difficult to understand. And there will be deeply committed death penalty partisans with angry resistance to the end of execution, in greater numbers in the United States than in Europe, in greater numbers in Texas than in Illinois.

There is some evidence that softening of commitment among death penalty supporters may have started to develop in the late 1990s, at least compared with the intensity and anger of 1994 (Ellsworth and Gross 1994, 2002). But intensity of support is not an easy phenomenon to measure in survey research. Further, there has not been a significant effort yet to focus on this aspect of public opinion. More measurement is needed.

THE STIGMA OF CAPITAL PUNISHMENT

The tactic of stigmatizing the execution process is important enough to merit its own heading. Doubts on the propriety of execution involve much more than theology and political theory. Even in an age of lethal injection,

the process of administering death as a punishment is vulnerable to association with the primitive, the brutal, and the undesirable. Social processes
can promote a stigma associated with the execution itself and with that a
view that the demand for execution is primitive and unprincipled.

There is also a potential for negative stereotyping of death penalty supporters by associating them with the execution process. Many who are sympathetic to abstract notions of serious punishment or homilies about victim
closure are put off by the primitive essence of the killing process. The
stigma of execution is one significant method of softening up significant
segments of death penalty support. A portrait of the death penalty supporter as a bloodthirsty version of Archie Bunker need not have a religious
component to carry a social message. Many supporters of capital punishment would not think highly of a person who would want to attend an
execution. There is of course also some risk of creating a culture war backlash by attacking the practice of execution as primitive.

Of further importance in a campaign of doubt is a relentless effort to
demythologize claims about the value of the death penalty in the United
States. How, exactly, does witnessing a lethal injection facilitate the psychological improvement of a victim's family? Would it be good for children too?

Elements of death penalty discourse that sow doubts in the moral self-
confidence of death penalty supporters can be of substantial importance in
creating an atmosphere where government officials can overcome their
fear of decisive action. Any sense that the end of capital punishment is
inevitable, any moral defensiveness among those who support the penalty,
creates political possibilities independent of the nominal support for a death
penalty in opinion polls.

Much of the political reputation of capital punishment in the United
States is based on a perception of unshakable public support. As soon as
that sort of bedrock commitment to a death penalty can no longer be assumed, the process of change in the politics of the death penalty will already be well under way.

Preaching to the Converted

Strengthening the intensity of commitment among those who oppose capital
punishment is as important as weakening the intensity of death penalty
supporters, and for many of the same reasons. The death penalty should
very soon become a much more important issue for many of those who
oppose it in the United States, a moral stand equal in importance to other
morally charged political issues of great moment. College and university
campuses, international human rights groups, liberal churches, prolife the-
ologies, minority and disadvantaged population interest groups, and left-

leaning political organizations should have levels of commitment and activity two or three times those found currently.

Execution in the United States is not protested by mass demonstrations even though the spoken prevalence of opposition to state execution is substantial on campuses and among many of the other groups usually associated with mass demonstrations and political protest. It is the intensity of commitment on capital punishment that has been lacking. There is irony in the fact that it is easier to organize a mass protest against a U.S. execution in Italy, Mexico, or France than in California or Pennsylvania. One would think that executions would provoke more student emotion in Texas or California, where the practice is carried out, than in Rome or Paris, but the opposite pattern has held since the mid-1990s. The lack of death penalty concern in centers of political activism in the United States is a political puzzle as well as a major defect in the abolitionist campaign.

In part, the low intensity of anti–death penalty activity on campuses and in left-oriented politics might be a product of the assumption that opposition will not change governmental behavior, particularly at the state level that generates execution policy. Yet the spectacular impact of a college-level journalism class in Illinois is a world-class counterexample to the presumed ineffectuality of student effort (Armstrong and Mills 1999).

A second significant deterrent to large-scale student involvement may be the large geographic divide between where liberal students go to college and where executions are clustered. Yet even when executions are scheduled at California's San Quentin prison, across the San Francisco Bay from San Francisco State University and the University of California at Berkeley, and an easy drive from several other colleges, capital punishment does not become a political event on college campuses. With both domestic and foreign recruiting efforts focused on college campuses, this should change quickly and to great effect. Campus activists on issues such as ecology and pollution tend toward a distrust of both the capacity and the will of those in government to do right and a healthy distrust of state-level electoral politics. The fact that execution is confined elsewhere in the modern world to violent and brutal regimes should be an easy sell on campus once potential activists start to care about the death penalty in America.

The power of committed activists to influence the capital punishment debate is not a question of either their numerical strength or their capacity to exert direct political influence. It is instead a question of the power of young activists without any pecuniary interest in the question of capital punishment to raise moral questions that make their elders uncomfortable with the absence of persuasive moral counterarguments. A visible and persistent activist presence within the community can serve as a stimulus to the moral uncertainties that destabilize the mainstream support for the death penalty. The key role of large-scale protest demonstrations is as a moral wake-up call to segments of the public who are quite comfortable not thinking about the death penalty. The inclusion in the activist community of

many moral and religious leaders who are from the mainstream denomina-
tions, as well as professional and intellectual leaders who are not found on
every other picket line, can be a significant attention-getting mechanism
in the broader community.

The second major contribution of morally committed activists would be
to reframe the issue of executions from one of criminal justice policy to a
matter of fundamental limits on state power. Any activism that is political
or rights-based comes from outside the ordinary scope of criminal justice
concerns. Human rights activists are not people principally concerned with
the punishment of criminals. Their prominent presence in the capital punishment debate would be a powerful push toward changing the subject of
that debate—reframing the issues that other citizens must confront when
taking a position on the death penalty. That kind of reframing of the issue
happened after abolition in Western Europe and has been a moving part of
the machinery of ending the death penalty only in Central Europe, Eastern
Europe, and South Africa. This perspective does not enter the debate from
the speeches of criminology professors, trial lawyers, or political analysts.
Rather, it makes a permanent impression on mainstream audiences as a result of the credible moral commitments of activists in the public discourse. A
forceful and sincere activist presence is thus an indispensable building block
in an American abolitionist campaign, a vehicle to transcend the traditional
categories and traditional limits that have been imposed in the question of
capital punishment in American thinking. For these purposes, it is the elo-
quence and intensity of the activists rather than their numbers that will determine results. Ethical credibility is leadership on the moral front: Jimmy
Carter, Nelson Mandela, Reuben "Hurricane" Carter, Ethel Kennedy, and
Coretta Scott King would be exemplary icons of moral leadership for such
a task, a wonderfully American public relations mix of two former Presidents, two criminal defendants, and two victim relatives.

Filling in the Blanks

The last section mentioned the ends of an abolition campaign; here I want
to sketch some means to those ends. When the priority targets for development mentioned in the previous section are measured against the current pattern of effort in the campaign against capital punishment in the
United States, there are a series of gaps in the current efforts that are worth
emphasizing.

One gap does not appear in current events. With respect to expansion of
public dialogue on the death penalty, there is no apparent need to invest in
raising the profile of capital punishment as a public issue in the United
States. Public attention is the one resource that is available in almost limit-
less quantity. Getting attention to particular problems, including practices

and effects in high execution states and the impact of procedural default rules on death penalty justice, will require supplementary public information campaigns, but there is no large gap in levels of general public interest between current circumstances and the conditions required for change.

At the high end of the intellectual food chain, however, there is a shortage of new ideas, spirited debate, and broad engagement in questions of capital punishment by professionals (other than lawyers), public intellectuals, civic interest groups, and mainstream religious organizations. The extensive involvement of lawyers and litigation in modern capital punishment seems to have been to the exclusion of other perspectives or interests. A modest investment in fostering high-level discussion and debate, perhaps with an intellectual foreign aid program from Western Europe and the Commonwealth, seems well worth its modest costs. The recruitment of women voters, artists and writers, professional organizations, and government watchdog groups to address questions generated by the death penalty will increase discussion and generate further controversy and inquiry. The larger the number of groups concerned with the death penalty, the more likely that the number of concerned groups will continue to grow.

Softening Support

The previous section argued that one important group to involve in thinking about the death penalty in America is the moderate supporters of a death penalty for murder, not the most extreme adherents of the death penalty but the next 30 percent or so of the population that stands in support of a death penalty but may be uneasy about executions. But who are these people, and how can they be approached? Particular targets might include the libertarian right and Catholic intellectuals with right-of-center political orientations. Protestant women with mixed feelings about the death penalty are a large and important group, as are African American and Hispanic conservatives, Catholic men and women, and the student groups and church youth groups in high-execution areas. The tactic is to make the death penalty a continuing concern, focusing on media and on special interest groups with high concentrations of target populations. Again, success here will be measured by the prevalence of doubt about the moral and instrumental virtues of execution.

Intensifying Opposition

The most obvious need in matching an abolitionist campaign to the needs of a moral crusade is to motivate an activist population to bear witness against the immorality and the political danger of state executions. Sub-stantial resources should be committed to finding and motivating activist campaigners on America's campuses and among activist groups on other issues and putting them to work in protest and social organizations. Out-side the legal community, capital punishment now is not high on the agenda of reform or protest issues among the young, among political activists, or among the broad community of organizations and individuals devoted to civil rights and the special concerns of minority populations. Yet the more the death penalty is recast as a limits-of-government issue, the more it becomes an issue both too broad and too important to be left exclusively to lawyers.

Tactics for the Long Run

While there is appeal in talking about an abolitionist *campaign* and focus-ing on explicit strategies of argument in the death penalty debate, there is also a substantial difference that must be recognized between campaigning for an election and creating a climate of opinion that supports government activity on an issue such as the death penalty. The abolitionist effort is long-term and not targeted at a single yes or no vote. Unlike an election, intensity of individual preferences counts for a great deal. Even more im-portant, a climate of opinion may be far less amenable to manipulation by advertisement and other media-driven efforts than an election.

The Limits of Rhetorical Influence

The strategic importance of an abolitionist campaign to the long-range future of the death penalty in America is easy to overstate. I suspect that special efforts to influence citizen attitudes about the death penalty can have some effect both on when state executions stop and on the level of resistance and hostility that abolition will provoke in the United States. In the long run, however, the larger continuing conflict that executions pro-duce and the incongruity of execution as a tool of government in an ad-vanced democracy will require the end of the death penalty. Sooner or later, both the executioner and the vigilante tradition will leave the Ameri-can scene, no matter the size of the media budget or the tactics of persua-sion used on either side of the debate.

Indeed, one reason the act of execution makes such a compelling case for public attention in the twenty-first century is its incongruity with so much of the rest of our civilization. State-run universal education and social insurance do not fit well with lethal injection. There is a sense of dissonance generated by the act of state killing in 2003 that is understood, at some level, even by many of those who support the death penalty. And that understanding of the incongruity of contemporary execution is embedded beyond the reach of public relations campaigns. Sooner or later, and most probably sooner, the death penalty will end as a function of the larger destiny of American society and government. In the context of that larger destiny, the return to executions in the last years of the twentieth century was more of a protest against the long-term shifts in government and society taking place in the United States than a successful attempt to change the nation's fate. So the eventual destiny of American capital punishment is not hostage to next year's elections or the effectiveness of a media campaign.

Conflict after Abolition

To the extent that the special circumstances of American capital punishment stem from a deeper conflict between widely held cultural values, the end of the death penalty, whenever it happens, will leave a bitter aftertaste in the mouths of those in government and society. Conflict over the death penalty will continue as long as the vigilante mythology and the values that support it have a significant constituency in the United States. So the end of the death penalty at any point in our experience will probably be the beginning of the end of conflicting images of punishment in our culture.

In this important sense, the question of capital punishment after its abolition nevertheless will still be present in the domestic politics of the United States as it was not in the other developed nations that abolished it. The death penalty has disappeared as an issue of domestic politics in every nation in Western Europe. But serious efforts to reinstate the death penalty will continue in the United States until our nostalgia for the popular democracy of the lynch mob has died down.

It may even be that the more quickly we end executions, the longer will be the postexecution conflict, because the expectation that executions can continue has been generated over the past two decades and will intensify opposition to any reversal of policy. Whereas postponing the end of executions now and allowing the debate and protest to grow more contentious might make the trauma after abolition less severe because the affection for vigilante values will have already been undermined as part of the primary processes that produce the end of execution. So a short and easy end to executions might have a longer and somewhat more contentious aftermath than would be the case if abolition itself requires a long and angry confrontation. On the other hand, the sooner that executions stop in the United States, the sooner the moral shifts that came only after abolition in Europe can start their ascent in America. On balance, sooner is better than later.

Could all of this angry conflict have been avoided if the Supreme Court had stayed its previous course in the mid-1970s? The immediate impact of the end of the death penalty would not have been great if it had come in 1976 because of the ten-year moratorium that was then in effect. The United States had broken its habit of executions; no withdrawal pains, no shift in expectations would have been necessary. But the resentment of federal power and the appetite for reintroduction of a death penalty would have been an important force in many parts of the United States for a long time.

Whether constitutional amendments or selected-to-reinstate-death-penalty Supreme Court appointments in the Reagan-Bush years would have actually taken place is unknowable. The anti–capital punishment ethos did not have the political constituency among feminists that (barely) saved *Roe v. Wade* in the early 1990s. But the high degree of ambivalence in the Northeast and North-Central states and the lack of any momentum of actual execution behavior might have stopped a restoration attempt short of legal success. In any case, the aftertaste of abolition in the 1970s would still have been a long-term phenomenon. Conflict and uncertainty would have continued. If a different judgment in *Gregg v. Georgia* in 1976 had closed out the American history of execution, the United States would have become a better country, but not a peaceful one on the question of capital punishment.

The true extent of the power of vigilante nostalgia to maintain resentment and provide resistance can be tested only by observing the persistence and intensity of resistance to the end of the death penalty when it happens. If we are lucky, the twenty-first century version of vigilante nostalgia will turn out to be a paper tiger, of lower intensity and shorter duration than there was reason to fear. Standing on its own merits, the death penalty would then pass from the American social and political landscape almost as quickly as it disappeared from Europe.

If, however, the deeper conflict takes a longer time to resolve, then the further unpleasantness that must be endured will be well worth its social cost. The vigilante image of state execution is a sinister illusion. It tempts citizens to remove legal barriers to the destruction of individuals by state machinery without ever admitting that it is the state as a political entity that is being invited to use this ultimate force. In the hard light of twentieth century history, the vigilante image of execution, by imagining that state and community are indivisibly unified in interests, has an oddly totalitarian flavor.

So the battle to end the era of killing as criminal punishment in the United States may be easy or difficult, but in either event it seems well worth the efforts to bring it to a close. If it proves easy, abolition will end a practice that is barbaric and inconsistent with high principles of legality and clear limits on government use of individuals. The end of executions would thus reinforce some of the defining virtues of due process in democracy. If the remaining vigor of a vigilante tradition makes the struggle longer and harder, then ending the death penalty in the United States will have required the defeat of a malignant mythology that now casts a wider shadow on law and culture. The benefits of abolition in the United States will climb in direct proportion to its costs.

How long will it take to exorcise both execution as a practice and the values that tempt us to it? The moment when conflicts that have been the subject of the last two chapters culminate in abolition, and the future date when this change is accepted, cannot be predicted now. But it does seem clear from review of the anger and contradiction of the 1990s that a process of social engagement with capital punishment that is without precedent in American history has already begun. The end game in the effort to purge the United States of the death penalty has already been launched. The length and the intensity of the struggle necessary to end the death penalty are not yet known, but the ultimate outcome seems inevitable in any but the most pessimistic view of the American future.

Appendix A

Statistical Materials on Lynchings and Executions

This appendix reports on the origins and relationship between the two long-term lynching reporting systems used in Chapter 5, as well as the statistical analysis of state-level data from one of these samples.

The Lynching Samples

The Tuskegee Archives track all lynchings by state and race between 1882 and 1968. Their data come entirely from newspaper accounts. The definition used to categorize an act as a lynching was taken from the Van Nuys Anti-Lynching Bill, which stipulates that the victim had to be accused of a crime by three or more persons, was denied due process, and was killed as a result. The NAACP records track lynchings occurring between 1889 and 1918. Their sources include press accounts, reports from their own investigations, Tuskegee Institute records, and *Chicago Tribune* records. The main difference between the two samples is that the NAACP record includes some murders that occurred in the context of a riot, while the Tuskegee Archives leaves out riot deaths.

The rank order correlation (Table A.1) took each sample individually and assigned a ranking to each state according to the absolute number of lynchings for the time period under study: 1882 through 1968 versus 1889 through 1918. The state with the highest number of lynchings was assigned the number one, the second highest was assigned the number two, and so forth all the way down to the forty-fourth state. Each state ended up with two assigned rankings, one from each sample, based on where it fell in terms of total lynchings compared with other

Table A.1.
Lynchings by State, Rank Order Correlation

State	1882-1968 Ranking	1889-1918 Ranking
Alabama	5	5
Arizona	25	30
Arkansas	6	6
California	21	17
Colorado	16	22
Delaware	42	40
Florida	7	8
Georgia	2	1
Idaho	31	29
Illinois	24	18
Indiana	20	21
Iowa	32	30
Kansas	18	19
Kentucky	9	9
Louisiana	4	4
Maine	42	40
Maryland	26	23
Michigan	35	32
Minnesota	34	32
Mississippi	1	2
Missouri	11	12
Montana	15	19
Nebraska	17	23
Nevada	38	32
New Jersey	40	40
New Mexico	22	26
New York	40	38
North Carolina	13	14
North Dakota	33	39
Ohio	28	28
Oklahoma	11	11
Oregon	30	32
Pennsylvania	35	32
South Carolina	10	10
South Dakota	27	26
Tennessee	8	7
Texas	3	3
Utah	35	43
Vermont	42	43
Virginia	14	13
Washington	28	25
West Virginia	19	16
Wisconsin	38	32
Wyoming	23	15

Source: Tuskegee Library Archives (1882–1968); National Association for the Advancement of Colored People 1919.

states in the sample. The two rankings for all forty-four states were then correlated resulting in an *r*-value of 0.9631. This signifies a very high degree of similarity in individual state rankings between the Tuskegee sample and the NAACP sample.

State-Level Lynching and Capital Punishment

The analysis of regional patterns of lynching and executions did not require any significance tests or formal statistical analysis, because the comparisons across regions were straightforward and the magnitude of the differences noted was quite high.

The data from individual states divide the same data into forty-eight instead of four categories. The first difference here is that a larger number of units are available for analysis, a statistical advantage. The second difference is that a smaller number of events per unit stand behind the state totals compared with regions. A few straightforward tests of association and significance were employed on these data.

Tables A.2 and A.3 reproduce two comparisons between the extreme lynching states (the top 14 and bottom 14) on the presence of a death penalty statute in 2001 (Table A.2) and executions during the period 1977–2000 (Table A.3). The two tables are not discrete measures of policy because a jurisdiction without a death penalty will not have any executions.

Table A.4 tests the execution variable using only states with death penalties in 2001, thereby shrinking the low-lynching total to seven jurisdictions. With only seven jurisdictions in the low extreme category, the chi-square value slips to 9.88 but is still significant at .01.

Table A.2.
Current Status of Death Penalty in High- and Low-Lynching History States

	Yes	*No*
Low-lynching	7	7
High-lynching	14	—

Note: Chi-square 9.33, significant at < .01.

Table A.3.
Executions in 1977-2000 in High- and Low-Lynching History States

	Yes	*No*
Low-lynching	3	11
High-lynching	14	—

Note: Chi-square 18.12, significant at < .0001.

Table A.4.

Executions in 1977–2000 in High- and Low-Lynching Death Penalty States.

	Yes	No
Low-lynching	3	4
High-lynching	14	—

Note: Chi-square 9.88, significant at < .01.

Eliminating the Potential "Southern Bias"

A second set of comparisons was designed to test the atypicality of low-lynching states when compared not merely with the high-lynching states but with all other American states that were in the original forty-eight-state lynching survey. The point of this was to test for an effect of lynching history that did not overlap with the all-South high-lynching history category. Tables A.5 and A.6 thus compare the low extreme states with the rest of the states in the Union. Deleting the South from these tables entirely (an unjustified move) would still leave a significant difference.

Correlations across All States

When middle-value states are mixed into correlations, the predictive value of lynching history drops. The correlation between the rank order of a state in lynching history and its modern executions is .45 (significant at < .01). The zero order correlation between rate of lynching historically and recent execution rate is .30 (significant at < .05). Both of these exercises use a state's 1900 census population to derive population rates, which introduces serious rate measurement error, particularly in the fast-growing West.

Table A.5.

Death Penalty Status in 2001 by Lynching History

	Yes	No
Low-lynching	7	7
Rest of United States	31	3

Note: Chi-square 10.19, $p < .01$.

Table A.6.

Execution Status 1977–2000 by Lynching History

	Yes	No
Low-lynching	3	11
Rest of United States	26	8

Note: Chi-square 12.56, significant at .001.

Population Estimates for Lynchings

The peak periods for lynching in the United States were also periods of high population growth. We estimated lynching and execution rates with one middle-of-the-period census for population. We also constructed two different estimates of rates of lynching at the regional level, one using the previous census as the population base for lynching estimates and one using the next census as the denominator for the previous decade's lynchings. Table A.7 shows the different estimates with these different methods.

Table A.7.

Lynching Rates per 100,000 Population.

	Lynchings 1889–1899		*Lynchings 1900–1909*		*Lynchings 1910–1918*	
	Rate Expressed over 1890 Population	Rate Expressed over 1900 Population	Rate Expressed over 1900 Population	Rate Expressed over 1910 Population	Rate Expressed over 1910 Population	Rate Expressed over 1920 Population
South	7.23	5.9	3.32	2.77	1.84	1.64
West	3.00	2.27	0.81	0.48	0.18	0.13

Sources: National Association for the Advancement of Colored People 1919; U.S. Census, 1920.

Appendix B

Reported Frequencies of National Death Penalty Policy, 1980 to 2001

Table B.1.

Reported Frequencies of National Death Penalty Policy, 1980–2001

Abolitionist for All Crimes

1980	1985	1990	1995	2001
Austria	Australia	Andorra (1943)	Andorra	Andorra
Cape Verde	Austria	Australia	Angola*	Angola
Colombia	Bolivia	Austria	Australia	Australia
Costa Rica	Cape Verde	Cambodia*	Austria	Austria
Denmark	Colombia	Cape Verde	Cambodia	Azerbaijan (1993)
Dominican Republic	Costa Rica	Colombia	Cape Verde	Belgium (1950)
Ecuador	Denmark	Costa Rica	Colombia	Bulgaria (1989)
Finland	Dominican Republic	Czech & Slovak Federative Republic*	Costa Rica	Cambodia
Federal Republic of Germany	Ecuador	Denmark	Croatia (1987)	Canada (1962)
Honduras	Finland	Dominican Republic	Czech Republic	Cape Verde
Iceland	Federal Republic of Germany	Ecuador	Denmark	Colombia
Luxembourg	France	Finland	Dominican Republic	Costa Rica
Nicaragua	Holy See	France	Ecuador	Cote D'Ivoire (1960)
Norway	Honduras	East Germany	Finland	Croatia
Panama	Iceland	West Germany*	France	Czech Republic
Portugal	Kiribati	Haiti (1972)	Germany	Denmark
Solomon Islands	Luxembourg	Honduras	Greece (1972)	Djibouti (1977) **
Sweden	Netherlands	Iceland	Guinea-Bissau	Dominican Republic
Uruguay	Nicaragua	Ireland (1954)	Haiti	East Timor (1999) **
Venezuela	Norway	Kiribati	Honduras	Ecuador

	Abolitionist for All Crimes			
1980	1985	1990	1995	2001
	Panama	Liechtenstein (1785)	Hong Kong*	Estonia (1991)
	Portugal	Luxembourg	Hungary (1988)	Finland
	Solomon Islands	Marshall Islands (1986)**	Iceland	France
	Sweden	Micronesia (1986)**	Ireland	Georgia (1994)
	Tuvalu	Monaco (1847)	Italy (1947)	Germany
	Uruguay	Namibia (1988)	Kiribati	Greece
	Vanuatu	Netherlands	Liechtenstein	Guinea-Bissau
	Venezuela	New Zealand (1957)	Luxembourg	Haiti
		Nicaragua	Macedonia*	Honduras
		Norway	Marshall Islands	Hungary
		Panama	Mauritius (1987)	Iceland
		Philippines (1976)	Micronesia	Ireland
		Portugal	Monaco	Italy
		Romania (1989)	Mozambique (1986)	Kiribati
		San Marino (1468)	Namibia	Liechtenstein
		Solomon Islands	Netherlands	Lithuania (1995)
		Sweden	New Zealand	Luxembourg
		Tuvalu	Nicaragua	Macedonia
		Uruguay	Norway	Malta (1943)
		Vanuatu	Palau (1994)**	Marshall Islands

Continued

Table B.1. (Continued)

Abolitionist for All Crimes

1980	1985	1990	1995	2001
		Vatican City State*	Panama	Mauritius
		Venezuela	Portugal	Micronesia
			Romania	Moldova (1989)
			San Marino	Monaco
			Sao Tome & Principe (1990)	Mozambique
			Slovak Republic	Namibia
			Slovenia (1957)	Nepal (1979)
			Soloman Islands	Netherlands
			Spain (1975)	New Zealand
			Sweden	Nicaragua
			Switzerland (1944)	Norway
			Tuvalu	Palau
			Uruguay	Panama
			Vanuatu	Paraguay (1928)
			Vatican City State	Poland (1988)
			Venezuela	Portugal
				Romania
				San Marino
				Sao Tome & Principe
				Seychelles (1976)**

Abolitionist for All Crimes

1980	1985	1990	1995	2001
				Slovak Republic
				Slovenia
				Solomon Islands
				South Africa (1991)
				Spain
				Sweden
				Switzerland
				Turkmenistan (1997)
				Tuvalu
				Ukraine (1997)
				United Kingdom (1964)
				Uruguay
				Vanuatu
				Vatican City State
				Venezuela
Total				
20	28	42	56	75

Continued

Table B.1. (Continued)

	Abolitionist for Ordinary Crimes Only			
1980	1985	1990	1995	2001
Brazil	Brazil	Argentina	Argentina	Albania (1995)
Canada	Canada	Brazil	Brazil	Argentina
Fiji	Cyprus	Canada	Canada	Bolivia (1974)
Guinea-Bissau	El Salvador	Cyprus	Cyprus	Bosnia-Herzegovina*
Israel	Fiji	El Salvador	El Salvador	Brazil
Italy	Israel	Fiji	Fiji	Chile (1985)
Malta	Italy	Israel	Israel	Cook Islands*
Mexico	Malta	Italy	Malta	Cyprus
Monaco	Mexico	Malta	Mexico	El Salvador
Nepal	Monaco	Mexico	Nepal	Fiji
Papua New Guinea	Nepal	Nepal	Paraguay (1928)	Israel
Netherlands	New Zealand	Papua New Guinea	Peru	Latvia (1996)
New Zealand	Papua New Guinea	Peru	Seychelles	Mexico
Spain	Peru	Sao Tome & Principe	South Africa (1991)	Peru
San Marino	San Marino	Seychelles	United Kingdom	
Switzerland	Spain	Spain		
United Kingdom	Switzerland	Switzerland		
	United Kingdom	United Kingdom		
Total				
17	18	18	15	14

1980	1985	1990	1995	2001
		Anguilla	Albania	Bhutan
		Bahrain	Bahrain	Brunei Darussalam
		Belgium	Belgium	Burkina Faso (1989)
		Bermuda	Bermuda	Central African Republic
		Bhutan	Bhutan	Congo
		Bolivia	Bolivia	Gambia
		British Virgin Islands	Brunei Darussalam	Grenada (1978)
		Brunei Darussalam	Burundi (1982)	Madagascar
		Cayman Islands	Central African Republic (1981)	Maldives
		Comoros	Congo (1982)	Mali
		Cote D'Ivoire	Comoros	Nauru
		Djibouti	Cote D'Ivoire	Niger
		Greece	Djibouti	Papua New Guinea
		Hong Kong	Gambia (1981)	Samoa
		Madagascar	Madagascar	Senegal
		Maldives	Maldives	Sri Lanka
		Montserrat	Mali (1980)	Suriname
		Nauru	Moldova (1989)	Togo
		Niger	Nauru	Tonga
		Paraguay	Niger	Turkey
		Samoa, Western	Papua New Guinea (1950)	

Continued

Table B.1. (*Continued*)

Abolitionist De Facto

1980	1985	1990	1995	2001
		Senegal	Philippines (1976)	
		Sri Lanka	Rwanda (1982)	
		Togo	Senegal	
		Turks &	Sri Lanka	
		Caicos Islands		
			Suriname (1982)	
			Togo	
			Tonga (1982)	
			Turkey (1984)	
			Western Samoa	
Total		25	30	20

Retentionist

1980	1985	1990	1995	2001
Afghanistan	Afghanistan	Afghanistan	Afghanistan	Afghanistan
Albania	Albania	Albania	Algeria	Algeria
Algeria	Algeria	Algeria	Antigua & Barbuda	Antigua & Barbuda
Angola	Angola	Angola	Armenia	Armenia
Antigua	Anguilla	Antigua & Barbuda	Azerbaijan	Bahamas
Argentina	Antigua & Barbuda	Bahamas	Bahamas	Bahrain
Australia	Argentina	Bangladesh	Bangladesh	Bangladesh
Bahamas	Bahamas	Barbados	Barbados	Barbados

Retentionist

1980	1985	1990	1995	2001
Bahrain	Bahrain	Belize	Belarus	Belarus
Bangladesh	Bangladesh	Benin	Belize	Belize
Barbados	Barbados	Botswana	Benin	Benin
Belgium	Belgium	Bulgaria	Bosnia-Herzegovina	Botswana
Belize	Belize	Burkina Faso	Botswana	Burundi
Benin	Benin	Burundi	Bulgaria	Cameroon
Bermuda	Bermuda	Cameroon	Burkina Faso	Chad
Bhutan	Bhutan	Central African Republic	Cameroon	China
Bolivia	Botswana	Chad	Chad	Comoros
Botswana	British Virgin Islands	Chile	Chile	Congo
British Virgin Islands	Brunei Darussalam	China	China	Cuba
Brunei	Bulgaria	Congo	Cuba	Dominica
Bulgaria	Burkina Faso	Cuba	Dominica	Egypt
Burma	Burma	Dominica	Egypt	Equatorial Guinea
Burundi	Burundi	Egypt	Equatorial Guinea	Eritrea
Cameroon	Cameroon	Equatorial Guinea	Eritrea	Ethiopia
Central African Republic	Cayman Islands	Ethiopia	Estonia	Gabon
Chad	Central African Republic	Gabon	Ethiopia	Ghana
Chile	Chad	Gambia	Gabon	Guatemala
China (People's Republic)	Chile	Ghana	Georgia	Guinea

Continued

Table B.1. (Continued)

Retentionist

1980	1985	1990	1995	2001
Comoros	China	Grenada	Ghana	Guyana
Congo	Comoros	Guatemala	Grenada	India
Cuba	Congo	Guinea	Guatemala	Indonesia
Cyprus	Cuba	Guinea-Bissau	Guinea	Iran
Czechoslovakia	Czechoslovakia	Guyana	Guyana	Iraq
Djibouti	Djibouti	Hungary	India	Jamaica
Dominica	Dominica	India	Indonesia	Japan
Egypt	Egypt	Indonesia	Iran	Jordan
El Salvador	Equatorial Guinea	Iran	Iraq	Kazakhstan
Equatorial Guinea	Ethiopia	Iraq	Jamaica	Kenya
Ethiopia	Gabon	Jamaica	Japan	Kuwait
France	Gambia	Japan	Jordan	Kyrgyzstan
Gabon	German Democratic Republic	Jordan	Kazakhstan	Laos
Gambia	Ghana	Kenya	Kenya	Lebanon
German Democratic Republic	Greece	North Korea	North Korea	Lesotho
Ghana	Grenada	South Korea	South Korea	Liberia
Greece	Guatemala	Kuwait	Kuwait	Libya
Grenada	Guinea	Laos	Kyrgyzstan	Malawi
Guatemala	Guinea-Bissau	Lebanon	Laos	Malaysia
Guinea	Guyana	Lesotho	Latvia	Mauritania
Guyana	Haiti	Liberia	Lebanon	Mongolia

		Retentionist		
1980	*1985*	*1990*	*1995*	*2001*
		Libya	Lesotho	Morocco
		Malawi	Liberia	Myanmar
		Malaysia	Libya	Nigeria
		Mali	Lithuania	North Korea
		Mauritania	Malawi	Oman
		Mauritius	Malaysia	Pakistan
		Mongolia	Mauritania	Palestinian Authority
		Morocco	Mongolia	Philippines
		Mozambique	Morocco	Qatar
		Myanmar	Myanmar	Russian Federation
		Nigeria	Nigeria	Rwanda
		Oman	Oman	St. Christopher & Nevis
		Pakistan	Pakistan	St. Lucia
		Poland	Poland	St. Vincent & Grenadines
		Qatar	Qatar	Saudi Arabia
		Rwanda	Russia	Sierra Leone
		St. Christopher & Nevis	St. Christopher & Nevis	Singapore
		Saint Lucia	St. Lucia	Somalia
		St. Vincent & Grenadines	St. Vincent & Grenadines	South Korean
Haiti	Hong Kong	Saudi Arabia	Saudi Arabia	Sudan
Hong Kong	Hungary	Sierra Leone	Sierra Leone	Swaziland
Hungary	India			
India	Indonesia			
Indonesia	Iran			
Iran	Iraq			
Iraq	Ireland			
Ireland	Ivory Coast			
Ivory Coast	Jamaica			
Jamaica	Japan			
Japan	Jordan			
Jordan	Kampuchea			
Kampuchea	Kenya			
Kenya	North Korea			
North Korea	South Korea			
South Korea	Kuwait			
Kuwait	Laos			
Laos	Lebanon			
Lebanon	Lesotho			
Lesotho	Liberia			
Liberia	Libya			

Continued

Table B.1. (*Continued*)

Retentionist

1980	1985	1990	1995	2001
Libya	Liechtenstein	Singapore	Singapore	Syria
Liechtenstein	Madagascar	Somalia	Somalia	Taiwan
Madagascar	Malawi	South Africa	Sudan	Tajikistan
Malawi	Malaysia	Sudan	Swaziland	Tanzania
Malaysia	Maldives	Suriname	Syria	Thailand
Maldives	Mali	Swaziland	Tadzhikistan	Trinidad & Tobago
Mali	Mauritania	Syria	Taiwan	Tunisia
Mauritania	Mauritius	Taiwan	Tanzania	Uganda
Mauritius	Mongolia	Tanzania	Thailand	United Arab Emirates
Mongolia	Monserrat	Thailand	Trinidad & Tobago	USA
Morocco	Morocco	Tonga	Tunisia	Uzbekistan
Mozambique	Mozambique	Trinidad & Tobago	Turkmenistan	Vietnam
Namibia	Namibia	Tunisia	Uganda	Yemen
Niger	Niger	Turkey	Ukraine	Yugoslavia
Nigeria	Nigeria	Uganda	United Arab Emirates	Zambia
Oman	Oman	USSR	USA	Zimbabwe
Pakistan	Pakistan	United Arab Emirates	Uzbekistan	
Paraguay	Paraguay	USA	Vietnam	
Peru*	Philippines	Vietnam	Yemen	
Philippines	Poland	Yemen	Yugoslavia	
Poland	Qatar	Yugoslavia	Zaire	
Qatar	Romania	Zaire	Zambia	
Romania	Rwanda	Zambia	Zimbabwe	

		Retentionist		
1980	*1985*	*1990*	*1995*	*2001*
Rwanda	St. Christopher & Nevis	Zimbabwe		
Saint Lucie	St. Lucia			
Saint Vincent	St. Vincent & the Grenadines			
Samoa	Samoa			
Sao Tome & Principe	Sao Tome & Principe			
Saudi Arabia	Saudi Arabia			
Senegal	Senegal			
Seychelles	Seychelles			
Sierra Leone	Sierra Leone			
Singapore	Singapore			
Somalia	Somalia			
South Africa	South Africa			
Sri Lanka	Sri Lanka			
Sudan	Sudan			
Suriname	Suriname			
Swaziland	Swaziland			
Syria	Syria			
Taiwan	Taiwan			
Tanzania	Tanzania			
Thailand	Thailand			
Togo	Togo			
Tonga	Tonga			
Trinidad & Tobago	Trinidad & Tobago			

Continued

Table B.1. (Continued)

		Retentionist		
1980	*1985*	*1990*	*1995*	*2001*
Tunisia	Tunisia			
Turkey	Turkey			
Uganda	Turks & Caicos Islands			
USSR	Uganda			
United Arab Emirates	USSR			
USA	United Arab Emirates			
Upper Volta	USA			
Vietnam	Vietnam			
North Yemen	North Yemen			
South Yemen	South Yemen			
Yugoslavia	Yugoslavia			
Zaire	Zaire			
Zambia	Zambia			
Zimbabwe	Zimbabwe			
Total				
130	130	94	93	86

Grand Total (All Countries)

167	176	179	194	195

Notes: Numbers in parentheses are dates of last execution.
*Missing data on date of last execution.
**No executions since independence.
Source: Amnesty International, *List of Abolitionist and Retentionist Countries.*

Appendix C

Death Row and Execution Statistics

Table C.1.

Death Row Population as of December 31, 1995, Number of Executions
1995–2000, and Rate of Execution per 100 Offenders on Death Row

State	Death Row Population Dec. 31, 1995	Total Number of Executions, 1995–2000	Rate of Executions per 100 Offenders on Death Row	Rank
Alabama	136	13	9.6	17
Arizona	121	19	15.7	12
Arkansas	37	14	37.8	5
California	386	6	1.6	26
Colorado	3	1	33.3	7
Connecticut	4	0	0	29
Delaware	14	7	50.0	2
Florida	353	17	4.8	23
Georgia	96	5	5.2	22
Idaho	20	0	0	29
Illinois	155	10	6.5	21
Indiana	47	4	8.5	19
Kansas	0	0	0.0	29
Kentucky	29	2	6.9	20
Louisiana	47	5	10.6	16
Maryland	13	2	15.4	13
Mississippi	50	0	0	29
Missouri	88	35	39.8	3
Montana	8	2	25.0	8
Nebraska	10	2	20.0	10
Nevada	65	3	4.6	24
New Jersey	9	0	0	29
New Mexico	1	0	0	29
North Carolina	111	10	9.0	18
Ohio	141	1	0.7	28
Oklahoma	130	27	20.8	9
Oregon	18	2	11.1	14
Pennsylvania	181	3	1.7	25
South Carolina	59	21	35.6	6
South Dakota	2	0	0	29
Tennessee	100	1	1.0	27
Texas	391	154	39.4	4
Utah	10	2	20.0	11
Virginia	55	57	103.6	1
Washington	9	1	11.1	15

Sources: Bureau of Justice Statistics, Capital Punishment 1995, Table 4 (Death Row Population), Bureau of Justice Statistics Data, available at http://www.ojp.usdoj.gov/bjs/cp.htm (Executions).

Appendix D

New Survey Analysis Materials

Included in this appendix are survey research data that have not been collected and published in the form that I use and cite in this volume. This new analysis covers one item in the National Election survey of 1996 study relating to the strength of belief in favor of and opposed to the death penalty and several questions relating to attitudes toward vigilante groups and behavior analysis from data provided at the Roper, Gallup, and Louis Harris archives.

Table D.1.
Support for Capital Punishment by Region and Intensity,
National Election Survey 1996

	Midwest	South	West	East
Strong support	59	59	53	54
Weak support	16	13	18	14
Strongly against	5	8	8	10
Weakly against	8	10	10	11
Ratio of strong to weak support	3.7	4.5	2.9	3.9

Source: Cross-tabulation provided by Merrill Shanks, University of California, Berkeley.

Vigilante Groups

We searched two survey research libraries for questions using the term "vigilante" in national public opinion polls: the Roper Center database, searched by Lois Timms-Ferrara, and the Louis Harris Archive at the University of North Carolina, searched by David Sheaves of the Howard Odum Institute for Research in Social Science.

The eight Roper Center items are reproduced below.

1. Gallup Poll [Aug. 15, 1937]
Do you approve of the citizen groups, called vigilantes, which have sprung up recently in strike areas?
  %
  24   Yes
  76   No
  Notes:
  Topics: Labor Ratings Groups
  Conducted by: Gallup Organization
  Field dates: July 21, 1937, to July 26, 1937
  Interview method: Personal
  Sample: National adult
  Sample Size: 1,500
  Study Note: Sample size is approximate.
  [USGALLUP.081537.R04]
Data provided by the Roper Center for Public Opinion Research, University of Connecticut, Storrs, Conn.

2. Harris Survey [Oct. 01, 1973]
(Let me ask you about different types of people in this country. For each, tell me if you feel they do more good than harm, more harm than good, or are neither helpful nor harmful?) . . . Vigilante groups such as the Minutemen, white citizens' councils, and the Ku Klux Klan
  %
  79   Do more harm than good
  21   Do more good than harm/Neither/Not sure
  Notes:
  Topics: Groups
  Conducted by: Louis Harris & Associates
  Field dates: Aug. 18, 1973, to Aug. 24, 1973
  Interview method: Personal
  Sample: National adult
  Sample size: 1,546
  [USHARRIS.100173.R1E]
Data provided by the Roper Center for Public Opinion Research, University of Connecticut, Storrs, Conn.

3. Gallup Poll [Feb. 14, 1985]
Do you feel that incidents like these—taking the law into one's own hands, often called vigilantism—are sometimes justified because of the circumstances, or are never justified?
%
72   Sometimes
17   Never
08   Always
03   No opinion
Notes:
Topics: Crime
Conducted by: Gallup Organization
Field dates: Jan. 25, 1985, to Jan. 28, 1985
Interview method: Personal
Sample: National adult
Sample size: 1,528
[USGALLUP.021485.R1]
Data provided by the Roper Center for Public Opinion Research, University of Connecticut, Storrs, Conn.

4. Gallup Report [Jan. 1985]
Do you feel that incidents like these (the recent incident in a New York City subway in which a man shot and wounded four teenagers who demanded money from him)—taking the law into one's own hands, often called vigilantism—are sometimes justified because of the circumstances, or are never justified?
%
72   Sometimes
17   Never
08   Always
03   No opinion
Notes:
Topics: Crime Values
Conducted by: Gallup Organization
Field dates: Jan. 25, 1985, to Jan. 28, 1985
Interview method: Telephone
Sample: National adult
Sample size: 1,528
[USGALLUP.232_6.R2]
Data provided by the Roper Center for Public Opinion Research, University of Connecticut, Storrs, Conn.

5. Gallup/Newsweek Poll [March 11, 1985]
Do you feel that taking the law into one's own hands, often called vigilantism, is justified by circumstances?
%
03   Always
68   Sometimes

23   Never
06   Don't know
Notes:
Topics: Crime
Source: Survey by *Newsweek*
Conducted by: Gallup Organization
Field dates: Feb. 28, 1985, to March 1, 1985
Interview method: Telephone
Sample: National adult
Sample size: 1,009
[USGALNEW.031185.R04]
Data provided by the Roper Center for Public Opinion Research, University of Connecticut, Storrs, Conn.

6. National Victims Week Study [March 26, 1991]
Sometimes when people lack confidence in the criminal justice system's ability to deal with a crime, they take the law into their own hands and attack the person who they believe is responsible for the crime. This is called vigilantism. Do you think that vigilantism in America has increased over the past 10 years, decreased over the past 10 years, or has remained the same?
%
39   Increased
09   Decreased
46   Remained the same
06   Not sure
Notes:
Topics: Crime Courts
Source: Survey by National Victim Center
Conducted by: Schulman, Ronca, and Bucuvalas
Field dates: March 8, 1991, to March 17, 1991
Interview method: Telephone
Sample: National adult
Sample size: 1,000
[USSRBI.VICTIM.R27]
Data provided by the Roper Center for Public Opinion Research, University of Connecticut, Storrs, Conn.

7. National Victims Week Study [March 26, 1991]
Do you think that vigilantism (sometimes when people lack confidence in the criminal justice system's ability to deal with a crime, they take the law into their own hands and attack the person who they believe is responsible for the crime) is ever justified?
%
33   Yes
61   No
06   Not sure

Notes:
Topics: Crime Courts
Source: Survey by National Victim Center
Conducted by: Schulman, Ronca, and Bucuvalas
Field dates: March 8, 1991, to March 17, 1991
Interview Method: Telephone
Sample: National adult
Sample size: 1,000
[USSRBI.VICTIM.R28A]
Data provided by the Roper Center for Public Opinion Research, University of Connecticut, Storrs, Conn.

8. National Victims Week Study [March 26, 1991]
(Asked of respondents who think vigilantism [sometimes when people lack confidence in the criminal justice system's ability to deal with a crime, they take the law into their own hands and attack the person who they believe is responsible for the crime] is ever justified) What might justify people taking the law into their own hands?

%
04   When a child is abused
03   When a child is murdered
01   When an adult family member is abused
03   When an adult family member is murdered
06   Rape/when someone is being raped
04   When person is murdered
10   When the police/law enforcement don't do their job (unspecified)
06   When family/family members is hurt/harmed (unspecified)
30   When the criminal justice system doesn't work/fails to give equal justice/bureaucracy doesn't work (unspecified)
04   When family/family member is murdered
04   When the law fails to protect the victim
17   When the criminal goes free/free on a technicality/gets a lenient sentence
03   When a child is hurt/harmed (unspecified)
12   Being present at the crime/self-defense/protection
04   Revenge
04   Build-up emotions/anger/stress
02   To protect their streets/neighborhood
02   To protect their home/property
04   All other mentions
07   Don't know/Not sure
Notes: Respondents feel vigilantism justified (33%)
Topics: Crime Courts
Source: Survey by National Victim Center
Conducted by: Schulman, Ronca, and Bucuvalas
Field dates: March 8, 1991, to March 17, 1991
Interview Method: Telephone
Sample: National adult

Sample size: 1,000
[USSRBI.VICTIM.R28B]
Data provided by the Roper Center for Public Opinion Research, University of Connecticut, Storrs, Conn.

Patricia Valderwolf of Schulman, Ronca, and Bucuvalas provided the only regional detail available by nine subregions to Question 7.

The Roper Center ran a cross-tabulation by region on the Gallup poll (item 3), which is reproduced in Table D.2.

The University of North Carolina provided cross-tabulation by region for 1970 and 1975 items, reproduced in Tables D.3 and D.4.

Table D.2.

Percentage of Public Believing That Vigilantism Is Justified

"Do you feel that incidents like these—taking the law into one's own hands, often called vigilantism—are sometimes justified because of the circumstances, or are never justified?"

	East	South	Midwest	West	Nation
Always	8	7	8	8	8
Sometimes	72	76	74	67	72
Never	18	14	16	21	17
No opinion	2	3	2	4	3

Source: Gallup Poll, January 25-28, 1985. Provided by Lois Timms-Ferrara, the Roper Center.

Table D.3.

Frequency of Support for Vigilante Groups, by Region

"Many different types of people with new viewpoints have sprung up in this country over the past few years. Tell me which of the following you feel to be helpful to the country, which ones are harmful, and which are neither helpful nor harmful —Vigilante Groups such as the Minutemen, White Citizens' Council, and the Like."

	East	*South*	*Midwest*	*West*	*Total*
Helpful					
Frequency	27	33	24	18	102
Percent	6	7	6	7	6
Harmful					
Frequency	268	238	247	174	927
Percent	61	53	58	63	58
Neither					
Frequency	63	42	52	29	186
Percent	14	9	12	11	12
Not sure					
Frequency	81	139	101	54	375
Percent	18	31	24	20	24
Total					
Frequency	439	452	424	275	1590
Percent	28	28	27	17	

Note: Frequency missing = 19.
Source: Harris 1970 Civil Liberties Survey, no. 2037 (August 1970). Provided by David Sheaves.

Table D.4.

Frequency of Opinion That Citizen Vigilante Groups
Are a Contributor to Violence, by Region

"Do you feel that Citizen Vigilante Groups Who Train People
to Handle Guns is a major contributor to violence in this country today,
a minor contributor, or hardly a contributor at all?"

	East	South	Midwest	West	Total
Major contributor					
Frequency	162	114	152	99	527
Percent	38	27	38	37	35
Minor contributor					
Frequency	122	133	127	95	477
Percent	29	31	32	35	31
Hardly contributes					
Frequency	83	94	77	55	309
Percent	20	22	19	20	20
Not sure					
Frequency	56	86	40	20	202
Percent	13	20	10	7	13
Total					
Frequency	423	427	396	269	1515
Percent	28	28	26	18	

Note: Frequency missing = 7
Source: Energy Shortage and Values Survey, no. 7586 (October, 1975). Provided by David Sheaves.

Appendix E

Justified Killings by Citizens and Police, by State

Table E.1.

Justifiable Homicide Rates (Citizen v. Police) by State,
1995–1998 (per 100,000)

State	Citizen Rate (CR)	Police Rate (PR)
Alabama	.28	.14
Alaska	.64	.48
Arizona	.92	1.48
Arkansas	.32	.28
California	.68	1.40
Colorado	.20	.80
Connecticut	.24	.075
Delaware	.00	.00
Florida	.08	.08
Georgia	.40	.36
Hawaii	.00	.58
Idaho	.16	.50
Illinois	.24	.36
Indiana	.48	.32
Iowa	.04	.04
Kansas	.00	.00
Kentucky	.12	.12
Louisiana	1.00	.56
Maine	.16	.08
Maryland	1.16	1.16
Massachusetts	.02	.04
Michigan	.52	.56
Minnesota	.04	.12
Mississippi	.12	.14
Missouri	.36	.60
Montana	.00	.12
Nebraska	.00	.06
Nevada	.72	1.24
New Hampshire	.00	.08
New Jersey	.40	.52
New Mexico	.36	.48
New York	.28	.56
North Carolina	.48	.22
North Dakota	.16	.00
Ohio	.08	.36
Oklahoma	.52	1.08
Oregon	.52	.62
Pennsylvania	.44	.28
Rhode Island	.12	.10
South Carolina	.60	.20
South Dakota	.00	.00
Tennessee	1.24	.72
Texas	.60	.56

Table E.1. *(Continued)*

Utah	.04	.36
Vermont	.36	.16
Virginia	.16	.56
Washington	.44	.44
West Virginia	.12	.16
Wisconsin	.28	.28
Wyoming	.20	.42

Sources: FBI Uniform Crime Index Supplementary Homicide Reports for 1995–1998 (Officer and Citizen Killings); U.S. Bureau of the Census (Population).

Appendix F

Review of Death Penalty Exoneration Data from the Death Penalty Information Center

Table F.1 shows: (1) the year a now-exonerated former death row inmate was convicted, (2) the year the state lost the power to execute him/her, and (3) the year the former death row inmate was actually released. The Death Penalty Information Center information used to draw up the "length of time between conviction and exoneration" chart (Fig. 7.1) was the length of time between conviction and *final* release (acquittal) (columns 1 and 3 on this table).

Table F.1.

Death Penalty Exoneration Data, Audit Sample

Name of exonerated individual	(1) Conviction	(2) No Death	(3) Release	State
James Robison	1977	1980	1993	Arizona
Muneer Deeb	1985	1991	1993	Texas
Andrew Golden	1991	1993	1994	Florida
Joseph Burrows	1989	1994	1994	Illinois
Adolph Munson	1985	1994	1995	Oklahoma
Robert Charles Cruz	1981	1995	1995	Arizona
Rolando Cruz	1985	1994	1995	Illinois
Alejandro Hernandez	1985	1995	1995	Illinois
Sabrina Butler	1990	1992	1995	Mississippi
Verneal Jimerson	1985	1995	1996	Illinois
Dennis Williams	1979	1996	1996	Illinois
Robert Miranda	1982	1996	1996	Nevada
Troy Lee Jones	1982	1996	1996	California
Ricardo Aldape Guerra	1982	1994	1997	Texas

Sources: Dieter 2002, Cases 53–69. Prepared by Tom Clifford.

References

ABC News/*Washington Post* poll. 1995, March 16–19.

ABC News/*Washington Post* poll. 1996, April 20–May 6.

American Bar Association. 1997. Report with Recommendations No. 107, from the ABA 1997 Midyear Meeting. Available at http://www.abanet.org/irr/rec107.html.

Amnesty International. *List of Abolitionist and Retentionist Countries* (April 1980, June 1985, September 1990, December 1995, and June 2001).

Amnesty London. 2000. "The Death Penalty" (pamphlet).

Amnesty USA. 2000. "The Death Penalty" (pamphlet).

Ancel, Marc (for the European Committee on Crime Problems). 1962. *The Death Penalty in European Countries*. Strasbourg: Council of Europe.

The Anti-terrorism and Effective Death Penalty Act of 1996. Public Law No. 104-132, 110 Stat. 1214 (codified as amended at 28 U.S.C. §§ 2241–2255 and adding 28 U.S.C. §§ 2261–2266) 2000. Eagan, Minn.: West.

Appeal of Presidents. 2001. Council of Europe, available at http://stars.coe.fr.

Armstrong, Ken, and Steve Mills. 1999, November 14. "Death Row Justice Derailed; Bias, Errors and Incompetence in Capital Cases Have Turned Illinois' Harshest Punishment into Its Least Credible." *Chicago Tribune*, p. 1.

———. 2000, June 12. "Gatekeeper Court Keeps Gates Shut; Justices Prove Reluctant to Nullify Cases" (Series: "State of Execution: The Death Penalty in Texas." Second of Two Parts). *Chicago Tribune*, p. 1.

———. 2002a, May 10. "Maryland Death Penalty on Hold; Governor Orders Moratorium Until Racial Study Done." *Chicago Tribune*, p. 1.

———. 2002b. "'Until I Can Be Sure': How the Threat of Executing the Innocent Has Transformed the Death Penalty Debate." In *Beyond Repair?*

America's Death Penalty, ed. Stephen P. Garvey. Durham: Duke University Press.

Armstrong, Ken, Steve Mills, and Douglas Holt. 2000, June 11. "Flawed Trials Lead to Death Chamber; Bush Confident in System Rife with Problems." (Series: "State of Execution: The Death Penalty in Texas." First of Two Parts). *Chicago Tribune*, p. 1.

Ashcroft, John. 2001, December 11. "Attorney General Transcript: News Conference Regarding Zacarias Moussaoui." Washington, D.C.: U.S. Department of Justice. Available at http://www.usdoj.gov/ag/speeches/2001/agcrisisremarks12_11.htm.

————. 2002, March 28. "Statement by Attorney General Ashcroft: Justice Department to Seek Death Penalty in Moussaoui Case." Washington, D.C.: U.S Department of Justice. Available at http://www.usdoj.gov/opa/pr/2002/March/02_ag_186.htm.

Ashmore, Harry. 1957. *An Epitaph for Dixie*. New York: Norton and Co.

Atkins v. Virginia. 2002. 122 S. Ct. 2242.

Bakst, Brian. 2001, July 2. "O'Connor Questions Death Penalty." Associated Press Online.

Banner, Stuart. 2002. *The Death Penalty: An American History*. Cambridge, Mass.: Harvard University Press.

Beccaria, Cesare. 1764. *On Crimes and Punishments*, 1st ed. Trans. David Young. Indianapolis: Hackett Publishing, 1986.

Bedau, Hugo Adam, and Michael L. Radelet. 1987. "Miscarriages of Justice in Potentially Capital Cases." *Stanford Law Review* 40: 21–180.

Booth v. Maryland. 1987. 482 U.S. 496, 107 S. Ct. 2529.

Brecht v. Abrahamson. 1993. 507 U.S. 619, 113 S. Ct. 1710.

Brown, Richard Maxwell. 1969. "Historical Patterns of Violence in America." In *Violence in America: Historical and Comparative Perspectives*, ed. Hugh Davis Graham and Ted Robert Gurr, 35–64. Staff Report to the National Commission on the Causes and Prevention of Violence. Washington, D.C.: U.S. Government Printing Office.

Brown v. Board of Education. 1954. 347 U.S. 483, 74 S. Ct. 686.

Brown v. Mississippi. 1936. 297 U.S. 278, 56 S. Ct. 2861.

Brundage, W. Fitzhugh. 1993. *Lynching in the New South: Georgia and Virginia, 1880–1930*. Urbana: University of Illinois Press.

Bureau of Justice Statistics, U.S. Department of Justice. Available at http://www.ojp.usdoj.gov/bjs/glance/tables/exetab.htm.

Burritt, Chris. 2000, July 2. "S.C. Moves Rebel Flag; Banner's Removal from Atop State Capitol Draws 1,500 in Protest." *Atlanta Journal Constitution*, p. 1A.

Buxton, R. J. 1973. "The Politics of Criminal Law Reform: England." *American Journal of Comparative Law* 21: 230–44.

California Penal Code § 3600 (West 2000).

Callins v. Collins. 1994. 510 U.S. 1141, 114 S. Ct. 1127 (Blackmun, J., dissenting from a memorandum denying petition for certiorari).

Cambridge Dictionary of American English (online). Available at http://dictionary.cambridge.org/search-default.asp.

Christoph, James B. 1962. *Capital Punishment and British Politics: The British Movement to Abolish the Death Penalty 1945–1957*. Chicago: University of Chicago Press.

Coker v. Georgia. 1977. 433 U.S. 584, 97 S. Ct. 2861.

Coleman v. Thompson. 1991. 501 U.S. 722, 111 S. Ct. 2546.

Combined U.S. News Sources (Lexis-Nexis).

Committee on Legal Affairs and Human Rights of the Council of Europe. 1999. "Europe: A Death Penalty-Free Continent." In *The Death Penalty: Abolition in Europe*, Appendix III, pp. 171–84. Strasbourg: Council of Europe Publishing.

Copeland, Larry. 2001, March 8. "3 States Wrapped Up in Flag Battle: 'Stars and Bars' an Incendiary Issue in S.C., Miss. And Ga." *USA Today*, p. 3A.

Council of Europe. 1999. *The Death Penalty: Abolition in Europe*. Strasbourg: Council of Europe Publishing.

Council of Europe, Protocol No. 6 to the Convention for the Protection of Human Rights and Fundamental Freedoms Concerning the Abolition of the Death Penalty. 1983, April 28. E.T.S. No. 114. Available at http://www.eurunion.org/legislat/DeathPenalty/CounEurProto6.htm.

Death Penalty Information Center. 2002. Available at http://www.deathpenalty info.org.

Dieter, Richard C. 2002. "Innocence and the Death Penalty: The Increasing Danger of Executing the Innocent." Death Penalty Information Center. Available at http://www.deathpenaltyinfo.org/inn.html.

Dray, Philip. 2002. *At the Hands of Persons Unknown: The Lynching of Black America*. New York: Random House.

Eddings v. Oklahoma. 1982. 455 U.S. 104, 102 S. Ct. 869.

Ellsworth, Phoebe C., and Samuel R. Gross. 1994. "Hardening of the Attitudes: Americans' Views on the Death Penalty." *Journal of Social Issues* 50: 19–52.

———. 2002. "Second Thoughts: Americans' Views on the Death Penalty at the Turn of the Century." In *Beyond Repair? America's Death Penalty*, ed. Stephen P. Garvey. Durham: Duke University Press.

Espy, M. Watt, and John Ortiz Smylka. 1988. *Executions in the United States, 1680–1987: The Espy File*. Inter-university Consortium for Political and Social Research Study No. 8451. ETS No. 14.

"European States Drop Wartime Exception to Ban on Death Penalty." 2002, May 3. *Agence France-Presse*.

Evans, Richard J. 1996. *Rituals of Retribution: Capital Punishment in Germany, 1600–1987*. Oxford: Oxford University Press.

Farrell, John Aloysius. 2001, June 2. "Judge Denies Bid for DNA Test to Verify Guilt of Executed Man." *Boston Globe*, p. A3.

———. 2001, June 26. "DNA Scrutiny Tests Judicial System." *Boston Globe*, p. A1.

FBI. Uniform Crime Reports. (See Appendix E.)

Forst, Michael. 1999. "The Abolition of the Death Penalty in France." In *The Death Penalty: Abolition in Europe*, 105–16. Strasbourg: Council of Europe Publishing.

"France to Limit Legal Links with US over September 11 Death Move." 2002, March 28. *Agence France-Press*.

Frank, Jerome, and Barbara Frank. 1957. *Not Guilty*. Garden City, N.Y.: Doubleday.

Furman v. Georgia. 1972. 408 U.S. 238, 92 S. Ct. 2726.

Gallup, George H., ed. 1976. *Gallup International Opinion Polls, Great Britain, 1937–1975*. New York: Random House.

The Gallup Organization. Available at http://www.gallup.com/poll/topics/
    death_pen.asp.
The Gallup Organization, cross-tabulation of May 10–14, 2001, poll, question
    19, by region. (See Appendix D.)
Gallup polls. 1985. (See Appendix D.)
Garland, David. 2001. *The Culture of Control: Crime and Social Order in Contempo-
    rary Society*. Chicago: University of Chicago Press.
Gregg v. Georgia. 1976. 428 U.S. 153, 96 S. Ct. 2909.
Harris Polls. 1970, 1975. Louis Harris Archive. University of North Carolina.
    (See Appendix D.)
Hastings, Deborah. 2001, August 29. "Testimony Doubted in Execution Case."
    Associated Press Online.
Herrera v. Collins. 1993. 506 U.S. 390, 113 S. Ct. 853.
Hertz, Randy and James S. Liebman. 2001. *Federal Habeas Corpus Practice and Pro-
    cedure*, Vol. 2, 4th ed. Charlottesville, Va.: Matthew Bender and Co.
Hood, Roger. 1996. *The Death Penalty: A World-Wide Perspective*. New York: Ox-
    ford University Press.
———. 1997. "The Death Penalty: USA in World Perspective." *Journal of
    Transnational Law and Policy* 6: 517–41.
Illinois Governor's Commission on Capital Punishment. 2002, April 15. Report.
    Available at http://www.idoc.state.il.us/ccp/ccp/reports/commission_
    reports/index.html.
Jennings, M. Kent. 1998. "Political Trust and the Roots of Devolution." In *Trust
    and Governance*, ed. Valerie Braithwaite and Margaret Levi, 218–44. New
    York: Russell Sage.
Jones, Jeffrey M. 2001. "Americans Closely Divided on Death Penalty Morato-
    rium." The Gallup Organization. Available at http://www.gallup.com/poll/
    releases/pr010411c.asp.
Jurek v. Texas. 1976. 428 U.S. 262, 96 S. Ct. 2950.
Kamin, Sam. 2000. "The Death Penalty Decisions of the California Supreme Court:
    Politics, Judging, and Death." Ph.D. dissertation, University of Califor-
    nia, Berkeley.
Kluger, Richard. 1977. *Simple Justice: The History of* Brown v. Board of Education
    and Black America's Struggle for Equality. New York: Vintage Books.
Krüger, Hans Christian. 1999. "Protocol No. 6 to the Convention for the Protec-
    tion of Human Rights." In *The Death Penalty: Abolition in Europe*, 69–78.
    Strasbourg: Council of Europe Publishing.
Langer, Gary. 2001. ABC News/*Washington Post* poll, taken April 20–24, 2001.
    (Random national sample of 1003 adults, 3% margin of error). Available
    at http://abcnews.go.com/sections/us/DailyNews/poll010504_death
    penalty.html.
Lichfield, John. 2001, September 21. "Europe Demonstrates Unity to Back Mili-
    tary Action: France." *The Independent*. Available at http://www.independent.
    co.uk/story.jsp?story=95225.
Liebman, James S., Jeffrey Fagan, Andrew Gelman, Valerie West, Garth Davies,
    and Alexander Kiss. 2002. "A Broken System Part II: Why There Is So
    Much Error in Capital Cases and What Can Be Done About It." Available
    at http://www.law.columbia.edu/brokensystem2/index2.html.

Liebman, James S., Jeffrey Fagan, Valerie West, and Jonathan Lloyd. 2000. "Capital Attrition: Error Rates in Capital Cases, 1973–1995." *Texas Law Review* 78: 1839–65.

Lockett v. Ohio. 1978. 438 U.S. 586, 98 S. Ct. 2954.

Loftus, Elizabeth F. 1996. *Eyewitness Testimony*. Cambridge, Mass.: Harvard University Press.

Lott, John Jr. 1998. *More Guns, Less Crime: Understanding Crime and Gun Control Laws*. Chicago: University of Chicago Press.

Markman, Stephen J., and Paul G. Cassell. 1988. "Protecting the Innocent: A Response to the Bedau-Radelet Study." *Stanford Law Review* 41: 121–60.

Marlowe, Lara. 2001, September 18. "French Back US Action but Politicians Steer Clear of a Military Crusade." *Irish Times*.

Masters, Brooke A. 2001, March 28. "New DNA Testing Urged in Case of Executed Man; Post, Others Ask Va. Court to Release Evidence in 1981 Murder." *Washington Post*, p. B1.

McKleskey v. Zant. 1991. 499 U.S. 467, 111 S. Ct. 1454.

Mills, Steve. 2001, March 25. "Texas Revisits Death Penalty: Legislators Weigh Reform in Nation's Execution Leader." *Chicago Tribune*, p. 1.

"A Mississippi Stuck in the Past." 2001, April 20. Editorial. *Washington Post*, p. A24.

Napolitano, Jo. 2002, April 20. "National Briefing—Midwest: Missouri: Stepfather Gets Life Term in 5 Killings." *New York Times*, p. A13.

National Association for the Advancement of Colored People. 1919. *Thirty Years of Lynching in the United States, 1889–1918*. New York: Arno Press.

National Election Survey. 1996. (See Appendix D.)

Noelle, Elisabeth, and Erich Peter Neumann, eds. 1967. *The Germans: Public Opinion Polls 1947–1966*. Allensbach, Bonn: Verlag für Demoskopie.

Packer, Herbert L. 1964. "Two Models of the Criminal Process." *Pennsylvania Law Review* 113: 1–68.

Payne v. Tennessee. 1991. 501 U.S. 808, 111 S. Ct. 2597.

Plessy v. Ferguson. 1896. 163 U.S. 537, 16 S. Ct. 1138.

Powell v. Alabama. 1932. 287 U.S. 45, 53 S. Ct. 55.

Pristavkin, Anatoly. 1999. "A Vast Place of Execution: The Death Penalty in Russia." In *The Death Penalty: Abolition in Europe*, 129–38. Strasbourg: Council of Europe Publishing.

Proffitt v. Florida. 1976. 428 U.S. 242, 96 S. Ct. 2960.

Radelet, Michael, Hugo Bedau, and Constance E. Putnam. 1992. *In Spite of Innocence: The Ordeal of 400 Americans Wrongly Convicted of Crimes Punishable by Death*. Boston: Northeastern University Press.

Radzinowicz, Leon. 1999. *Adventures in Criminology*. London: Routledge.

Ravaud, Caroline, and Stefan Trechsel. 1999. "The Death Penalty and the Case-law of the Institutions of the European Convention on Human Rights." In *The Death Penalty: Abolition in Europe*, 79–90. Strasbourg: Council of Europe Publishing.

Resolution No. 1179. "Honouring of Obligations and Commitments by Ukraine." Available at http://stars.coe.fr/ta/ta99/eres1179.htm.

Roberts v. Louisiana. 1976. 428 U.S. 325, 96 S. Ct. 3001.

Rosenberg, Gerald N. 1991. *The Hollow Hope: Can Courts Bring About Social Change?* Chicago: University of Chicago Press.

Royal Commission on Capital Punishment. 1953. *Royal Commission on Capital Punishment 1949–1953 Report.* London: Her Majesty's Stationery Office.

Salter, Stephanie. 1998, January 27. "Closure, Politics, and Justice." *San Francisco Examiner,* p. A13.

Sarat, Austin. 2001. *When the State Kills: Capital Punishment and the American Condition.* Princeton: Princeton University Press.

Scheck, Barry, Peter Neufeld, and Jim Dwyer. 2000. *Actual Innocence: Five Days to Execution and Other Dispatches from the Wrongly Convicted.* New York: Doubleday.

Schwarzchild, Henry. 1982, December 23. "Homicide by Injection." *New York Times,* p. A15.

Shenon, Philip, and Neil A. Lewis. 2002, March 28. "France Warns It Opposes Death Penalty in Terror Trial." *New York Times,* p. A1.

Smith, Tom W. 2000. *1999 National Gun Policy Survey of the National Opinion Research Center: Research Findings.* Chicago: National Opinion Research Center.

Snell, Tracy L., Bureau of Justice Statistics. 1996, December. *Capital Punishment 1995.* Washington, D.C.: U.S. Department of Justice.

———. 2001. *Capital Punishment 2000.* Washington, D.C.: U.S. Department of Justice.

Stanford v. Kentucky. 1989. 492 U.S. 361, 109 S. Ct. 2969.

Tax Foundation. Available at http://www.taxfoundation.org.

Teague v. Lane. 1989. 489 U.S. 288, 109 S. Ct. 1060.

Texas Penal Code § 19.03 (West 2000).

Thompson v. Oklahoma. 1988. 487 U.S. 815, 108 S. Ct. 2687.

Tison v. Arizona. 1987. 481 U.S. 137, 107 S. Ct. 1676.

Toscano, Roberto. 1999. "The United Nations and the Abolition of the Death Penalty." In *The Death Penalty: Abolition in Europe,* 91–104. Strasbourg: Council of Europe Publishing.

Toussaint, Philippe. 1999. "The Death Penalty and the 'Fairy Ring.'" In *The Death Penalty: Abolition in Europe,* 29–34. Strasbourg: Council of Europe Publishing.

Tysver, Lobyan. 1999, May 26. "Moratorium Vetoed Death Penalty Timeout Is Poor Policy, Johanns Says." *Omaha World Herald,* p. 1.

United States Census Bureau. 1900, 2000, 2002. United States Census Data.

United States Department of Justice, Bureau of Justice Statistics. Available at http://www.ojp.usdoj.gov/bjs/glance/tables/exetab.htm and http://www.ojp.usdoj.gov/bjs/glance/tables/drtab.htm.

Wainwright v. Sykes. 1977. 433 U.S. 72, 97 S. Ct. 2497.

Walsh, Edward. 2000, December 8. "Clinton Stays Killer's Execution; Delay Prompted by Need to Complete Study on Disparities." *Washington Post,* p. A12.

Watts, Jonathan. 2000, November 30. "Japan's State Execution 'Obscure and Arbitrary.'" *Guardian Unlimited World Dispatch.*

Weisberg, Robert. 1983. "Deregulating Death." *The Supreme Court Review* 1983: 305–95.

"When Death Is Appropriate." 2002, March 30. Editorial. *Boston Herald,* p. 16.

Wicker, Tom. 1983, July 15. "Refusing the Rope." *New York Times* (Late City Final Edition), p. A23.

Witt, Howard. 1987, July 1. "Canada Refuses to Bring Back Death Penalty." *Chicago Tribune*, p. 3.

Woodson v. North Carolina. 1976. 428 U.S. 280, 96 S. Ct. 2978.

Zimring, Franklin E. 1991. "Ambivalence in State Capital Punishment Policy: An Empirical Sounding." *New York University Review of Law and Social Change* 18: 729.

———. 1999. "The Executioner's Dissonant Song: On Capital Punishment and American Legal Values." In *The Killing State: Capital Punishment in Law, Politics, and Culture*, ed. Austin Sarat, 137–45. New York: Oxford University Press.

Zimring, Franklin E., and Gordon Hawkins. 1986. *Capital Punishment and the American Agenda*. New York: Cambridge University Press.

———. 1991. *The Scale of Imprisonment*. Chicago: University of Chicago Press.

———. 1996, January. "Toward a Principled Basis for Federal Criminal Legislation." *Annals of the American Academy of Political and Social Sciences* 543: 15–26.

———. 1997. *Crime Is Not the Problem: Lethal Violence in America*. New York: Oxford University Press.

Index

*Note: Page numbers in *italics* refer to charts and graphs.

Asia, 35, 37–38
assumption of innocence, 121–22
Atkins v. Virginia, 180, 184, 185
Attorney General appointment, 188, 191
Australia: abolition of capital punishment, 24,
    37, 113, 135, 194; executions and
    execution policy, 118; public support for
    capital punishment, 23

Badinter, Robert, 28
Beccaria, Cesare, 17, 25, 34
Bedau, Hugo, 157–58, 160
Belarus, 36
Belgium, 19, 27, 31
Bill of Rights, 68–69, 123
Blackmun, Harry, 150, 185
Booth v. Maryland, 53, 58
Brecht v. Abrahamson, 148
Britain. *See* England; Great Britain
Brown v. Board of Education, 131, 132–33
Brown v. Mississippi, 69
Bulgaria, 36
bureaucracy of capital punishment, 71
Burger, Warren, 52–53
Bush, George H. W., 183–84
Bush, George W., 4, 163, 188
Bush v. Gore, 186

California: executions and execution policy, 7,
    68, 74–75, 80–81, 85, 120, 189; Kaczynski
    case, 61–62
Callins v. Collins, 185
Cambodia, 37
Canada: abolition of capital punishment, 24,
    113, 135, 181, 194; public support for
    capital punishment, 10, 23, 127, 128, 136,
    193
Carter, Jimmy, 200
Carter, Reuben "Hurricane," 200
Cassell, Paul, 157–58, 163–64
China, 38
Chirac, Jacques, 42–45
civil rights activism, 183, 185
Clinton, William Jefferson, 188
closure associated with capital punishment: as
    consideration in sentencing, 58–63;
    influence, 176; media coverage
    mentioning, 60, 60; for prosecutors, 146;
    witnessing executions, 198
Coker v. Georgia, 82
Coleman, Robert, 169–70
Coleman v. Thompson: evidence review denied,
    169–70; operational impacts, 187;
    procedural defaults, 149–50, 154, 176,
    183
college campus activism, 199, 202
Colorado, 74
Committee of Legal Affairs and Human
    Rights of the Council of Europe, 27
Commonwealth nations: abolition emphasis,

17, 19, 127; compared to U.S., 14;
    influence on U.S., 183; public opinion,
    11; trends, 181–82
community effort, execution as, 120, 121, 176
concealed weapons laws, 104–5, 120
Confederate flag issue, 128–29
conflict, inevitability of, 15, 194, 203–5
Congress, 148, 180, 191–93
constitutional errors, restrictions on, 148
constitutional limits and values, 125
contract killings, 9
Convention for the Protection of Human
    Rights and Fundamental Freedoms, 31
costs of executions, 47
Council of Europe, 27, 39–40
courts. *See* federal government; state
    governments; Supreme Court
crime investigation, 121–22
Crimes and Punishments (Beccaria), 17
criminal records, 166
cruel and unusual punishment: *Furman v.
    Georgia* decision, 9, 70; *Herrera v. Collins*
    decision, 152; methods of capital
    punishment, 50; standard disregarded,
    180
cultural influences on capital punishment: in
    Asian countries, 38; culture of
    punishment, 116–17; culture of violence,
    116; international influence on U.S., 183
Czechoslovakia, 36, 37, 134

deadlines, effect on exonerations, 175
Death Penalty Information Center (2002), 7,
    161, 164–65
death row: backlog, 143–44, 228; ratio of
    condemned to executed, 7–8, 8; regional
    distribution, 87
debates: human rights issues, 28–33, 194–96;
    lack of intellectual debate, 47, 194–96, 200
defense counsel: dependence of inmates on,
    169; exonerations, 175; quality, 166, 171–
    72, 173; selection, 148–49
Delaware, 97, 98, 117
delays in death penalty administration:
    appellate process, 78–80; effects, 81–82;
    efforts to expedite executions, 176;
    exonerations, 174–75, 175; functions, 80–
    81; *Furman* decision, 71; opposition to
    appeals, 144, 150; as source of frustration,
    8; time limits on, 148
democracy, 39
Denmark, 18
Dent, Alfred, 133
Department of Justice, 191
deterrence factors in capital punishment, 58
"Dilemma of Diversification," 189–90
dissatisfaction with death penalty, 144
distrust of government. *See* trust and distrust
    of government
Djandoubi, Hamida, 16